Developing Faculty in Liberal Arts Colleges

The American Campus

Harold S. Wechsler, Series Editor

The books in the American Campus series explore recent developments and public policy issues in higher education in the United States. Topics of interest include access to college, and college affordability; college retention, tenure, and academic freedom; campus labor; the expansion and evolution of administrative posts and salaries; the crisis in the humanities and the arts; the corporate university and for-profit colleges; online education; controversy in sport programs; and gender, ethnic, racial, religious, and class dynamics and diversity. Books feature scholarship from a variety of disciplines in the humanities and social sciences.

Gordon Hutner and Feisal G. Mohamed, eds., *A New Deal for the Humanities: Liberal Arts and the Future of Public Higher Education*

Adrianna Kezar and Daniel Maxey, eds., *Envisioning the Faculty for the Twenty-First Century: Moving to a Mission-Oriented and Learner-Centered Model*

Scott Frickel, Mathieu Albert, and Barbara Prainsack, eds., *Investigating Interdisciplinary Collaboration: Theory and Practice across Disciplines*

Jillian M. Duquaine-Watson, *Mothering by Degrees: Single Mothers and the Pursuit of Postsecondary Education*

W. Carson Byrd, *Poison in the Ivy: Race Relations and the Reproduction of Inequality on Elite College Campuses*

Vicki L. Baker, Laura Gail Lunsford, Meghan J. Pifer, *Developing Faculty in Liberal Arts Colleges: Aligning Individual Needs and Organizational Goals*

Developing Faculty in Liberal Arts Colleges

Aligning Individual Needs and Organizational Goals

VICKI L. BAKER, LAURA GAIL LUNSFORD,
MEGHAN J. PIFER

RUTGERS UNIVERSITY PRESS

NEW BRUNSWICK, CAMDEN, AND NEWARK, NEW JERSEY, AND LONDON

Library of Congress Cataloging-in-Publication Data

Names: Baker, Vicki L., 1978– author. | Lunsford, Laura Gail, author. |
Pifer, Meghan J., 1978–author.
Title: Developing faculty in liberal arts colleges : aligning individual needs and
organizational goals / Vicki L. Baker, Laura Gail Lunsford, Meghan J. Pifer.
Description: New Brunswick, New Jersey : Rutgers University Press, 2017. |
Series: The American campus | Includes bibliographical references and index.
Identifiers: LCCN 2016056602| ISBN 9780813586816 (hardback) |
ISBN 9780813586809 (pbk.) | ISBN 9780813586823 (e-book (epub))
Subjects: LCSH: Universities and colleges—United States—Faculty. | Education,
Humanistic—United States. | College teachers—Professional relationships—United
States. | College teachers—In-service training—United States. | BISAC: EDUCATION /
Higher. | EDUCATION / Professional Development. | EDUCATION / Leadership.
Classification: LCC LB2331.72 .B35 2017 | DDC 378.00973—
dc23 LC record available at https://lccn.loc.gov/2016056602

A British Cataloging-in-Publication record for
this book is available from the British Library.

∞ The paper used in this publication meets the requirements
of the American National Standard for Information Sciences—
Permanence of Paper for Printed Library Materials, ANSI Z39.48–1992.

www.rutgersuniversitypress.org

Manufactured in the United States of America

We dedicate this book to current and future faculty members in liberal arts colleges, which are special places, and to the people who support them.

CONTENTS

PART THREE
Aligning Resources: Supporting
Faculty Members and Academic Work

PART FOUR
At the Intersection: A Space for
Innovation and Competitive Advantage

FOREWORD
LIFE AT A SMALL LIBERAL ARTS COLLEGE

While the past decade has seen the burgeoning of professional literature about supporting faculty teaching and learning at small liberal arts colleges, too little has been written about faculty life at such institutions. Yes, there is a long history of fictional depictions of life on a small college campus, from Nathaniel Hawthorne's *Fanshawe* (1828), based on his experiences at Bowdoin College, to the movie *Liberal Arts* (2012), set on Kenyon College's campus. These provide interesting (and hopefully entertaining) views into life on such campuses. But despite a recent spate of books about the value of a liberal arts education and the future of liberal arts colleges, most current literature—like the fictional depictions of life on those institutions' campuses—provides little insight into what goes into creating a successful faculty career at liberal arts colleges.

Before we examine the nature of such a career, it is important to note the true variety of institutions hidden behind the label "liberal arts colleges." To the uninitiated, that group of schools may seem essentially indistinguishable from each other, and one might guess that faculty careers at such institutions are essentially the same. Certainly these small colleges have similarities: they rarely have more than 3,000 students (often fewer than 2,000); they usually have fewer than 200 full-time faculty members; almost all are primarily undergraduate; they emphasize teaching and student engagement; and most are residential and view the cocurricular experiences outside of the classroom as an essential part of a student's education. But it is difficult to make universal claims about liberal arts colleges beyond those general characteristics.

A closer look reveals significant differences among liberal arts colleges. Most are private, but some are public. Some have religious roots that continue to influence their daily campus life even today, while others have always been decidedly secular. Some had their genesis in the commitment to the education of women and continue that tradition today, while less than a handful focus on educating men. Although all grant at least 50 percent of their degrees in arts and sciences, many offer business and professional degrees, some offer master's degree programs, and one or two even grant the occasional doctorate.

And the financial resources of these schools—resources that can affect the nature of faculty work—vary tremendously. Some small liberal arts colleges have endowments worth over $2 billion. With a rule of spending 5 percent of the endowment each year, that can amount to endowment income upward of $50,000 per student per year. Others have close to no endowment and rely almost exclusively on tuition and annual fund-raising to meet their budgeted expenses.

The level of faculty work on these colleges' campuses varies, too. Faculty members at top-ranked, national liberal arts colleges may teach just two courses per semester (or fewer), while at other schools faculty members might teach four courses a semester (or more). Requirements for scholarly activity and creative work for tenure can also differ markedly: some of the top "research colleges" can require faculty members to have published more than one book—or multiple articles per year—to earn tenure, while other schools with higher teaching loads might ask little more of their faculty members than some kind of professional engagement, such as the occasional presentation at a conference.

What all liberal arts colleges have in common, I would argue, is their claim that faculty teaching and student learning is central to their mission, with full-time faculty members focusing on educating undergraduate students. This focus on teaching undergraduates often influences how a faculty member engages with the other two parts of the typical triumvirate of faculty responsibilities: scholarship and service. Furthermore, the typical doctoral education, even one that emphasizes teaching, does not do enough to prepare a future faculty member for the demands of a career at a liberal arts college.

What Is Distinctive about Having a Career at a Small, Residential Liberal Arts College?

At the risk of overgeneralizing, I would argue that being a faculty member at such a school offers specific advantages and challenges.

Teaching, Advising, and Mentoring

The advantages of a teaching life at a liberal arts college are many, especially when compared to teaching at a large university. The majority of courses at such colleges usually have fewer than twenty students, and upper-division courses are even smaller. This more intimate learning environment allows faculty members to work closely with and mentor undergraduates, and to share their enthusiasm for their discipline with students who are usually eager to learn.

There are smaller departments, which means that even early in their careers, faculty members have the opportunity to teach courses in their specific area of expertise. In addition, because many liberal arts colleges have transdisciplinary first-year seminar programs or writing across the curriculum, faculty members are often asked to teach outside of their traditional fields—for example, it is not uncommon to have a mathematician or chemist teaching critical reading and academic writing as part of their courses. Because all students have curricular "general education" requirements that cut across academic departments, both faculty members and students have opportunities to become conversant with multiple disciplines, and both come to appreciate the value of diverse disciplinary perspectives.

In addition, the model of advising at many liberal arts colleges often involves intensive one-on-one work to help guide a student not only in his or her major, but also through the general liberal arts curriculum—one that offers a great deal of options, including the many individualized opportunities available for students (for example, language study, community learning, study abroad, research, and specialized programs). Advising and mentoring undergraduate students is often considered part of teaching (or service), and new faculty members may feel unprepared to act in this role of enhanced advisor.

The more intimate and interdisciplinary nature of the teaching life at a liberal arts college can present many challenges. For some faculty members, teaching outside one's area expertise may not be appealing, or it may be something they feel they need a great deal of support to do effectively. And at many institutions, the teaching load is heavier than at research-focused universities—in terms not only of the number of courses taught per year but also of the variety. It is not uncommon for a faculty member to teach three different courses in any given term, or six different courses per year. Simply put, effective teaching matters. And as I have argued elsewhere, any college that claims to care about good teaching needs to support it intentionally and concretely, with resources and programs that focus on effective faculty teaching (Reder 2007 and 2010; Reder and Gallagher 2007).

Scholarship and Creative Work

The pace of scholarship and creative work on a liberal arts campus is often different from that at a research-intensive university. This is particularly true in the sciences, where labs are often smaller at a liberal arts college and are staffed by undergraduates. Yet at many such colleges the scholarly requirements for tenure may equal—or even exceed—those at larger institutions.

Ideally, a faculty member's research and creative interests inform his or her teaching. In many disciplines at liberal arts colleges, students are involved in a faculty member's research, and it is not uncommon for a student and a professor to present their work together at conferences or coauthor publications. This approach poses challenges for faculty members who have just left the research model of graduate school and find that their research and creative work are now closely related to the teaching and mentoring of students. Additionally, because departments are small, faculty members can sometimes feel intellectually isolated. The demands of teaching, especially on faculty members early in their careers, can make accomplishing scholarly and creative work difficult. As Robert Boice points out in his work on new faculty members, if an early-career faculty member's teaching is not going well or is taking too much time, other dimensions of his or her life—such as participation in the college community, personal life, and scholarship—suffer (Boice 1992 and 2000). This makes it even more important for liberal arts colleges to systematically support faculty members in their teaching and beyond.

Service and Community

Perhaps the least anticipated aspect of a faculty career at a liberal arts college is the amount and variety of required service, as well as the never-ending opportunities to engage with the larger campus community. Shared governance is the norm, and there are myriad committees on which to serve and dozens of campus leadership positions (departmental, programmatic, and senior administrative) to fill. Almost all liberal arts colleges emphasize their residential experience, and faculty are encouraged to participate not just in course-based learning but also in the intellectual and social life outside of the classroom (including lectures, symposiums, discussions, informal social events, clubs, athletics, and the arts, to name but a few).

   The nature of service at such institutions has the potential to affect the ways in which faculty members pursue their scholarship, research, and creative work. The potential to connect with colleagues across disciplines and throughout the institution, sometimes leading to unexpected collaborations and friendships, is one of the many positive aspects of such institutionwide involvement. All of these factors make a liberal arts college career different from one at any other type of institution and create different needs for faculty support.

   Even among faculty members who naturally gravitate toward this type of engagement, few are prepared during their graduate training to undertake it effectively. Service opportunities usually begin during a faculty member's first or second year, often in one's department, and then expand outward into the larger college community. The rewards of such service are a greater understanding of the educational enterprise as a whole and the sense that one person can help make real change and improvements. But the demand on one's time, particularly for early-career pretenure faculty members, is often a challenge.

Effectively Supporting Faculty Careers at Liberal Arts Colleges

While elements of these advantages and challenges of faculty life are not unique to liberal arts colleges, I believe they come together on such campuses in a distinctive manner. A successful career at a liberal arts college requires of faculty members a mix of commitments and skills that need to be developed and supported by colleagues and administrators in myriad ways.

Liberal arts college faculty members are constantly negotiating relationships—teaching across disciplinary boundaries, mentoring students, and service with colleagues. Early-career faculty who are diversifying their departments and the campus, not only in terms of academic interests but also often in terms of individual identity, need specific supports. And there are multiple demands on faculty members' time and priorities, not only in the early stages of one's career, but throughout one's teaching and professional life.

This book offers unprecedented insights into the challenges and needs of faculty members at small colleges and offers concrete suggestions on how best to support them in their careers. This study of thirteen schools, all in the Midwest but nonetheless varied in terms of resources and faculty life, includes the voices of a wide range of faculty members. Unlike any previous study of liberal arts colleges, this book focuses on the experiences of faculty members at such institutions across their careers.

This work reveals the complicated and sometimes conflicted nature of faculty life at liberal arts colleges, and the many ways such colleges attempt to support faculty careers and improve teaching and learning. Not all of these efforts are effective, and this study also highlights the importance of intentional, effective programming to support faculty members. Additionally, it draws our attention to the different dimensions of programming needed to support faculty success, including, importantly, aligning faculty work and support with overall institutional goals and values. Thinking about support for faculty across multiple dimensions—focusing on the people, the institutional context, and the evidence that informs such practices—as well as on different institutional levels (those of the individual, the department, and the institution as a whole) allows for the effective and intentional allocation of resources (Felten et al. 2013).

The book offers insights into the many, sometimes conflicting, forces at small liberal arts colleges and makes helpful suggestions about how to best support faculty members, in the interest of advancing their teaching and professional careers and making those careers as happy and fulfilling as possible. And a successful faculty life, of course, supports the ultimate goal of improving student learning—which is at the center of every liberal arts college's mission.

Michael Reder
Connecticut College

NOTE ON THE TEXT

The opening vignettes featured in several chapters use direct quotes from faculty focus groups and interviews. Names and disciplines were changed to protect the featured faculty members' identities.

Developing Faculty in Liberal Arts Colleges

INTRODUCTION

Developing Faculty Members in Liberal Arts Colleges

Aligning Individual Needs with Organizational Goals

Imagine driving down a rural back road in small-town America. As you round the bend, you see a quaint downtown that reminds you of another era. Coffee shops and local businesses now inhabit historic buildings that once housed the town pharmacy, the five-and-dime store, or maybe an old post office or school building. The town hall is prominent in the square, and just past it are majestic trees flanking a green, well-manicured lawn. Historic plaques adorn the impressive architecture. Students and professors are walking down stone pathways, presumably going to their next class or to the iconic library next to the campus chapel. You imagine students sitting on the bench you just spotted, perfectly located for shade under the canopy of an ancient tree, discussing their professor's latest intriguing lecture. The bell tower or grand water fountain in the quad is surely where seniors congregate for graduation photos. You park your car and begin strolling toward the center of the campus, catching snippets of rich intellectual debates with learned professors who are masters of both their fields of inquiry and the classroom space. You find yourself wishing that you were here for the weekend, when there is sure to be a magnificent play or ballet in the theatre building you just passed.

The idyllic scene above is the stereotypical view of the liberal arts college (LAC) experience. Indeed, there are places and times in which this scene actually plays out. Yet it is also an image that belies the complexity of what success looks like for today's LACs, how it is achieved, and at what costs.

In fact, this scene is in stark contrast with news headlines that describe the "death of the liberal arts," as students leave LACs with mounting student debt. The same news stories highlight the plight of the unemployed humanities major (Kiley 2012), the insinuation being that faculty members at LACs do not impart skills that help their graduates find gainful employment after graduation. Fueling the negative publicity faced by LACs are the recent closings (followed, in some cases, by reopenings) of institutions such as Antioch College and Sweet Briar College due to financial mismanagement and lack of leadership. One may speculate that these closings are a harbinger of the end of LACs as students and parents start to prefer a more vocation-focused degree to a costly liberal arts education.

Further exacerbating this negative perception of LACs is their seeming inability to describe to prospective students and the public at large what differentiates a liberal arts experience from other educational choices. This communication failure only helps institutional competitors that seek to replicate the liberal arts experience, such as honors or residential colleges in large research universities.

The liberal arts model continues to be idealized, yet it is often criticized. Public accountability and demands for transparency are increasing. Metrics such as time to degree, college costs, admission procedures, and alumni employability are now deemed necessary and appropriate for shaping assessments of the value of these institutions. Higher education institutions are struggling to win the war for the holy trinity of professional relevance, economic value, and transformative educational experiences. In this book, we attempt to reduce this information deficit. We provide a closer look at the experiences and needs of the labor force that provides a key component of the student experience and fulfillment of institutional mission at LACs—their faculty members.

The Critical Role of Faculty Development

There are at least four barriers to the ability of institutional leaders (for example, presidents, provosts, and associate deans) to support faculty in LACs. First, researchers have revealed a disconnect between doctoral training and the realities of academic careers, particularly in types of institutions such as LACs, where the mission and focus are notably different from those of the research training emphasized in graduate education (Austin 2002). Such a focus leaves new faculty members ill-prepared for the variety of roles (teacher, advisor, and mentor) and responsibilities (assessment, recruitment, and community engagement) they must engage in regularly.

Second, tension exists between a faculty member's loyalties to his or her institution and discipline. Liberal arts faculty members are expected to put teaching first and to support students within and beyond the classroom, as well as to engage in service to the department and college. Resources—including the priceless resource of time—are allocated according to those priorities. If faculty members also have active research agendas, they may struggle to identify the support, mentoring, resources, and time for that component of their scholarly identities.

Third, LACs are lagging behind in faculty development beyond teaching and learning, such as leadership development and challenges specific to various career stages that are critical to successfully navigating the professoriate in this institutional setting.

Fourth, the academic employment landscape is changing. Traditionally, conversations about the academic career have been organized around the three ranks of assistant, associate, and full professor. Recently, however, the national shift toward the use of contingent faculty members has introduced a new majority into the academic labor force, thus making it more difficult for aspiring professors to secure full-time academic work, promotion, and tenure. A broader perspective is needed in decision making about faculty work in LACs.

Furthermore, there is a need to support leaders in making such decisions in ways that align with institutional programming and policies, administrative perspectives and goals, and faculty efforts. Effective faculty development will equip faculty members in LACs with the knowledge, skills, and resources to help fulfill the institutional mission and student learning goals, as well as to find success and satisfaction in academic careers and professional contexts.

Of course, these processes will be viewed from various perspectives. Thus, we examine slices of institutional priorities and faculty needs through the human resources concept of alignment, described below and throughout the chapters in this book. We present examples from LACs to illustrate effective and ineffective models of faculty development, as well as effective and ineffective strategies used by faculty members. The concept of alignment situates our work at that critical intersection where decisions are made in the understudied LAC context.

We provide a framework and resources to enable stakeholders to first assess, and then improve, faculty work and related outcomes at their institutions. As a team of scholars, we share an interest in and passion for effective organizational administration that uplifts rather than burdens; successful and satisfying faculty careers; and the fulfillment of higher education's potential for the individual learner and the public good. Leaders will benefit from knowing more about current trends in faculty development practices and institutional programs, and considering what may be possible in cultivating successful academic careers in LACs.

Past to Present: The American Liberal Arts College

"The past isn't over, it isn't even past."
—William Faulkner, *Requiem for a Nun*

A Brief History

As William Faulkner suggested, an understanding of the past informs the present and perhaps the future. The American LAC is one of the most successful educational enterprises to be undertaken thus far and has been characterized as one of the icons of American higher education (Miller and Skinner 2012). The residential LAC provided the original model of undergraduate education in the United States, with many institution types seeking to replicate that model (Chopp, Frost, and Weiss 2013). Defining features such as a broad-based curriculum grounded in the arts and sciences, small class sizes, and strong faculty-student interactions have made the model one that is gaining in prominence around the world (Baker and Baldwin 2015). LACs are credited with cultivating the first-year experience, developing living and learning communities, implementing writing across the curriculum, and supporting undergraduate research experiences (Baker, Baldwin, and Makker 2012).

The origin of the liberal arts curriculum is in the seven areas of knowledge that guided inquiry in the early middle ages: the trivium (grammar, rhetoric, and logic) and the quadrivium (arithmetic, geometry, astronomy, and music) were the original liberal arts (Haskins 1965). References to the *artes liberales* date back to Cicero's use of the term in the first century B.C.E. (Kimball 1986). The original colleges of the United States, eight of which were founded before the American Revolution, called for professors who taught within the seven liberal arts and who cultivated the moral character of their students (Knapp 1965). As President Thomas R. Dew implored in his 1836 address to the students of the College of William and Mary, "now is the time to imbibe the great lessons of morality and to study the general and elementary doctrines of government and politics" (quoted in Thelin 2014, 60). Victor Ferrall praised LACs' special contributions to educating citizens: "The thesis here is simple. Society needs well and broadly educated citizens. The more liberally educated citizens it has, the stronger it will be. . . . Liberal arts colleges, while not the only vehicles for producing liberally educated citizens, are among the best" (2011, 16).

As a viable and attractive model of postsecondary education, the LAC thrived—at times through adaptation—before the United States became a nation. LACs did not disappear even when the competing model of the great research university emerged. In the postwar expansion period of the 1950s, LACs continued to enjoy a position of status and relevance in the postsecondary education landscape, specifically in relation to undergraduate education (Thelin 2011). By the 1960s, they were viewed as what John Thelin referred to as the "antidote" to the large and impersonal university (ibid., 296).

Over the decades, LACs have continued to fulfill their institutional missions, though they are again in a period of turmoil that requires careful attention to new models of institutional strength and success. Despite the waxing and waning of institutional resources, LACs have clearly influenced the intellectual and civic development of the United States. For example, LACs have educated nearly 20 percent of all US presidents and 20 percent of all Pulitzer Prize winners in drama, history, and poetry from 1960 to 1998. Furthermore, compared to other academic institutions, LACs produce nearly twice as many students who go on to earn doctorates in the sciences (Kanter 2010).

The faculty members who create learning spaces, faithfully teach the curriculum, and mentor students are the core resource of the successful LAC. It is the faculty members who develop future leaders and thinkers, through their disciplinary and pedagogical knowledge and creativity and through their commitment to a career situated in the liberal arts model.

Liberal Arts Colleges Today

Today, the LAC is under fire, criticized as either a quaint has-been or an expensive waste of potential (Baker, Baldwin, and Makker 2012; Jaschik 2012a). Some people question the relevance of a liberal arts education in today's competitive global economy, while others argue that the price of such an educational experience is too high, beyond the reach of a large number of people, and not worth the return on investment (Ferrall 2011). Other detractors suggest that the faculty members at LACs, despite their educational pedigrees, chose to be teachers and mentors rather than true scholars in their respective fields. This narrow view ignores the many contributions of liberal arts faculty members and is not an accurate depiction of their professional activity or how they allocate their time, as we will demonstrate. Some (such as Ferrall 2011) have encouraged LACs to invest in improved teaching excellence as a necessary strategy for maintaining (or regaining) relevance, while others (such as Zemsky 2013) have called for an approach that combines the institutions' traditional roots with innovative entrepreneurialism and expansion. Educational innovations add to the ever-increasing price tag at LACs, rather than holding them constant or lowering them (Miller and Skinner 2012), and critics contend that these institutions cannot compete on economies of scale with their larger counterparts in terms of providing opportunities to students. Yet it is challenging to put a price on increases in learning outcomes and skill development for students, and the long-held view that LACs provide an imitable value to their graduates' lives and careers. We agree with Martha Kanter's assessment in her remarks at the Annapolis Group Conference related to the critiques of LACs: "These beliefs are misguided, if not counterproductive. Yet those critiques do contain kernels of truth" (2010).

The trend David Breneman (1990) identified two decades ago continues today—there is a decline in the number of true LACs, as many morph into professional colleges and turn away from an arts and sciences core. This evolution in LACs continues to be newsworthy (see, for example, Kiley 2012; Lane 2013). However, this may simply be a transitional period in higher education overall (Baker, Baldwin, and Makker 2012) rather than the end of the road for LACs. This transition is prompted by external forces such as rapidly evolving technologies, changing approaches to teaching and learning, students' increased vocational interests, and reduced funding (Baker and Baldwin 2015; Baker, Pifer, and Lunsford 2015; Kezar 2001). Leaders of LACs must respond to challenges such as rising tuition rates and market pressures for vocation-oriented programs while continuing to preserve their colleges' defining features. Again, we note that institutional leaders need to engage faculty members in these changes if they hope to fulfill their institutional mission, as well as strengthen and sustain LACs as an institution type in the current era.

Engaging the Liberal Arts Faculty

How might campus administrators and faculty members dispel misguided perceptions about LACs? How can institutions focus on effective faculty development as a strategy for improving institutional reputation and student outcomes, while also paying attention to responding effectively to criticism and reduced resources? How might faculty members become better informed about the realities of academic work in liberal arts contexts, and cultivate careers that offer success and satisfaction in such challenging times?

To answer these questions, some researchers (Baker and Baldwin 2015; Baker, Baldwin, Makker 2012; Breneman 1990) have taken a big-picture view of evolutionary change as a means of examining this sector of higher education. Other scholars (for example, Mooney and Reder 2008; Reder 2010; Reder, Mooney, Holmgren, and Kuerbis 2008), have narrowed their view to examine LACs and other small colleges from an institutional perspective, focusing on the attributes of successful faculty development programs and the ways in which institutions can better support their faculty in teaching, learning, and other scholarly endeavors. Still others (Baldwin and Blackburn 1981; Baldwin and Chang 2006) have opted to take an individual faculty perspective as a means of learning about the realities faculty members face in this institution type as a means of better understanding the assumptions made about LACs and the pressures faculty members face. While this work has laid the foundation, this singular focus—whether it be the big-picture, institutional, or individual faculty perspective related to faculty development—has yet to offer effective responses to the questions posed above and is an ineffective approach for two reasons.

First, faculty development continues to develop as a professional field. The work of the scholars noted above has made a contribution to our understanding of LACs by identifying the needs of faculty members and the role of institutional efforts for faculty development. However, it takes time for a new field to coalesce. Thus, faculty development is limited in its ability to provide immediate and refined solutions.

Second, to best support faculty work in LACs, we need to do more than improve faculty development. Rather than defaulting to models in which faculty activity and institutional programming operate on parallel tracks, LACs need to align institutional priorities and faculty development programming with the realities of academic work and faculty members' needs. The nature of faculty work is changing, and institutions are the central context in shaping faculty members' goals and experiences. Indeed, Judith Gappa, Ann Austin, and Andrea Trice have noted that "many institutions have not seriously considered how support for faculty must evolve to better enable them to accomplish their work" (2007, 4). LACs are at a crossroad, and institutional leaders need to leverage their core resource—the faculty members—to help maintain their valued place in higher education.

The pressures faced by LACs affect their faculty members across career stages, disciplines, and personal characteristics. Disconnects between their academic preparation and the realities of the liberal arts context for early-career faculty members create job stress and a steep learning curve as they move from a research focus in doctoral training to faculty work that includes teaching, research, and service. Midcareer and senior colleagues must adapt to the changing model of an LAC that is different from the one under which they earned tenure. They are now expected to take on leadership and mentoring roles—often, we have found, with little training or support. Across institutional contexts, there have been calls for more attention to the unique career-stage needs faculty members have and how those needs are influenced by institutional context (Austin 2010). Kim Mooney and Michael Reder noted a paucity of work that specifically addresses "the professional experiences, programming goals, and other potentially distinctive issues and concerns of faculty development at liberal arts and other small colleges" (2008, 159). Until now we have lacked a larger framework that examines the intersection of institutional priorities and academic work to address these concerns. As Ferrall (2011) wrote, improved training and support for faculty work must include efforts from both administrators and the faculty body.

We believe that the field of faculty professional development needs to include a close consideration of the faculty experience, specifically in LACs and beyond the research university—which is typically studied in the field. Approaches are needed that carefully integrate administrative and faculty perspectives to paint a nuanced and complete picture of the faculty experience and the factors that contribute to it. Investigating the presence and degree of alignment between the perspectives and actions of these two populations is crucial for achieving individual and organizational outcomes. There is a dearth of research on the complexity of the faculty experience that might guide college leaders. We acknowledge that it is challenging to consider all the factors relevant to faculty work. However, we argue that approaches to faculty development are needed that consider—in honest, realistic, and data-driven terms—essential factors such as academic rank, departmental environments, field of study, and faculty members' personal characteristics and family structures.

The Alignment Framework for Faculty Development in Liberal Arts Colleges

Over a decade ago, KerryAnn O'Meara and Eugene Rice (2005) highlighted a growing concern about the misalignment between the priorities of faculty members and the central missions of the institutions where they work. The authors' recognition of this misalignment foreshadowed what has become an incomplete model of faculty development and support within LACs. To date, however, their call for attention to the consideration of alignment has gone largely unanswered. In this book, we give close consideration to this specific concept as a framework for understanding and improving institutional and individual efforts to improve faculty success and satisfaction.

We expand on Lynda Gratton and Catherine Truss's (2003) three-dimensional people strategy to situate our findings and recommendations at the intersection of institutional priorities and academic work. Thus, we extend the authors' model to what we will refer to as the alignment framework for faculty development in liberal arts colleges (AFFD-LAC). We use alignment as a framework to "focus on the connection between people strategy and organizational performance" (ibid., 75), with the goal of creating and promoting a competitive advantage for LACs through the effective development of their key resource—the faculty.

The alignment framework consists of vertical alignment, horizontal alignment, and implementation. Vertical alignment is a macro-level consideration, in that it accounts for the ten-thousand-foot view of the link between the organizational strategies as a whole and the organization's people-management strategy. "Organizational strategy" refers to the goals, missions, objectives, and values of an organization. "People-management strategy" refers to the organization's approach to managing people. Horizontal alignment is a micro-level consideration focused on individual areas of human resource policy. The goal of horizontal alignment is the development of a coherent, consistent approach to people management that permeates all activities of human resources staff members and the other functional areas across the organization at the policy level. Lastly, implementation is the action, or practice, component of the framework. As Gratton and Truss noted, it is not enough to have organizational and people-level (vertical and macro-level) strategies and specific policies (horizontal and micro-level) that speak to those strategies. Those strategies and policies need to be implemented, supported, and assessed equitably.

We note, however, that Gratton and Truss (2003) developed their three-dimensional people strategy based on a ten-year study of large corporations. We adapt and reenvision their work by proposing the AFFD-LAC to assess institutional strategies for supporting faculty work in higher education. Such an adaptation acknowledges that human resources managers in LACs are not responsible for personnel development for faculty members, unlike those managers' peers in other organizational settings. An important question emerges: Who is responsible for faculty development? We provide answers to this question, with related recommendations for action, throughout this book.

The AFFD-LAC provides guidance for academic leaders to situate strategies for improved practices at the intersection of institutional priorities and academic work. We complement this framework with the work of Gappa, Austin, and Trice (2007), which provides an effective model to enhance understanding of faculty work in LACs. In their framework, these authors identified the essential elements of the faculty work experience, which fall in two broad categories: faculty characteristics (including demographic characteristics and appointment types) and institutional characteristics (such as culture, mission, and leadership). In addition to these two categories of elements, we closely examine core contexts of academic work in LACs, such as the role of the academic department and faculty members' mentoring models and key relationships.

The AFFD-LAC enables both faculty members and administrators to examine the intersection of faculty needs and behaviors, institutional priorities, and administrative programming and policies. Such an examination, facilitated by both exemplary and problematic examples and trends from the field, can equip stakeholders to understand and support both institutional and individual goals with the aim of improving LACs' fulfillment of both their mission and the potential of academics within them.

How Will This Book Support My Work?

This book is written for you if you wish to know more about how to lead or navigate (or help others navigate) the complexities of managing and supporting faculty work in LACs. We have written this book for administrators and faculty members (both present and future) who are interested in improving LACs by leveraging their core resource—the faculty. You may be a campus administrator worried about stretching institutional resources to meet competing needs and wondering how to differentiate your institution from its competition. Perhaps you are a department head thinking about fulfilling students' curricular needs, supporting a newly hired member of your department, and developing your leadership skills. You may be a faculty member at an LAC who is struggling to make sense of your own experience and wondering whether it is typical and how to improve it. Or you may be a doctoral candidate who is preparing for the academic job market and wondering if an LAC will enable you to make good use of your talents.

In this book we present an in-depth, practical, research-informed perspective about the faculty experience and faculty development priorities in LACs. We draw on various views of faculty careers and professional development in higher education, psychology for the science of mentoring and positive relationships, and business for human resource management strategies.

The Initiative for Faculty Development in Liberal Arts Colleges

The book draws on our mixed-methods study of the faculty experience in a consortium of thirteen LACs (the Great Lakes Colleges Association, or GLCA), titled the Initiative for Faculty Development in Liberal Arts Colleges. We present the experiences reported by liberal arts faculty members across career stages, academic disciplines, and institutional and departmental contexts; and with different personal characteristics and life circumstances. The perspectives of campus leaders, policy documents, and other resources at these institutions are also discussed to highlight the alignment between administrative knowledge of and approaches to supporting faculty experiences on campuses.

The genesis of this research was in conversations with faculty members and academic deans within the GLCA and the broader Global Liberal Arts Alliance, an international partnership of liberal arts institutions around the world modeled after the American LAC. The goal of the alliance is to support transnational excellence in liberal arts education. Administrators and faculty members from this alliance gathered in Athens, Greece, in summer 2011. During that time, faculty partners from member institutions in attendance met to develop co-shared undergraduate course experiences to be delivered that fall semester. When the faculty teams provided updates on their planning efforts, discussions arose related to the ways in which faculty members are socialized into the LAC environment, given disconnects in graduate school training related to faculty roles in institution types beyond research universities, and how faculty members can be better supported in their work given these disconnects and the evolving nature of an LAC education. Data from the Initiative for Faculty Development in Liberal Arts Colleges were collected in the period 2012–16 through surveys of and interviews with faculty members, as well as interviews and focus groups with administrators at LACs. For study details, see Appendix A.

How to Approach This Book

The chapters build on each other to make the case for the recommendations (in sections titled "What Can I Do?") presented in chapters 1–6. We provide a discussion of the AFFD-LAC in chapter 7. However, the chapters also stand alone as they relate to particular subcontexts of academic work, and thus they may be read independently to suit the reader's needs and interests. For example, a department head might be most interested in part 1, which focuses on the role of contexts as important influencers of faculty development and academic work. And an early-career or prospective faculty member might be most interested in part 2, which is about what it means to be a faculty member at an LAC and the kinds of support to expect (or request). Therefore, they may focus on the second section of the book.

The parts and chapters are organized by content area as they relate to faculty development and academic work. In part 1, the importance of context as a critical influencer of faculty development and academic work is emphasized. Chapter 1 focuses on the institutional context by highlighting the factors that contribute to the creation and management of the faculty development portfolios at the thirteen LACs in our study. Chapter 2 focuses on the academic department as a critical yet understudied contributor to the faculty experience and a missed opportunity for faculty development programming.

The individual or people perspective is the focus of part 2, which provides a more holistic view of the faculty experience in today's LAC. Chapter 3 discusses the daily roles and responsibilities as well as the challenges and areas of opportunity for the faculty members across the thirteen LACs. Chapter 4 illustrates the need to involve administrators and faculty members in the development and implementation of faculty development programming. We examine the intersection of institutional priorities, faculty members' needs, and faculty development practice to illuminate a disconnect in priorities and practice.

Part 3 shows the types of support institutions provide, the faculty development programming faculty members do (and do not) participate in and the associated outcomes, and what strategies faculty members use to support their own career development. Chapter 5 presents a broader view of professional relationships, including faculty mentoring and engagement in professional development beyond the departmental context. Formal institutional efforts as well as informal faculty engagement in mentoring are discussed. Chapter 6 documents trends in institutional strategies for supporting faculty work, as well as when, how often, and why faculty members make use of these sources of support. We highlight exemplary programs.

And finally, part 4 consists of chapter 7, in which a more comprehensive model of the faculty experience in LACs—the AFFD-LAC—is described in more detail. Future directions and strategies are considered for how to improve the faculty experience at your current or future institution.

PART ONE

Contexts of Academic Work in Liberal Arts Colleges

Inside Institutions and Departments

1

Institutional Structures,
Support, and Evaluation

*It's eight o'clock on a Tuesday morning, and the members of a strategic plan-
ning committee—consisting of faculty members, the associate provost (the chair of
the committee), and the provost—have gathered for one of their biweekly meetings. A
faculty member questions how the institutional priorities will change in the current
revision process. The associate provost responds, "I think our institutional priorities
are driven from our strategic plan, which was developed seven years ago. I think
they're very clearly articulated. They're very public. Updates were provided annually
to the institutional community, and feedback and assessments were collected to
ensure goals and initiatives were achieved."*

*As members review the data from the past seven years and benchmark the col-
lege's accomplishments against its aspirations, the main pillars of the new strategic
plan begin to emerge. The usual suspects appear: community engagement, global
partnerships, and student learning. One faculty member asks: "Do any of these programs connect to faculty explicitly? We worry about excellence at the student and
programming levels, but what about faculty?" Another faculty member asks the provost, "How do you define faculty excellence, and what does that mean to us?"*

*The provost responds: "My use of the term 'faculty excellence' is probably much
more of a 'campaign' way of talking about faculty excellence. Of course faculty development is a priority of the institution, but it's not explicitly accounted for in strategic
planning and hasn't been in the past."*

This disconnect between strategic planning and supporting faculty members
caused us to wonder how institutional leaders conceptualize faculty development as part of their strategy for improving institutional reputation and

student outcomes. Furthermore, how might they do this while offering meaningful responses to critics and adjusting to reduced resources? Most important, how might leaders equip their faculty members to fulfill their institutions' priorities, while also signaling that liberal arts colleges (LACs) support their faculty members' careers?

A main premise of this book is that campus leaders, other administrators, and faculty members at LACs can do more to align institutional aspirations and goals with professional development opportunities for faculty members. Before exploring the components of alignment in faculty development, we present an overview of what institutions do in this regard. Then we consider how to make improvements that may strike a better balance between LAC faculty members' needs and institutional priorities in the changing higher education landscape. In this chapter, we specifically focus on the institutional infrastructure that underpins faculty development in the Great Lakes Colleges Association (GLCA). We organize this discussion into three categories: structures, supports, and evaluations. We reviewed the faculty development portfolio of each institution in the consortium to provide the context for faculty professional development opportunities within LACs. We then consider institutional themes and outliers related to faculty professional development strategies and their influence on the nature and outcomes of faculty work in LACs.

Institutional Structures for Faculty Development

We all know that academic institutions today are expected to do more with less. How do the GLCA institutions manage this challenge and support faculty development as a means of using available resources to the greatest advantage? It is easy to overlook institutional structures in seeking to understand faculty work. We are reminded of the saying that the fish can't see the water. Yet academic leaders need to see the water—their institutional structures—to conceptualize their faculty development efforts. In the GLCA, we found three types of structural approaches to assigning responsibility for faculty development: administrative positions, faculty committees, and centers for teaching and learning.

Administrative Positions for Faculty Development

"I was happy to step into the associate dean position responsible for faculty development. But talk about drinking from a fire hose those first two years, in all honesty!"

　　　　　　　　　　　　　—An associate dean

There are many models for administrative oversight of faculty development efforts, each of which has benefits and drawbacks. The GLCA institutions reflect this range of models (see table 1.1). Three categories of administrative positions exist: full time permanent; full time renewable; and half time. Most GLCA institutions rely on a combination of positions, ranging from full time to half time, to serve as the primary points of contact for supporting faculty work.

TABLE 1.1

Summary of Administrative Positions for Faculty Development at Institutions in the Great Lakes Colleges Association

Institution	Administrative Positions
Albion College	Provost
	Associate Provost
	Director for Teaching and Learning
Allegheny College	Associate Provost for Faculty Development
Antioch College	Dean
	Associate Dean
Denison University	Associate Provost for Faculty Affairs
DePauw University	Faculty Development Coordinator
Earlham College	Associate Academic Dean
Hope College	Associate Dean for Teaching and Learning
	Associate Dean for Research and Scholarship
Kalamazoo College	Associate Provost
	Director of Teaching and Learning
	Director of Faculty Grants
Kenyon College	Associate Provost
	Faculty Development Coordinator
Oberlin College	Associate Dean of the Faculty
	Director of the Center for Teaching Innovation and Excellence
Ohio Wesleyan College	Provost
	Associate Dean for Faculty Development
Wabash College	Dean of the College
	Faculty Development Coordinator
College of Wooster	Dean for Faculty Development

Full-Time Permanent Positions for Faculty Development

Albion, Antioch, Earlham, Kalamazoo, Kenyon, Ohio Wesleyan, and Wabash have full-time permanent positions dedicated to faculty development. The executive titles are at the director, dean, or provost level. At Albion College, the provost and associate provost share this responsibility, spending approximately 10 percent and 20 percent of their time, respectively, on faculty development. Similarly, at Antioch College the dean spends approximately 25 percent of his or her time engaging in faculty development, and the associate dean spends roughly 25 percent of his or her time on mentoring faculty and scheduling courses. Faculty development at Earlham College is the responsibility of the associate academic dean, who works with the academic dean. The academic dean/provost has primary responsibility for faculty development at Ohio Wesleyan University. At Wabash College, the dean of the college has primary responsibility for the development of the faculty and is supported by the faculty development coordinator. Kalamazoo has a director of faculty grants, an administrative position, who provides support for faculty members seeking external support for their scholarship. The associate provost is the primary point of contact for faculty development at Kenyon College.

BENEFITS. Having a full-time permanent position responsible for faculty development sends a message to faculty members about the importance of having clear and direct administrative support for them as they engage in academic work. In most of these LACs, the dean is the position on campus most connected to faculty development. The person in a full-time permanent position becomes the faculty development advocate as he or she works to ensure that faculty development is an institutional priority. Ideally, faculty members are able to build a strong working relationship with a full-time staff member, helping to foster continuity in programming, consistency of message, and ownership of faculty development work.

DRAWBACKS. The reality is that faculty development is one of many areas of responsibility assigned to staff members in the dean's or provost's office. Although the position is a full-time permanent one, its predominant focus is not on faculty development. Furthermore, most deans and associate deans have had their primary training within their disciplines and professional societies, which often results in their having a steep learning curve to understand faculty development more generally—including all that encompasses the professional field and as it pertains to individual faculty members. Lastly, the average tenure of a dean is 4.7 years, according to an American Council of Education study titled *The American College President 2007* (King and Gomez 2007), and thus leadership turnover makes it difficult to achieve the continuity in programming, consistency of message, and ownership of faculty development work that we noted above. Finally, relying on just one administrative position to oversee faculty development leaves LACs vulnerable to person-specific politics and personalities that could help or hinder faculty buy-in for that person's ability to support and develop the faculty effectively.

Full-Time Renewable Positions for Faculty Development

Several of the colleges have full-time renewable positions, which are typically occupied by full-time members of the faculty. At Allegheny College, the associate provost is responsible for faculty development and spends approximately 25 percent of his or her time on such efforts. This position is a four-year renewable term. At Denison University, the associate provost for faculty affairs is responsible for all faculty development programs. This is a three-year appointed position, filled by a teaching faculty member who reports to the provost; it can be renewed for a second term. DePauw University has a faculty development coordinator appointed for a three-year term from the faculty by the vice president for academic affairs and dean of faculty, on the recommendation of the faculty development committee. At Kalamazoo College, the associate provost, a member of the faculty, has a three-year term. Faculty development is part of the portfolio of the associate dean of the faculty at Oberlin College. The position of associate dean normally rotates every three years, and the associate dean reports directly to the dean of arts and sciences. And lastly, the College of Wooster has a dean for faculty development, which is a full-time cabinet (that is, senior administrative) position. In all of these colleges, these roles are filled by faculty members, who typically return to their faculty roles after their appointments expire.

BENEFITS. The benefit of a full-time renewable position appointed from the faculty is credibility. Faculty members are more likely to see a single point person with faculty development responsibilities as the face of faculty development. If this person also comes from the faculty, he or she is likely to have established relationships with colleagues, understand the institutional culture, be aware of institutional opportunities and challenges, and have personal experience with faculty work, needs, and even challenges related to the potential divide between faculty and administrative styles and perspectives.

DRAWBACKS. The reality is that members of the faculty do not have formal training in faculty development, given that their training is rooted in their disciplines. This creates a steep learning curve that could minimize the effectiveness of such a position in the short term as the appointee learns how to do his or her job. Depending on term limits, by the time one person hits his or her stride, it may be time for another faculty member to learn the ropes. One associate dean illustrated the learning curve and the cycle of inconsistency and leadership turnover for renewable positions: "I was happy to step into the associate dean position responsible for faculty development. But talk about drinking from a fire hose those first two years, in all honesty! As I end my second term, it's bittersweet. I was just getting my feet under me and am now passing the torch."

Deans and associate deans also noted the challenge of having administrative responsibility for faculty development, which meant that their perspective was decidedly different from that of their former faculty peers. Professionals are able to manage such tensions, but the added element contributes to the learning curve and the types of support needed by those who are responsible for faculty development. In addition, within the small contexts of LACs, the loss of a full-time faculty member to such an administrative appointment is a disruption for any department, which likely does not receive support to cover the teaching, advising, and service duties that the selected individual had been performing.

Half-Time Positions for Faculty Development

Several of the colleges have employees who support faculty development on a part-time basis. Albion College's director of the Center for Teaching and Learning is a member of the faculty and works with the center on a half-time basis. At Hope College, the associate dean for teaching and learning supervises the Initium program, which provides faculty development for new faculty members and manages the mentoring program. The associate dean for teaching and learning is a half-time position, appointed from among the teaching faculty by the provost, and has nine direct reports. The director of teaching and learning at Kalamazoo College is a member of the faculty who spends half of his or her time directing programming in the Teaching Commons and on teaching and learning (T&L) generally. At Wabash College, special responsibility is also placed on the faculty development coordinator, a faculty member appointed by the dean and released from teaching a course to attend to issues of faculty development—including meeting individually with faculty members and promoting discussions of issues of T&L. Kenyon College has two positions that promote faculty development. The McCoy–Bank One Distinguished Teaching Professor is an endowed chair released from one course to supporting mid-career faculty members. Kenyon also has a faculty development coordinator, which is a faculty member released from one course to work on faculty development for posttenure faculty members.

BENEFITS. This type of appointment raises the question: If this is the only option, is having a half-time position better than having no position at all dedicated to faculty development? That depends on the particular college and faculty members involved. A half-time position may serve as a learning opportunity for the person who occupies that role and may be viewed as a career development opportunity, for faculty members considering administrative career paths. Such a position also allows the faculty developer to engage in that work while still staying grounded in the classroom and having personal experiences with and knowledge of students' needs—and thus of the types of T&L supports that might be of interest and helpful to students.

DRAWBACKS. The reality is that, as with the other positions, half-time appointments result in a steep learning curve and additional responsibilities on top of existing duties. Despite the position officially being half-time, the person in it might well feel as if he or she has two full-time positions without the requisite supports or compensation and is thus unable to fully contribute to supporting faculty in their work. Turnover is also a challenge with a half-time appointment, particularly if the position is underresourced and not a desirable or effective use of faculty members' time and talents.

Committees Responsible for Faculty Development

"I'm really pleased with how engaged our faculty members are in terms of supporting committee work."

–An associate dean

Committees are important structures at every GLCA institution, as they supplement and support administrative appointments related to faculty development. Committees connect faculty governance to faculty development, particularly at LACs (Lee 2010). The primary foci of the standing committees related to faculty development are scholarship, teaching, and faculty affairs. Tenured and tenure-track faculty members across divisional representation (the natural sciences, humanities, social sciences, and fine arts) elected to serve on those committees make up the majority of their members. In a few instances, faculty members are appointed to the standing committees. Terms are three years on average and are staggered to ensure continuity in committee composition. The three primary committee models that support faculty development in the GLCA are a scholarship committee, a curriculum and teaching committee, and a personnel and faculty affairs committee. While the committees may not have these particular titles at each institution, all thirteen GLCA institutions have committees that address these three primary areas.

The charge of a scholarship committee is to review, approve, and award institutional research and development resources, including grants and awards internal to the institution. Additionally, scholarship committees may review and approve sabbaticals, endowed professorships, and the internal research grant applications process and approvals.

Curriculum and teaching committees are primarily responsible for reviewing and approving courses, course descriptions, and syllabi. Members also review and approve degree, major, and program requirements. In some instances, curricular committees also evaluate program review and assessment documentation. T&L committees are charged with creating pedagogical and course design initiatives that support teaching development and subsequently student learning. In addition, members of these committees organize campus events such as symposiums centered on T&L. If an institution has a center for teaching and learning (CTL), the committee works in support of and with the CTL director to support overall programming focused on T&L.

The primary focus of committees related to personnel or faculty affairs is general policies related to the employment and support of the faculty members in the institution. These committees address such matters as compensation, employee handbook language, and conditions of employment. Their members work closely with faculty members elected or appointed to faculty development committees, given that resources provided to faculty members through faculty development opportunities relate to personnel matters.

Other noteworthy committees that support faculty development in the GLCA include Oberlin College's Community-Based Learning Committee, which ensures support for pedagogy-based learning, and Wabash College's McLain-McTurnan-Arnold (MMA) Research Scholar Committee which reviews proposals for the MMA Fellowship, an honor awarded to a faculty member whose scholarship makes an important contribution to his or her respective field.

BENEFITS. The primary benefit of using a committee to support faculty development is faculty ownership of and engagement in this important work. Committees support faculty development by giving the faculty a voice in professional development and related resource allocation and programming. As one associate dean said, "I'm really pleased with how engaged our faculty members are in terms of supporting committee work. It's so vital to us as an institution as we seek to assist faculty as they engage in academic work and with students." Engaging faculty members in the process across divisions and departments provides a diversity of viewpoints and frequently results in important disciplinary insights about needed faculty development supports. This process creates an opportunity for committee members to provide developmental feedback to their peers and learn more about the types of work other faculty members are engaged in through their disciplines in support of the institution. A committee has minimal start-up costs and supports alignment between the faculty and the administration.

DRAWBACKS. Turnover is the biggest challenge with committees, despite staggered terms. Term appointments are generally for three years and not renewable in most cases. Steep learning curves result, given that faculty members are not typically skilled in faculty development. Other challenges that stem from turnover include changing committee chairs (most chairs serve a one-year term), lack of consistent documentation, institutional memory, and committee member training.

Centers for Teaching and Learning

"Having a physical presence [on campus] has made a big difference."

–A director of a CTL

CTLs and associated support, such as teaching workshops and related resources, play an important role in faculty development in LACs. These centers can be particularly effective when their programming focuses on innovation rather than remediation of poor behaviors (Cook and Marincovich 2010). Ideally, these centers, particularly in the context of liberal arts and other small colleges, are one important way in which the strategic vision of the institution is implemented, and the faculty members are supported in honing their craft. For example, we agree with Michael Reder's assertion, "Just as faculty members are asked to be critical practitioners in their scholarly and creative endeavors, faculty development focused on teaching asks them to do the same with their teaching" (2010, 297).

Six of the thirteen GLCA institutions have dedicated CTLs (table 1.2). Interestingly, their budgets vary from $6,000 to $60,000 and support a range of activities including workshops, conference attendance, faculty travel for professional conferences, and brown-bag lunches. In terms of staffing, the CTL at Kenyon College has a full-time director, while Albion, Denison, DePauw, Kalamazoo, and Oberlin support their centers with faculty members who are released from teaching courses, receive a stipend, or both.

The allocation of physical space for CTLs is not the only way institutions provide resources for faculty development. The seven GLCA institutions that do not have on-campus centers for faculty development all offer comparable supports through other means. At Allegheny College, the associate provost responsible for faculty development also serves as the director for the Allegheny Gateway, a center that supports student, faculty, and staff programming that fosters intellectual enrichment, cross-cultural and global engagement, civic and social responsibility, ethical development, career exploration, and personal growth. Antioch College has a teaching and learning collaborative, a grassroots faculty group that meets for events related to T&L. Topics are selected by the faculty members and/or linked to themes covered in the quarterly faculty

TABLE 1.2
Centers for Teaching and Learning (CTLs)

	CTL	CTL annual budget	Budget use	CTL staff	Teaching load
Albion College	Yes	$10,000	Programming Faculty travel	Full-time faculty member (no course release; stipend only)	3-3
Allegheny College	No	$8,000	Workshops Travel Books and supplies	Associate Provost for Faculty Development or Director of Allegheny Gateway (same position currently)	3-3
Antioch College	No	~$6,000	Programming Books and resources Workshop	—	2-2-2
Denison University	Yes	$60,000	Workshops Onsite conferences Honorariums Brown-bag lunches Faculty travel Faculty stipends Mentoring seminars	Director of the CTL (member of the faculty, 1–1 course load during academic year)	3-2

	CTL	CTL annual budget	Budget use	CTL staff	Teaching load
DePauw University	Yes	$12,275	Roundtables Faculty forums Research colloquia Staff salary support	Faculty Development Coordinator	3-3
Earlham College	No	No dedicated budget	Academic year programming	T&L consultant (half-time, member of the faculty; two-year term)	3-3
Hope College	No	$16,000 (T&L) $2,000 (mentoring)	Outside speakers Books Food Workshops	Associate Dean for T&L (50/50 split between teaching and administrative responsibility; 12-month appointment) Shared admin asst.	3-3
Kalamazoo College	Yes	$35,000	Faculty stipends T&L grants Professional activities Related programming	Half-time coordinator	2-2-2
Oberlin College	Yes	$7,000–$10,000	Workshops Brown-bag lunches (four per term) Conference travel Guest speakers	Director of the CTL (member of the faculty, two course reduction during academic year)	4.5 per year, on average

(continued)

TABLE 1.2
Centers for Teaching and Learning (CTLs) (*continued*)

	CTL	CTL annual budget	Budget use	CTL staff	Teaching load
Ohio Wesleyan College	No	No dedicated budget	—	Supported through various committees	3-3
	CTL	CTL annual budget	Budget use	CTL staff	Teaching load
Wabash College	No	9,000	Workshops Travel Lunches	Coordinator of Faculty Development (member of the faculty; one course reduction per year)	3-3
College of Wooster	No	No dedicated budget	—	Supported by the Office of the Dean for Faculty Development	5.5 per year

Notes: Institutions with no CTL provide comparable support in other ways. Some cells are blank because related programming is supported in other ways, as discussed throughout the chapter.

development retreat organized by the Office of Academic Affairs. At Earlham College, faculty members are supported by a T&L consultant, which is a half-time rotating faculty position with a two-year term. The consultant supports faculty development through faculty consultations and academic year programming. This position has no formal budget, but the programming is supported and administered by the academic dean. Hope College supports T&L through efforts of the associate dean for teaching and learning, who has eight direct reports—including the director of academic computing, director of college writing, and the five staff members of the Academic Success Center. The associate dean also helps plan and organize much of the Pre-College Conference and the faculty mentoring program to support newly hired faculty members. Ohio Wesleyan University supports T&L through several related committees. At Wabash College, T&L support is facilitated by the coordinator of faculty development. The coordinator is given a reduction of one course in his or her teaching load and has access to funds to help support faculty travel to conferences about the scholarship of T&L, acquire related resources and materials, and supplement the activities of the T&L Committee. The Committee (which has a modest budget) works closely with the coordinator to support an annual faculty workshop in August and monthly teacher talk lunches. The College of Wooster supports T&L through the office of the dean for faculty development. Corresponding programming is supported through endowed funds, the faculty development fund, the faculty conference fund, and distinguished scholarship awards.

BENEFITS. CTLs are likely to become more prevalent to support faculty members at LACs and other small colleges, given their missions and emphasis on teaching. As one director of a CTL said during an interview, "I am thrilled we now have an actual center on campus. Having a physical presence has made all the difference." The GLCA schools offer programming throughout the academic year to support faculty as they seek to educate the students in their classrooms. Support, particularly for new faculty members, is paramount.

DRAWBACKS. Syllabi development workshops and microteaching workshops are effective faculty development supports, yet having a CTL does not mean learning is happening (Reder 2007). Although learning does happen in the classroom, that learning is only one component of the residential LAC education experience. Experiential learning, for example, occurs through volunteer activities under the direction of faculty members and through conversations with them in the quad. These are the experiences that dominate the four-year student experience in a GLCA (or comparable) institution, and thus CTLs need to appropriately support faculty members who play an essential role in these types of learning experiences. Given that this is the type of learning administrators and campus leaders advertise to help recruit (and retain) students, faculty members need to be supported beyond the traditional classroom learning activities.

Institutional Supports for Faculty Development

"There is a bias for funding towards junior faculty members."
–An associate professor in the natural sciences

GLCA institutions offer a variety of resources to support faculty members across their career stages. These resources can be divided into three categories: monetary support, nonmonetary support, and onboarding and orientation.

Monetary Supports

A small sum of money may make an important difference in faculty development when deployed effectively. Our work suggests that the most effective ways to use money are as travel funds, research grants, and start-up funds. Some institutions also fund summer research support, and two GLCA colleges provide stipends for faculty members to mentor early-career colleagues.

TRAVEL FUNDS. All of the GLCA institutions offer travel support for faculty members to engage in professional development. A few of the institutions (for example, Albion College) support travel to conferences only if the faculty member is on the program, whereas other institutions (such as Allegheny College) provide travel funds, at a reduced rate, to support conference attendance. Funding levels range from $1,000 to $2,000 for meetings in the United States and from $1,200 to $2,200 international conferences. Some of the institutions allow faculty members to apply for funds to attend a second conference during the same academic year, ranging from $1,000 to $1,800 (at Albion College and Wabash College, for example). Denison University and Kenyon College provide individual annual faculty development accounts for faculty members. At Denison, faculty members are granted $3,000 annually and are able to use those funds as needed within guidelines. Kenyon College provides each tenure-track faculty member with an individual faculty development account of $2,250 annually, and each faculty member may accrue up to a maximum of $6,750.

RESEARCH GRANTS. All of the GLCA institutions also have an internal grants program to support faculty research. As noted above, some of these programs are administered by a committee, such as Earlham College's Professional Development Committee and Oberlin College's Research and Development Committee, or by the person responsible for faculty development. Others are managed at the departmental level. All internal grants programs require faculty members to submit a proposal for review. Internal funds range from $1,700 to $5,000 during the academic year.

START-UP FUNDS. And all of the GLCA institutions provide start-up funds ranging from $3,000 to $8,000. Typically, the funds must be used within the first one to two years of a faculty member's employment at the college (Kalamazoo College is an exception). On occasion, those funds are larger, based on the faculty member's discipline (for example, to buy equipment in the sciences) and career stage (for example, to serve as a signing bonus). Start-up funds may be used for professional dues, computer hardware and software, research materials like a digital recorder, journal subscriptions, and professional development programming.

SUMMER SUPPORT. Ten of the GLCA institutions provide summer support for faculty each year. Almost all of this support is to facilitate the engagement of faculty members and students in undergraduate research. Summer support is awarded through a formal proposal review process, and stipends range from $1,500 to $5,000, on average. Kalamazoo and Antioch Colleges do not provide summer support, given they operate on a trimester and quarter system, respectively. And while Kenyon College does provide some summer support, it does not do so every year.

MENTOR STIPENDS. All of the GLCA institutions offer some type of formal mentoring program (which will be discussed in more detail in chapter 5), yet such supports are nearly all focused on early-career faculty. However, Allegheny and Hope Colleges are the only two institutions to provide stipends to their mentors.

Benefits and Drawbacks of Monetary Supports

BENEFITS. A diversified portfolio of monetary supports for faculty members provides more options for faculty members to get what they need to support their academic work. Also, having funds available throughout the academic year, including the summer, provides continuous support for faculty members to engage in scholarship individually or in collaboration with peers and students. Given that most funds are awarded through a proposal process, this provides an opportunity for peers—at least those on the committees that review such proposals—to learn more about what their colleagues are doing outside of the classroom.

DRAWBACKS. Our research shows that most monetary supports are targeted at early-career faculty members. In the words of one faculty member, "There is a bias for funding towards junior faculty members. And I get that—we want to see them get tenure. However, [there is] not a lot of support to get your agenda going again after supporting the college administratively for X amount of time." Start-up funds benefit newly hired faculty members, but providing such funds only to them neglects the needs of mid- and late-career faculty members.

Nonmonetary Supports

Academic leaders also provide nonmonetary support for faculty development, which is an important aspect of the institutional resources devoted to faculty development. The most effective deployment of these resources is in the form of sabbaticals, formal mentoring programs, workshops, and brown-bag lunches. Some institutions also used pretenure course release and administrative support for pursuing external funding for research activity.

SABBATICALS. All thirteen GLCA institutions have a sabbatical program that operates on a six- to seven-year rotation. All thirteen require faculty members to apply for a sabbatical. Several of the colleges have a rigorous review process in which a faculty member could be denied a sabbatical, though this is rare. In addition, faculty members must submit a summary of their sabbatical's outcomes when they return to campus the following semester.

FORMAL MENTORING PROGRAM. All thirteen institutions also offer a formal mentoring program for early-career faculty. Mentors either volunteer or are invited to join the program by the academic dean, provost, or associate provost who administers it. The formal mentoring programs range from covering just the first year of employment for an early-career faculty member to extending through his or her interim review after three years. Hope College created a mentoring program called Continuum to help faculty members in their third and fourth years with the promotion and tenure process. This is in addition to the college's Initium program, which focuses on first- and second-year faculty members.

WORKSHOPS AND BROWN-BAG LUNCHES. And all thirteen institutions offer a series of workshops or brown-bag lunches related to T&L, scholarship, and critical issues in the faculty career. Some notable examples include Kalamazoo College's annual Teaching and Learning Workshop for new faculty members and its topic-specific brown-bag lunches, such as the one called "Managing Hot Moments in Class." Kalamazoo also has a "Great Ideas for Teaching" webpage, where individuals post articles and other support resources for faculty members. Denison University has an Early Career Faculty Learning Community, which focuses on faculty members in their second year through their tenure review year. This program supports monthly meetings, common readings and discussions, and individual support as early-career faculty members develop and implement a new teaching activity or strategy. Albion College offers "What Matters to Me and Why" dinners, which are open to faculty and staff members and students. These events feature a speaker affiliated with the college and encourage a dialogue about topics and issues important to the campus and surrounding community.

GRANT WRITING SUPPORT. Ten of the GLCA institutions have a full-time position dedicated to providing support to faculty members seeking external funding.

PRETENURE COURSE RELEASE. Ten of the GLCA institutions support a pretenure course release. Typically such a release is available the year after interim review at the institution. Course releases range from a reduction in the teaching load by one course to a full semester release from teaching (which in most cases would mean a three-course reduction in a given academic year). In the GLCA tenure decisions are most commonly made during a faculty member's sixth year at the institution, with a interim review during the third year, at the assistant professor level. The only three institutions that do not offer a pretenure course release are Antioch College, Wabash College, and the College of Wooster.

Benefits and Drawbacks of Nonmonetary Supports

BENEFITS. While monetary supports aid faculty members in their work, so do nonmonetary supports. One of the greatest nonmonetary supports that administrators and other campus leaders can provide to their faculty members is time—provided through pretenure course release and sabbaticals. We recommend the proposal process if it allows for developmental feedback on both the proposal and the postsabbatical report. This is an excellent opportunity for the institution to assess alignment between institutional and individual outcomes.

DRAWBACKS. All of the GLCA institutions have a mentoring program, but only Allegheny and Hope Colleges provide stipends to mentors. Mentoring takes time away from other academic work, and mentors should be rewarded and acknowledged appropriately. Institution-supported mentoring needs to be accompanied by mentor training and postmentoring program assessments related to the achievement of intended outcomes as well as insights into overall satisfaction with engagement in the mentorship for the mentor and protégé (for more details, see chapter 5). In our conversations with deans and provosts, we learned that little to no formal training or assessment is conducted in relation to formal mentoring programs, which means that an opportunity to make critical connections between institutional and individual outcomes is being missed.

Onboarding and Orientation

Onboarding, the adjustment period during which a new employee learns what social and performance standards he or she is expected to meet, is one of the most important activities for an educational institution to invest in newly hired faculty members. Most institutions socialize their new faculty members through a faculty orientation. Orientation, the first event in an ongoing onboarding effort, is of particular importance since new faculty members need to balance institutional and departmental demands, while learning critical policies and processes to enact the various and sometimes conflicting roles they play on a daily basis. All thirteen GLCA institutions offer orientation programs for new faculty members. The programs range in length from half a day (at the College of Wooster) to three weeks (at Antioch College). Topics addressed include institutional infrastructure, students, faculty development supports (such as those for teaching and scholarship), and human resources issues. We provide some specific examples from the GLCA institutions below.

As noted, at Antioch College orientation is a three-week period that includes multiple workshops about the history and mission of the college, an update on accreditation status and progression through the accreditation process, an explanation of the curriculum, a discussion of key initiatives for the coming academic year, and more role-specific information about such topics as syllabus development, assessment, student advising, and degree audit completion. The three-week period culminates with a town and gown reception for new and retired faculty members and community contacts. At Wabash College, new faculty members are given a robust orientation program that lasts four days. New faculty members are introduced to the culture of the college, important offices, and corresponding supports. Sessions include learning about the student body, syllabus construction, preparation for the first day, and the community. Albion College has a one-day orientation for new faculty members. Much like the other GLCA schools, Albion provides information about the mission and vision of the college and an introduction to the surrounding community. Senior colleagues who have received awards such as teacher or Phi Beta Kappa scholar of the year share their experiences with new faculty members and offer guidance on managing careers and accessing more focused faculty development supports on syllabus creation and classroom management, for example.

All GLCA institutions offer onboarding activities to support new and early-career faculty members, as administrators seek to socialize and retain talented faculty members. These activities include formal mentoring programs, workshop series throughout the first year (and in some cases, the second year as well), and brown-bag lunches. Onboarding can be an important way to engage early-career faculty in the academic and campus community. While most onboarding efforts focus on retention, they can also be developmental in nature, which we advocate. Below we feature some exemplary onboarding programs.

Denison University has a three-year early-career mentoring program, which focuses on teaching, service, and scholarship. Denison also has a first-year faculty learning community, administered by the CTL, and an early-career learning community, which is a yearlong course for second- and third-year faculty members administered by the CTL. At Hope College, all new faculty members participate in the Initium program, which consists of a three-day workshop before the beginning of the fall semester, two ninety-minute meetings a month through the first year, a one-day midyear retreat, and a one-on-one faculty mentoring program that begins in the second semester and continues for two more years (until the end of the third year). To help faculty members manage their new responsibilities, they have a course reduction each semester in the first year. The College of Wooster organizes regular meetings for new faculty members (for example, once a week for the first six weeks of the term), a mentoring program for new faculty members, a peer teaching network program, a course design workshop at the end of the year, and monthly brown-bag lunches in series called "Teaching Matters" and "Research Matters". Kenyon College offers topic-specific monthly events for new faculty members and provides all of them with a three-member mentoring committee for their first two years.

BENEFITS. A comprehensive onboarding program including orientation allows administrators and other campus leaders to stay in touch and be engaged with new faculty members. Onboarding socializes new faculty members to the institutional culture and creates a cohort of faculty members who participate at the same time. Early establishment of networks of support, both professional and personal, may provide psychosocial and career benefits as faculty members navigate the vagaries of the tenure and promotion process as well as the unwritten rules of campus life.

DRAWBACKS. While onboarding is a critical organizational tool, most efforts focus only on newly hired faculty members. Institutional missions rarely change, but visions and strategic initiatives do. Given changes in leadership and institutional priorities, it makes sense to engage in onboarding-type efforts to reengage and resocialize all faculty members throughout their careers. Typical onboarding does not do this.

Institutional Evaluations of Faculty Development

Evaluation and assessment are increasingly part of academic life. While faculty members may groan when they hear these terms (often because of poorly implemented or communicated strategies), leaders must engage in strategic assessments. We now take a brief look at faculty evaluation strategies at the GLCA institutions. We focus on annual reports and interim reports at the level of the individual faculty member. These institutional activities provide additional insights into the priority and visibility of faculty development.

As shown in table 1.3, Denison University and Earlham College are the only two institutions without traditional annual reports. At Denison, however, such evaluative information is gathered and submitted by academic departments to the annual university fact book. Each faculty member's teaching, scholarship, and service is reviewed every three years. At Earlham College, the academic dean (who is also vice president for academic affairs) receives an annual activity report from all faculty members in January, covering the preceding calendar year. Earlham College does not have annual reports from departments.

For the GLCA institutions that do have an annual review process, reviews are submitted to the provost or academic dean. At DePauw University, for example, untenured faculty members send annual reports to the Office of Academic Affairs, and these are included in faculty members' personnel file where they undergo interim reviews and are considered for tenure. In other years, the

TABLE 1.3

Evaluations of Faculty Professional Development

	Annual reports	Interim reports
Albion College	Yes	No
Allegheny College	Yes	No
Antioch College	Yes	No
Denison University	No	No
DePauw University	Yes	Yes
Earlham College	No	No
Hope College	Yes	No
Kalamazoo College	Yes	No
Kenyon College	Yes	No
Oberlin College	Yes	No
Ohio Wesleyan College	Yes	No
Wabash College	Yes	Yes
College of Wooster	Yes	Yes

annual reviews are examined by the dean of the faculty and the vice president for academic affairs. After receiving tenure, faculty members provide their updated curriculum vitae each year, documents that are added to their personnel files and reviewed by the dean of the faculty and the vice president for academic affairs. At Hope College, every department chair writes an annual report about teaching, as well as many other things, which goes to the appropriate divisional dean and provost. Albion College follows a similar process: department chairs submit a yearly evaluation on each departmental faculty member, and each department undergoes program review on a three-year rotational basis (including data on faculty development). At Kalamazoo College, faculty members provide individual reports, called professional updates, to the provost, reporting on their teaching and advising, service to the college, and professional activities and achievements. The provost and associate provosts at Kenyon College review similar annual reports. In addition, individual faculty members' teaching evaluations are reviewed by their mentoring committees and the provost and the Tenure and Promotion Committee during reviews. The review process at Allegheny College consists of each faculty member submitting an annual report to the department chair and the provost. These reports are reviewed and used to assess merit. Given the lack of traditional departments at Antioch College, there are no reporting requirements or structure. However, scheduling and assessment reports are submitted to (and reviewed) by the associate dean.

There are also annual or biannual review processes for individual faculty members. At Wabash College, all faculty members produce an annual activity report that discusses their teaching, research, and service. The report is reviewed by the department chair, who writes an annual salary letter. The report and letter are the subject of a discussion with the division chair, and subsequently the personnel committee (consisting of the dean of the college and three division chairs) reviews all annual reports. Finally, at the College of Wooster, faculty members also complete annual reports on their work, which are submitted to the provost's office and reviewed by the promotion and tenure committee. Only three of the GLCA institutions (DePauw University, Wabash College, and the College of Wooster) have institutionwide interim reviews. All thirteen institutions have interim reviews for individual early-career faculty members on the tenure track.

What Can I Do?

The effectiveness of faculty professional development depends on the proper allocation of resources to support it and academic work. Administrators, faculty members, and faculty developers must consider what are the best sources and models of investing in faculty success at their institutions. Examining the models of faculty development at the GLCA schools suggests possible steps to take. To help you reflect on the current faculty development portfolio at your institution, as well as on your own role in shaping future strategies for supporting faculty success and satisfaction, we return to the three main areas of structures, supports, and evaluations.

We draw on the alignment framework for faculty development in LACs to organize this section of the chapter, using its structure of: vertical alignment (links between the organization's strategies overall and its people-management strategy), horizontal alignment (individual human resource policy areas), and implementation (action or practice).

Advancing Faculty Work through Institutional Structures

Within the GLCA, we found three structural approaches to assigning responsibility for faculty development: administrative positions, faculty committees, and CTLs.

ADMINISTRATIVE POSITIONS. There are three categories of administrative positions dedicated to faculty development: full-time permanent positions, full-time renewable positions, and half-time positions. Ask the following questions to help stakeholders determine if there is vertical alignment in your institution's approaches to faculty development:

1. How does your institutional mission align with faculty development?
2. How does the institutional vision align with faculty development?
3. How does the institutional strategic plan align with faculty development?
4. What is the vision for faculty development programming at the institution? How does that vision align with current (and future) institutional initiatives?

The next set of questions may help leaders and stakeholders pursue horizontal alignment in institutional approaches to faculty development, working toward a coherent and consistent approach that permeates all activities and policies across functional areas (Gratton and Truss 2003). Consider asking these questions:

1. What skills and experience are needed by the person responsible for faculty development?
2. What kinds of supports (for example, training, money, and authority) do we provide to the individual(s) responsible for faculty development?
3. How is ongoing professional development for the individual(s) encouraged?

Having a full-time permanent position responsible for faculty development not only sends a signal, but it also provides both continuity and clarity about who is responsible for supporting faculty members in their work. Faculty members expressed frustration over the presence of seemingly disparate committees, offices, and positions tasked with faculty development, and they reported being unsure about who provided specific areas of support. However, we realize that it may not be possible to have a full-time permanent position for faculty development, particularly at smaller institutions. It is not advisable to make faculty development part of the academic dean's portfolio, given the range of other responsibilities of this person. Instead, we recommend having a dean or associate dean for faculty development. If that is not possible, we suggest giving the responsibility for faculty development to two people in full-time renewable positions. One person would focus on T&L programming, and the other would focus on supporting scholarship—which would mean that there would be individuals specifically responsible for supporting faculty members in these areas.

Take a lesson from human resources. Faculty development efforts that are truly strategic and focused on innovation rather than remediation (Cook and Marincovich 2010) should draw on the tenets of succession planning. Steve Bates (2015) offered three critical questions that all organizational leaders should ask when planning for the next leader to assume a critical campus position:

1. Who could step in today in an emergency?
2. Who might be ready in one to five years?
3. Who might be a good fit in five or more years?

Faculty members are the key human resource of any college, and therefore plans to support them need to be at the forefront of all leadership conversations. Should whoever is responsible for faculty development suffer a personal or professional hardship, who will step in to manage that portfolio? If administrators and other campus leaders are unable to answer that question, that should raise a red flag.

The last two questions are where human resources and the notion of alignment can add value by helping you to think about future needs. In nearly all of our conversations with deans and presidents in the GLCA, the topics of preparing the next generation of global leaders dominated strategic planning efforts.

We asked ourselves why such efforts aren't replicated or considered at the faculty level. If it's the faculty members who deliver the educational experience that prepares students to be global leaders, then why aren't administrators and other campus leaders thinking about what kinds of supports are needed to prepare the faculty leaders of 2020, 2025, and 2030? If the answer is "I don't know" to the last two questions, it's time to start thinking about them in a very deliberate and strategic way and identifying faculty members who—with the appropriate training and supports—could fill such positions within the desired timeframes.

FACULTY COMMITTEES. The committee structure is an effective component of faculty development programming, given the importance of faculty governance and engagement in institutional decision making. However, committees can be ineffective due to the inconsistency inherent in the inevitable turnover of their memberships. Here, we offer vertical alignment questions to support maximum institutional benefit from the committee structure:

1. What committees currently support faculty development?
2. Are all the facets of academic work addressed by these committees?
3. Does our institution even have knowledge management systems to support committee work?
4. Are we effectively using knowledge management systems to streamline committee initiatives and other efforts?

As administrators and other campus leaders seek to support the development of committee members and the efficiency of the committee structure, the questions below will support horizontal alignment:

1. What kinds of training do we provide to committee members, particularly committee chairs?
2. Are all faculty members aware of the committees that support faculty development, their charges, and how to engage with the committees?

We recommend that institutions invest in knowledge management systems to ensure the achievement of organizational and individual outcomes. We offer this recommendation based on our conversations with deans and the frustrations expressed by faculty members about the lack of consistency and clarity related to the committee structure. Such systems support decision-making capabilities by organizing overwhelming amounts of information and clarifying what is and is not important. Knowledge management systems support organizational (and individual) learning by helping institutions routinize the learning process, which is of particular importance when the composition of a committee changes annually. Knowledge management systems help stimulate cultural change and innovation through the identification of trends, the exchange of ideas, and open dialogue. Open dialogue is important internally to the committees, but it also creates a conduit for communication between committees and the administration (particularly with administrators who are not part of a given committee). Lastly, knowledge management systems support consistency among committee members.

Although knowledge management systems help organize critical information and support the notion of a learning organization, they are ineffective if people are not trained how to use them. We suggest adapting the notion of interrater reliability from statistical analyses, which refers to the level of agreement among raters, when developing training. Specifically, we suggest making committee training part of the faculty retreat or welcome back that kicks off the academic year. Such training could be part of the afternoon activities. All members of any given standing committee might meet for two hours to review the primary charge of the committee, any known tasks for the coming academic year, and examples of the committee's actions in the previous year. Engaging in such activities would set the tone for the academic year, ensure that all members of the committee were clear about their responsibilities, and—through the discussion of previous actions—allow the members to maintain a degree of consistency across years and as committee membership changes. And when we say all members should attend this two-hour meeting, we mean new committee members but also those who are leaving the committee, who could provide insights into previous actions. Those individuals likely wouldn't need to be present for the entire meeting but could be there for some part of it as they pass the torch.

CENTERS FOR TEACHING AND LEARNING. We believe that CTLs can be vitally important to the mission of LACs and other small colleges, if administrators and other campus leaders are willing to support them by investing in physical space, human resources (for example, a full-time director, whether permanent or renewable), and finances (such as funds to support programming). We focus our attention on the big-picture view of the role CTLs can and should play at these colleges by offering the following questions, which are aimed at achieving greater vertical alignment with this critical resource:

1. Is our CTL a source of competitive advantage for our institution?
2. Is the CTL's mission aligned with the institution's mission?
3. How does CTL programming and related supports help us attract and retain a talented and diverse faculty body across the ranks?
4. Does CTL programming support the relationship between teaching and research?

We also believe that CTLs can be a way to rejuvenate faculty members and allow them to build communities. In that spirit, the following questions help ensure horizontal alignment:

1. Are program assessments focused on behaviors rather than simple measures of satisfaction?
2. Does our CTL programming support faculty engagement in the life of the college?

3. Does it help faculty members understand and support their development as aligned with individual goals?

We recommend investing in a CTL by providing a physical space in which faculty members can interact around issues of T&L. We suggest this based on insights gleaned from conversations with deans. At institutions with an actual, physical center, we heard about its symbolic importance for faculty members, as it serves as a safe space in which teaching practices can be tested, programming can be supported, and resources made available. The lack of such a space sends a message to faculty members about the priority (or lack thereof) of such supports. To that end, we also suggest investing in at least a full-time renewable position to support the CTL and manage associated programming. Having a half-time faculty appointment does not allow this person to focus on T&L to the level that is needed, particularly at LACs and other small colleges.

IT IS ALSO IMPORTANT TO FOCUS ON AND SUPPORT BEHAVIORS. Presidents, provosts, and academic deans spend a great deal of time, energy, and money to support student learning and to assess academic experiences and connect them to outcomes at the student level, yet such efforts are not matched at the faculty level. A true learning organization, one focused on organizational and individual thriving, realizes the importance of investing in its human capital. While assessing faculty members' satisfaction with CTL programming is important, we believe that such programming needs to focus on supporting behavior changes. For example, programming geared toward leadership development at the level of midcareer faculty members might include creating an individualized leadership development plan. Six months later, the CTL staff could engage participating faculty members in an assessment to determine if the plan milestones were met or if participants assumed informal or formal leadership roles on their campus as a result of participation.

Advancing Your Institution through Supports

The biggest disconnect we consistently saw was between what is valued—or at least what campus leaders say is valued through promotion and tenure (P&T) assessments—and the institution's investment in corresponding supports. In other words, there is an opportunity for campus leaders to better align their strategies by "putting their money where their mouth is." Engaging more frequently in a candid review of what is valued and rewarded on campus might help leaders determine if faculty members have the supports they need to be successful in those areas. We offer the questions below with the goal of achieving vertical alignment between institutional priorities and faculty member supports:

1. Do you offer a variety of monetary and other supports and incentives that line up with the institutional mission (for example, developing leaders and fostering community engagement)?
2. Do you regularly assess institutional goals and faculty development programming to ensure that the programming aligns with changing goals and institutional vision?
3. Do staff members from Institutional Advancement or Development work to engage alumni and other donors in supporting faculty development programming as part of their fund-raising goals?

At the individual level,

1. Are expectations for each career stage clearly articulated? Do those expectations correspond with a diversified portfolio of available supports?
2. Do the available supports cover the primary areas in which faculty members regularly engage (such as teaching, scholarship, advising, mentoring, and service), and are those supports specific to different career stages?

Recommendations for Using Monetary And Nonmonetary Supports

CREATE AWARENESS. Monetary and nonmonetary supports are only helpful if faculty members are aware of their availability. E-mails from the office of the academic dean informing faculty members of such supports does not seem to be enough. Engaging faculty members directly in supporting activities like brown bag lunches sets an example for them to apply for available research grants. For example, the chair of the internal grants committee could talk about the proposal guidelines, the review and revision process, and details about funds. Common mistakes in applying for a grant, a review of projects supported in the past, and their outcomes could be discussed.

REDUCE ROADBLOCKS. We are strong advocates of tying the receipt of monetary and nonmonetary supports to developmental opportunities. It is simply good stewardship to expect faculty members to submit proposals that include explanations of how they plan to use the requested funds or a sabbatical, as well as a report on the outcomes afterward. However, it may be possible to eliminate or reduce roadblocks to accessing such funds. Examine carefully and annually, together with faculty members, policies and procedures related to accessing resources. At some of the GLCA schools, for example, research grants could not be used as salary support even when funds were requested to support the development of a new course or to engage in interdisciplinary research with a faculty colleague in the summer. Salary support through stipends appeared to be permissible when connected to summer research experiences with students. We believe that interdisciplinary work with colleagues or developing a new course may be worthy of a salary stipend, depending on the nature of the proposed project. We also read proposal guidelines from the GLCA institutions and discovered instances where faculty members could not apply for funds related to a line of research that had been supported in the past. We found this surprising, especially for faculty members engaged in longitudinal research. Such policies may be counterproductive and stifle faculty work.

ONBOARDING AND ORIENTATION. A comprehensive orientation and an ongoing onboarding effort are essential. Such an effort requires a dedicated plan, training, and engaged team to involve new faculty members from day one. We offer the following questions to help provide a more comprehensive and strategic onboarding effort that serves as a conduit for supporting and communicating institutional priorities and values (vertical alignment):

1. How, if at all, do onboarding efforts align with the institution's mission and strategic vision?
2. What types of learning experiences are wanted for students, and are corresponding onboarding supports available to ensure that faculty members are equipped to provide those experiences?
3. Are onboarding efforts progressive in nature? If not, what can be done to create such a progression?
4. Do onboarding efforts enable faculty members to navigate the college system effectively?
5. Are onboarding efforts reevaluated and reenvisioned as part of strategic planning processes and updated accordingly?

Onboarding efforts are, in effect, the first faculty development programming that new faculty members engage in. The programming sets the tone for career development, as campus leaders and administrators seek to build a solid professional development foundation through horizontal alignment.

1. Are you aware of primary offices, committees, and centers that support faculty development work on campus?
2. How do existing onboarding efforts help lay a solid foundation for teaching, scholarship, and service?

Next we offer specific onboarding programming recommendations to support the development of a more comprehensive and strategic onboarding effort.

Orientation is often newly hired faculty members' first formal introduction to the institution, the senior colleagues who participate in the orientation, and the importance of faculty development to the college's overall life.

Orientation needs to address common human resources areas such as the faculty handbook, benefits, and employment expectations. Orientation should also include sample syllabi development, advising tips, advice on how to manage the first year, a tour of campus, an overview of how to access key faculty resources (such as internal grants), and a session with upperclassmen at which insights into student expectations are shared. Equally important, orientation is the time to orient new faculty to the invisible rules by connecting them with senior faculty members and mentors to learn about how "things really work around here."

Most faculty members do not have training or experience in the behind-the-scenes workings of a college. Understanding the operating budget or endowment investments, for example, helps faculty members connect the dots across all major offices, initiatives, and strategic decisions. We recommend hosting topic-specific workshops such as introductions to finance, admissions, and institutional advancement as a means of featuring important offices (and functions) on campus, and of illustrating the types of programming and challenges managed by these offices. Our faculty informants talked about wanting to learn more about the institutions in which they worked as a way to understand "the bigger picture."

For teaching and learning to be viewed as a strategic imperative, we suggest that T&L be envisioned, implemented, and described as an important component of the overall faculty development portfolio. That would signal the important role of T&L, rather than presenting it as something separate that a center supports, for example. Throughout our interviews with faculty members and campus leaders, we heard that while teaching is of the utmost importance, scholarship is becoming increasingly important and critical to earning tenure and promotion. Given that trend, we suggest a conversation between tenure-track faculty members and those key individuals or committees charged with personnel matters to discuss expectations related to scholarship as well as a discussion of available resources that support it. Senior faculty members who have been successful at managing teaching and scholarship should be involved in the session, as they could offer tips or advice to new faculty members on strategies for succeeding in both areas.

P&T procedures and guidelines create a lot of anxiety for faculty members, and we might argue that much of it is unnecessary. We encourage administrators and other campus leaders to organize sessions related to organizing and preparing P&T materials. For example, an initial discussion of P&T could be facilitated by the current or past chair of the personnel committee. During this session, big-picture ideas could be shared, organizational tips offered, procedural steps explained, and sample materials disseminated. Given differences between work in the natural sciences and that in the social sciences, for example, subsequent sessions could be more tailored, perhaps to specific divisions, and more details could be shared about what constitutes good teaching, scholarship, and community engagement. The more uncertainty that can be removed from this process, the greater the likelihood of supporting faculty members' successful navigation of the P&T process.

Advancing Your Institution through Evaluations

Annual and Interim Reports

Regardless of how strong or diverse your faculty development portfolio is, it will fail if you are not consistently collecting and using data on the outcomes of these efforts to communicate your and faculty members' successes internally and externally. Furthermore, you are missing opportunities to expand and improve on existing efforts and to identify those members of the faculty who can be advocates and future leaders (through succession planning) of faculty development. Keeping these ideas in mind, we suggest you ask these questions to help achieve vertical alignment:

1. Do we have a streamlined evaluation system related to faculty development? Or is there redundancy in the system?
2. What kind of knowledge management system is in place to capture data on faculty development outcomes?
3. Are we investing as much in mechanisms to collect data on faculty members' outcomes as we are in mechanisms to collect such data for students?
4. Do all main offices on campus have appropriate access to faculty outcomes data? For example, can the development office use it to share faculty members' work with possible donors?

The following questions are intended to help you think about how the evaluation process at your institution supports career development there (horizontal alignment):

1. How, if at all, is collected information used to support collective and individual faculty development programming?
2. Does our current system account for divisional and disciplinary differences in teaching, scholarship, and service?
3. How, if at all, does current faculty development programming align with faculty handbook language in terms of roles and responsibilities and expected performance?

Recommendations

Although we focused predominantly on annual reports, since very few of the GLCA institutions employ interim reviews beyond the early-career stage, we suggest that interim reviews might play a more developmental role beyond that stage. Much as early-career faculty members engage in an interim review on the path to tenure, we argue that such a review might benefit those faculty members working toward promotion to full professor. Our mid-career faculty participants, for example, talked about how such a process would help them be clear about what is expected for promotion and serve as an opportunity to prepare materials in an ongoing fashion. A process such as the one we suggest here would help create clear milestones for those aspiring faculty members to work toward.

Conclusion

Faculty development strategies in LACs need to equip faculty members with the knowledge, skills, and resources to contribute to the fulfillment of the institutional mission and the achievement of student learning goals, as well as success and satisfaction in academic careers in the liberal arts. In this chapter, we provided an overview of faculty development structures, supports, and evaluations within one consortium of LACs. By describing and comparing the faculty development models of these thirteen institutions, we identified trends in institutional approaches to supporting faculty work. In spite of institution-specific idiosyncrasies, we found certain common themes in these approaches. We applaud these institutions for their current efforts, but we see many missed opportunities to develop a faculty development portfolio that aligns institutional and individual outcomes.

2

Academic Departments

Rachel, a newly minted PhD, was delighted yet surprised to receive an offer of a tenure-track position at a liberal arts college (LAC). During her job interview, she had felt unprepared to answer questions about pedagogy, student diversity, and teaching with technology. In addition, one search committee member had made a comment about her research not being relevant to departmental needs.

She consulted with her mentor and advisor, who encouraged her to negotiate for a reduced teaching load. The hiring dean, however, noted that the department had postponed this faculty search for several years due to unanticipated budgetary constraints. In addition, the dean noted she would already be short one full-time person, as one faculty member would be on paternity leave in the fall semester and another would be on sabbatical in the spring semester. The dean observed that she really wanted Rachel to join the faculty but needed her to teach at least seven courses a year.

Relieved that her job search was over, Rachel accepted the position. At last she would fulfill her dream of being a professor, she thought. She looked forward to the opportunity to support other students as she herself had been mentored as an undergraduate.

She soon found herself being toasted by her colleagues at her annual disciplinary conference, although she could tell that some were a little jealous about her landing a position fresh out of graduate school. A few declared that her research agenda was dead in the water, and that she shouldn't expect institutional support for her scholarship.

Others told tales about colleagues in LACs who had received merciless critiques of their teaching in student evaluations but assured her that would never happen to her. One friend shared a cautionary word: "I don't know anyone in your department, but I have a buddy in the humanities at that college. From what she says, you'd better *watch your back at that place." Elation gave way to self-doubt as Rachel began to wonder what she would have to report at the next year's conference.*

Hearing about experiences like Rachel's led us to ponder three questions. First, what is the structure and role of the academic department in LACs? Second, how does the departmental environment shape faculty experiences in LACs? And finally, what are the opportunities for faculty support and development related to that departmental context? In this chapter, we explore whether faculty members receive the information, resources, and support they need to engage in their departmental roles successfully, and we show how faculty members spend their time at work

Achieving Strong Vertical Alignment

Vertical alignment is present when the policies, practices, and strategies for supporting faculty members are aligned with the overall mission and vision of the college and the priorities of its administrators. Being committed to strongly supporting academic departments is an opportunity for an institution to fulfill its mission. Ideally, both the institution and the department are informed about and prepared to support faculty work. In their comprehensive study of faculty work, Robert Blackburn and Janet Lawrence (1995) investigated whether there was congruence between administrative and faculty views of the changing higher education climate as it relates to faculty work. The faculty members we surveyed were much less likely than administrators to believe that institutional resources were shared equally across departments and units. In particular, faculty members believed that they had much less influence in departmental matters than administrators believed they did. Administrators may overestimate their knowledge of faculty needs, which at times is incongruent with faculty members' perspectives. And administrators whose views differ from those of the faculty may not try to understand the realities of faculty work at the ground level within departmental contexts, which leads to misinformed decisions about departmental priorities, policies, and resources. When institutional supports for faculty work are lacking, departments have some ability to compensate and provide local support. But when both the institution and the department fail to support faculty work effectively, it is challenging for faculty members to obtain the guidance and resources they need.

Departmental Characteristics

"At my prior university, teaching was viewed by the department as a whole as something that had to be done—a little bit like housework. At this college, it's different. The reason we're here is to teach undergraduates. We also do research, and scholarship is important. But the main thing people are excited about is the courses they're teaching and the students they're working with."

—A professor in the natural sciences

Having an understanding of the academic department is required to understand faculty development activities and to assess the alignment between institutional efforts and faculty needs. Scholars (for example, Blackburn and Lawrence 1995) have emphasized the importance of context—institutional, disciplinary, and departmental—in understanding academic work. Through the collaborative efforts of its chair and faculty members, the academic department plays a central role in the faculty experience in postsecondary institutions (Hearn and Anderson 2002; Hendrickson, Lane, Harris, and Dorman 2013). The department constitutes the day-to-day context of faculty work and is an important location for influencing what Blackburn and Lawrence (1995) refer to as the environmental conditions that help motivate faculty work.

The department is particularly important in LACs in ways that it may not be at other types of institutions. At LACs, faculty members' main responsibilities are to their students through formal tasks such as teaching and advising and informal ones such as mentoring and supporting. Departments are the institutional subunits that most directly organize faculty teaching, research, and service (Carpenter-Hubin and Snover 2013). One of the hallmarks of LACs is their attention to the student experience, through low student-faculty ratios (on average, 11:1 across the Great Lakes Colleges Association [GLCA]), small class sizes, and close relationships of students with instructors and advisors.

Table 2.1 provides an overview of the key characteristics of the departments we studied and helps us begin to think about the departmental context of academic work. Individual faculty members' characteristics and experiences are of course a critical component of departmental experiences (see chapter 3). LAC departments are typically quite small. On average, they have five to seven full-time faculty members; some have as few as one, and some have around ten. Within each department, the faculty may include professors with dual appointments or half-time appointments, non-tenure-track (NTT) instructors or lecturers, and others.

TABLE 2.1

Key Characteristics of Great Lakes Colleges Association (GLCA) Institutions

	Students	FTE faculty members	Student-faculty ratio	Teaching load	Departments
Albion College	1,360	106	11:1	6.0	23
Allegheny College	1,930	171	11:1	6.0	8
Antioch College	270	38	7:1	6.0	NA
Denison University	2,150	233	9:1	5.0	46
DePauw University	2,264	227	10:1	6.0	21
Earlham College	1,019	110	10:1	6.0	47
Hope College	3,455	246	13:1	6.0	29
Kalamazoo College	1,443	103	13:1	6.0	39
Kenyon College	1,651	159	10:1	6.0	18
Oberlin College	2,961	302	9:1	4.5	50
Ohio Wesleyan University	1,675	146	11:1	6.0	33
Wabash College	868	97	10:1	6.0	34
The College of Wooster	2,058	171	11:1	5.5	50
Combined	23,104	2,109	NA	NA	398

Notes: Teaching load is per academic year. Figures included in this table are based on self-reported figures as noted on institutional websites. FTE is full-time equivalent. NA is not available.

About 34 percent of the departments are in the natural sciences, 29 percent in the humanities, 26 percent in the social sciences, about 6 percent in the fine arts, and about 5 percent included faculty members with dual appointments across disciplines. For the 360 faculty participants who indicated their department, the responses represented thirty-six different departments, and 6 of the participants worked in departments not listed in the survey response options because of idiosyncratic institution-specific areas of study.

The structuring of academic work and the allocation of resources are two important functions served by departments in LACs. A closer examination of the academic department in LACs reveals that it provides an organizing context and resources for faculty teaching, research, and service; an organizational culture based on policies, colleagueship, and leadership; and a clearer understanding of faculty development needs and strategies.

Departmental Components: Teaching, Research, and Service

"Well, I think the teaching load is really heavy. The student demands are high, which is okay. I think there's a huge amount of service. So between the service and the large teaching load, it can be very hard to do research."

–A professor in the humanities

We were curious about the specific ways in which departmental contexts influence faculty work in LACs. The fact is that, regardless of challenges or characteristics, the work must get done. Thus, we examined the time faculty members in LACs invested in fulfilling department-specific responsibilities to see how much time was devoted to the three main components typically used to structure academic work: teaching, research, and service. It is useful to consider activities that don't fall neatly into one of those three categories, such as time spent chatting with colleagues about upcoming accreditation visits or commiserating with a peer about grading over coffee or a cocktail. Therefore, we wanted to know how faculty members spent time informally and socially that was related to cultivating a sense of collaboration and community, as well as time spent on tasks directly related to fulfilling their professional responsibilities to the institution and department.

As one might expect, faculty members in LACs spend a lot of time on department-based activities such as advising, teaching, and committee work and other service. Figure 2.1 summarizes the average time our respondents reported spending on tasks per week as organized by teaching, research, service activities, and collegial interactions, as indicated by column shading. These time allocations follow a long-established pattern of faculty work in LACs.

The majority of faculty time is spent teaching and working with students. Efforts to support the department and its students add up to about thirty-two hours per week, on average much more than time spent on research, scholarship, and service combined. Next, we explore how faculty members fulfill their departmental responsibilities for teaching, research, service, and that fourth category that ties everything else together—colleagueship.

Teaching, Preparing, Grading, and Advising

It is primarily within the department that faculty members fulfill their teaching load requirements. Full-time faculty members in most of the colleges we studied had teaching loads of six courses per academic year. In other words, faculty members typically taught three courses each fall and spring semester. As figure 2.1 shows, faculty members spent an average of nine hours a week teaching, with another sixteen hours spent on teaching-related tasks such as preparing to teach, grading, and course development. We considered advising to be a teaching-related task. Faculty members spent five hours a week advising students and an additional two and a half hours supervising undergraduate research. As noted above, most LACs have a teaching load of six courses a year, which is intended to take up 60 percent of a faculty member's time. Yet we found that about 80 percent of that time (thirty-two and a half hours out of a forty-hour work week) was actually devoted to teaching and teaching-related activities.

Given the small department sizes and high priority placed on teaching at LACs, faculty members invest an inordinate amount of time in managing, preparing for, and implementing this component of academic work. As one study participant said of his institution, "Here, we would say that teaching is 60 percent of our job, but realistically, if it weren't for the summer, it would be 95 percent of our job." Many faculty members pointed to high teaching loads as something that was both rewarding and challenging.

Related to teaching, departments assign faculty members in various fields of study to guide students earning degrees in those fields through their curricular plans. Unlike some large universities and community colleges, LACs do not outsource academic advising to a professional staff of advisors in a centralized advising center. Departmental faculties also bear the responsibility for developing and accessing discipline-specific curricula, including both courses and academic majors and minors.

There are at least three challenges for faculty work in LACs related to teaching: insufficient resources, a heavy teaching load, and advising responsibilities. We discuss them next.

INSUFFICIENT RESOURCES. The relationship between departmental resources and faculty work related to teaching is clear. Institutions and departments are best prepared to support their students when they are informed about, and able to provide, the proper amount of support needed to facilitate faculty work related to teaching and advising students. The obvious resource is money. Departmental budgets include line items for faculty and staff positions, as well as compensation for instructional overload. They also include money for the physical resources needed to teach effectively, from chalk to smart boards and laboratory equipment. There may be budgetary limits on incidental expenses, such as the cost of printing materials for students or out-of-class activities related to experiential learning. As one professor put it, "The problem with this school is that your time is actually all about money. There isn't money right now to hire faculty. Without hiring faculty, I gotta teach those courses."

HEAVY TEACHING LOAD. Excessive teaching loads are often a source of stress in departments in LACs, where a few faculty members are responsible for offering the right combination and sequence of courses. Of course, teaching also includes developing curricula, preparing lesson plans, responding to student questions, and grading student work and providing feedback. The extra work required can be a barrier to faculty members' engagement in other aspects of their jobs.

ADVISING RESPONSIBILITIES. Faculty members also viewed advising as a challenge, in both large and small departments. One member of a science department noted that advising students was a less efficient use of faculty time than he would have preferred: "We haven't figured advising out. We're one of the largest departments, and so we have many more advisees than anyone else." Yet faculty members in smaller departments faced a different version of the same problem: they had fewer students, but also fewer faculty members to advise them. Faculty members overwhelmingly reported that they enjoyed interacting with their students through teaching and advising, but our findings on the resourcing and structuring of academic work in LAC departments highlighted opportunities for improvement.

Research, Scholarship, and Creative Inquiry

Faculty members in GLCA institutions spend an average of six hours per week on research and scholarship. They reported spending less than one hour per week on grant writing and seeking funding for research, and less than one hour preparing for conferences and professional presentations (figure 2.1). We may conceptualize faculty development as happening at the institutional level, and in many ways that is the case. However, it is typical for allocations for faculty professional travel to come from departmental budgets, which provide a very important component of faculty professional development resources. This can

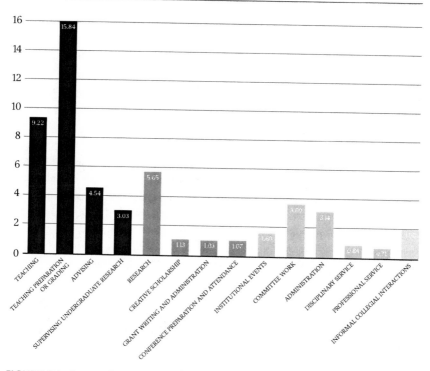

FIGURE 2.1. Average Hours per Week Spent by Faculty Members at Institutions in the Great Lakes Colleges Association, by Task

include funds for presenting at or attending professional or academic conferences, collecting data, accessing technical equipment, and meeting with collaborators or potential funders. Requests for lab equipment and space, instructional technology resources, research software, and other research-related expenses often are first made at the department level.

Just as with resources for teaching, we found that requests for resources related to faculty research were not always easily fulfilled. In the small departments of LACs, whose missions emphasize teaching first and foremost, departmental resources for research may be limited. We identified physical, personnel, and time resources as critical to LAC faculty engagement in research and inquiry. They are most often conceptualized as being managed by the institution (especially physical resources), but in fact the department is instrumental in providing all three.

PHYSICAL RESOURCES. Faculty members have different discipline- and inquiry-based needs in terms of materials and supplies for conducting their research. A scientist may need lab space or equipment, while a historian may need time to spend in an archive. Faculty support at the institutional level in LACs may not include sufficient funds for travel to research sites or purchases of hardware, software, or other materials, given the need to invest limited resources in the high-priority tasks related to teaching and mission fulfillment. Departments may pick up the slack to provide additional resources for faculty engagement in research, but if they cannot, faculty members' motivation and ability to complete their research, scholarship, or creative inquiry may be affected. One person we interviewed lamented the effects of resource limitations on the scholarly work in his department. He explained that he was unable to make sufficient progress with his research because of the time he had to spend maintaining and setting up his lab equipment, a task often completed by a lab manager or graduate assistant at larger universities. He said: "Even if a handful of us in the department could share a technician, with the little time we have to get research done. . . . If I could dream big, I would have a technician to help me out, but that's unlikely at a school like this."

PERSONNEL RESOURCES. Faculty members rely on several different types of personnel to aid them in their research and related work. One key distinction of scholarly activity at LACs is the absence of doctoral research assistants, a common component of the research labor force at large universities. Using undergraduates for research help can yield rewards for faculty members, but those tend to be psychosocial rewards related to mentoring and supporting students, and they often come with costs caused by frequent student turnover, higher training and supervision demands than would be the case with doctoral students, and inconsistent student ability and availability (Baker, Pifer, Lunsford, Greer, and Ihas 2015). Other personnel needed might include lab technicians and managers; support staff to help manage projects; budget officers, technology support staff, and development officers; and faculty collaborators. Compared to research universities, LACs have smaller organizational structures and fewer personnel dedicated to such support. This puts pressure on departments to come up with their own solutions to meet resource needs for faculty members' research and scholarship.

THE RESOURCE OF TIME. Many faculty members we spoke with noted that one of their biggest challenges was effectively managing their time so they could fulfill their many roles, and that an inordinate amount of time was invested in teaching-related tasks. Course releases or summer stipends for research activity may be less likely at LACs than overloads for teaching assignments. LACs may be particularly wary of outsourcing teaching to adjunct instructors, at least relative to other types of institutions. This is because of the skyrocketing trend of using adjunct labor in higher education, their teaching missions, and the dependence of their brand on student interaction with highly qualified faculty experts. All of this also contributes to prioritizing the use of faculty members to fulfill or exceed teaching requirements over opportunities to free up faculty time for research activity.

Service Activities and Governance

The third branch in the typical conceptualization of academic work is service. Precise definitions of service roles elude us because of the multitude and duration of activities in this category. Particularly in LACs, which are so dependent on faculty engagement across roles, service activities include a range of contributions and efforts, from volunteering for a recruitment event to being a member of an institutional governance committee or chairing a departmental committee. Some service activities are incidental and require relatively small investments of time, but they may interrupt a faculty member's work flow in a given day or week. Other service activities involve elected or appointed responsibilities that extend over several semesters or even years.

Perhaps uniquely at LACs, faculty members spend an average of two hours per week on institutional events such as athletic events or fund-raising activities. They also spend about four hours a week on meetings and committee work. Faculty members at LACs may also experience a sense of responsibility for advancing the institution, through administrative service, fund-raising, mentoring, and participating in the life of the college. It is hard to determine precisely, but easy to guess, how many of these service activities are related to serving departmental needs and students as much as to serving the institution.

Academic departments must coordinate the service responsibilities within their units, as well as monitor the need for departmental representation within institutional governance. Service roles may be more short-term than research projects or, of course, continuous teaching responsibilities, so faculty workloads related to service tend to fluctuate over their careers. Faculty service roles extend outside of the department to the institution and their disciplines, and often their communities and other social spaces. However, service is also an important piece of faculty work in the department.

We learned of several ways in which service responsibilities contributed to challenges for conducting and supporting faculty work in LACs.

THE NEED FOR COMMITTEES TO BE STAFFED. Again, for LAC departments, the distribution of service duties among a small group of faculty members can be overwhelming. Department members are already responsible for maintaining their major and minor degree programs and supporting students through academic (and often nonacademic) advising, not to mention their own scholarly activities.

DEPARTMENTAL REPRESENTATION WITHIN THE INSTITUTION. Effective departmental representation on college-level committees and in institutionwide discussions is important, as it relates to faculty shared governance and affects the competition of academic departments for institutional resources. This is particularly true when there are political or financial implications of that representation. In colleges with complex faculty governance structures, this can create challenges for department members who desire a seat at the table but must also fulfill their other responsibilities.

OVERRELIANCE ON THE EFFECTIVE FEW. A complete view of the challenges presented by service responsibilities within departments must include consideration of human factors such as ability, willingness, and politics, which we found to be important components of departmental realities in LACs. One faculty member summed the challenges this way: "There are people who don't do service at all. Then there are the people you don't want to do it. I think there are questions around . . . what service means and how do people take stewardship of the institution seriously without being burdened by it."

Together, the departmental tasks of teaching, advising, research, and service contributed to a sense among faculty members that they were dedicating a great deal of their time to work on behalf of the institution and students. In fact, having a heavy workload was among the greatest challenges reported in a departmental context (and as related to participation in faculty development activities; see chapter 6), and the single greatest challenge preventing faculty members from engaging in professional development.

Having considered the tasks that structure academic departments in LACs, we now turn our attention to the roles that people play in implementing or impeding those tasks—as colleagues and as shapers of departmental cultures. These were the greatest reported strengths and the greatest reported challenges of departmental life.

Departmental Cultures: Policies, Colleagueship, and Leadership

"If I came into this department and didn't have a model of experienced faculty members who were very active in their research areas, it would be really hard to push myself. And then there are role models in different ways in terms of service or teaching. Nobody was a single role model in every aspect that I was aspiring to. But that culture was important."

—An associate professor in the social sciences

Academic departments are one of the professional communities that Kerry-Ann O'Meara, Aimee Terosky, and Anna Neumann (2008) wrote about as being vital for faculty learning, growth, and contribution, through the meaningful relationships formed there. In fact, as one liberal arts faculty member put it, "community really begins at the department level" (Hughes 2014). The faculty composition of various departments affects the experiences of those who work in them, and faculty members evaluate their departmental colleagues' commitment to their various roles through their words and actions. A sense of consensus among, and support from, colleagues is likely to help motivate faculty members to engage in their various roles (Blackburn and Lawrence 1995). The ways that departmental culture affects faculty members' experiences include practices related to departmental policy and personnel, relationships with colleagues in the department, and the leadership of the department chair.

Departmental Policy and Personnel

As noted above in the chapter, near peers in the department amount to a team of professionals dedicated to working together to fulfill the department's goals and meet student learning, advising, and mentoring needs. A department's context is characterized by formal policies and informal practices. Examples of formal policies might include those that dictate instructor assignments for courses and promotion and tenure guidelines. They might also provide structure to the incidental factors that influence faculty work in departments, such as how maternity or paternity leaves may affect a semester's teaching schedule or what happens when an underenrolled course is canceled.

Related to both incidental and typical tasks, there is a crucial component of academic work that affects liberal arts faculty members at the department level. Faculty staffing is rooted in the department. From a financial perspective, departmental budgets include lines for faculty salaries. The college president and provost share the authority, at times acting on behalf of the board of trustees, to offer or terminate faculty employment, grant tenure, convert faculty lines from NTT to tenure track, and approve salary increases. These decisions, however, are driven by department-level evidence and recommendations. It is in the department that search committees are formed and chaired, merit awards and salary increases are made, and requests for promotion and tenure are put forth. These critical responsibilities for building, supporting, retaining, and promoting liberal arts faculties fall largely on academic departments, in addition to their other roles outlined here. These larger departmental issues related to policy and personnel can lead to challenges for faculty members individually and collectively in the department—such as managing time, supporting the onboarding and socialization of new faculty, and policy underdevelopment and inconsistency.

Challenges Related to Policy and Personnel

FACULTY RECRUITMENT AND SELECTION. In addition to teaching, conducting research, and performing service activities, faculty members are responsible for managing their department and collectively working for its development and continued success. For example, think of the stages of an academic search. The department must identify and justify a need for a new professor (perhaps because a faculty member is retiring or moving on, student enrollment is increasing, or academic programming is being restructured), obtain approval to conduct a search, work with the human resources staff to draft the position description, select and train a search committee, develop and post advertisements in the appropriate outlets, field inquiries and review applicant materials, hold meetings and several rounds of interviews, conduct background checks, and prepare recommendations for offers. And that's just the hiring process. Departments must also conduct annual reviews, make tenure and promotion decisions, and manage other aspects of the peer review process on which faculty careers are built. Faculty searches also involve a financial cost to the department, which often includes advertising positions, arranging for funds to cover candidates' airfare and accommodations, and group meals with each candidate, as well as start-up costs for new hires.

FACULTY ONBOARDING. The department chair and others must invest time in onboarding new department members, assigning courses and office space to them and providing social and collegial support as they establish themselves in the institution and region. Asked how LACs can support newly hired faculty members, one person replied: "I think it's very department-specific. I ended up in a department with fantastic mentors who really cared about my success and were willing to invest their time in it."

POLICY UNDERDEVELOPMENT AND INCONSISTENCY. Lastly, we observed challenges related to policy and personnel in academic departments when policies were not written down and therefore were perceived to be too flexible and customized. This left room for inconsistency in who was informed about policies and how these policies were interpreted and implemented. We also observed cases in which faculty members sought information about departmental policies or practices to provide guidance about how to request leave or manage conflict, for example, but clear information was unavailable.

Issues related to departmental personnel and policies can present challenges to the success of departments and their faculty members. In some ways, these issues focus on the formal aspects of departmental management and interactions. There is an equally important informal factor in the functioning of departments—departmental colleagueship.

Departmental Colleagueship

As noted, time spent in departments and the roles that departments play in shaping faculty work and development include incidental and informal interactions that do not belong in any particular category. What happens (or does not happen) in the department signals the institutional values and expectations. This signaling is crucial for new faculty members at LACs but is also important for their colleagues. Information about cultural norms, political and strategic relationships, and the way faculty work gets done in the institution is communicated to faculty members through their relationships with near peers in their department (Fries-Britt 2000). Judith Gappa, Ann Austin, and Andrea Trice framed faculty autonomy as going hand in hand with faculty members' "responsibility for their actions with regard to the well-being of their students, departmental colleagues, the faculty as a whole, and the respect with which they and their colleagues are viewed within and beyond the institution" (2007, 164). This framing can be translated to a call for collegiality for academics in their departments.

Departmental colleagues are among the most influential sources of support for departmental peers' teaching, research, and service activities. In fact, among the various levels of academic organization, departmental colleagues are more influential than everyone but disciplinary colleagues outside of the institution (see chapter 6 for a related discussion). Socially, faculty members reported spending an average of two hours per week interacting with colleagues informally, including those within and outside of their departments. Asked to describe the top two strengths of their departments, LAC faculty members overwhelmingly indicated their colleagues and the departmental culture. Interestingly, those were also the most often reported challenges. This evidence that faculty members' peers are most influential in both their department and discipline is interesting. Collegial relationships with faculty members in different academic fields or institutions were less significant, though also important.

In the best cases, we heard faculty members describe their departments as rewarding places to work, where they enjoyed spending time among powerful mentors and close friends. It is not hard to imagine how the benefits of such environmental conditions would spread to students. Departmental colleagues can provide near-peer support for many aspects of faculty work through a variety of relationship types such as mentoring, collaboration, advice seeking, networking, and facilitating connections outside of the department and institution, and social support and friendship. Faculty members tended to view their departments positively, as components of their professional work experience that provided a mentoring culture where they could seek advice from both senior and peer colleagues. This included leaning on department chairs in their formal leadership roles and receiving informal support from colleagues.

Effective departments demonstrated a collective commitment to their members' success and satisfaction, and a willingness to work collaboratively to generate solutions to problems.

COLLEAGUESHIP CHALLENGES. Jack Schuster and Martin Finkelstein (2006) reported that faculty members at LACs were likely to report better departmental relations with colleagues than those at other institution types. In the relatively small academic departments of LACs, those relationships are key. What we learned about departmental colleagueship in LACs suggests there are areas for improvement on this front. We noticed challenges related to bullying and other noncollegial behavior, isolation, and general fatigue and stress.

BULLYING AND OTHER NONCOLLEGIAL BEHAVIOR. Not all departmental cultures were described positively. It is not hard to imagine how hostile, ineffective, or isolating environments would influence the experiences of faculty and students spending time in departmental offices, hallways, and classrooms. One person described the situation within his department: "I would say my department culture is very unhealthy, and would probably be widely recognized as such, as one of the most dysfunctional departments on campus. So that's been pretty—pretty difficult."

ISOLATION. Problems can arise when a faculty member feels isolated within his or her department. This can happen at any educational institution, but we suspect that it may be relatively more common at LACs, where faculty members have fewer departmental colleagues and thus fewer opportunities to identify a like-minded peer. This may also be a particular problem for early-career academics entering departments where most or all their colleagues are at a different career stage and have different perspectives about faculty work in LACs, such as the role of research in one's career or the best ways to develop and teach the curriculum. For example, one LAC faculty member noted: "I'm the only statistician here, and being in isolation is a problem. Most faculty routinely interact with the people who study and teach . . . what they study and teach, and I haven't had that."

GENERAL FATIGUE AND STRESS. Challenges can also arise even when faculty members have a good fit with departmental colleagues if the department overall is overworked and underresourced. As discussed in chapters 4 and 6, heavy workloads are a major challenge for faculty members in LACs. The academic department—the location of one's teaching and advising responsibilities and disciplinary scholarship, and much of one's service activities—is likely to become the physical and organizational source of high expectations for faculty work. Negative feelings related to being overworked may be exacerbated when coupled with academics' sense of loyalty to their students, colleagues, and department, and the demands faculty members often make of themselves to be all things to all people.

Not all faculty members experience their departmental contexts in the same ways. Professional characteristics such as research interests, rank, and approaches to teaching, as well as personal characteristics such as race, gender identity, and sexual identity, can influence faculty members' experiences in their departments and those crucial collegial relationships. We delve into those individual characteristics and experiences in chapter 3. In this chapter, we focus on academic departments as work sites. One important component of the departmental environment is departmental leadership.

Departmental Leadership

When trying to understand the academic department and the role of colleagues and collaboration in shaping its work, the significance of effective departmental administration and leadership becomes clear. Departments are led by a department chair (typically elected by departmental peers) or by a department head (appointed by the dean or other senior administrators). Whether elected or appointed, the leader typically has a limited term and must meet criteria set at the institutional or departmental level (Gappa, Austin, and Trice 2007; Hendrickson et al. 2013). Traditionally, a department chair is selected from among the senior members of the department (Gappa, Austin, and Trice 2007) who have earned tenure—and often hold the rank of full professor—and are at a point in their careers where they can provide leadership to the institution and their colleagues through the role.

When it comes to facilitating the work of their colleagues, department chairs have many roles. Chairs influence departmental cultures and oversee formal policies, and they can have a strong influence on the daily work lives of faculty members. Chairs are instrumental in securing resources for their departments, in competition with their fellow chairs, in the form of faculty salary lines, professional travel and merit pay pools, office space and materials, and classroom or lab assignments. In the current environment of scarce resources and competing initiatives in LACs, the ability to garner institutional or other resources for departmental purposes is paramount for a chair. Departmental budgets must be stretched to cover instructional costs through faculty salaries or adjunct payments, as well as supplies and other resources.

Chairs also develop, implement, and oversee departmental policies and procedures and play the same role in the application of institutional policies and procedures as they relate to the work of the department. Perhaps the most important among these is the chair's role in the selection, retention, and promotion of faculty members. Effective chairs advocate for their faculty members; properly, fairly, and sometimes creatively manage budgets and allocate resources; keep the focus on supporting student learning; advocate for the department to institutional administrators; mentor and support colleagues; and manage conflict within the department and between the department and the administration.

Challenges Related to Leadership

We identified challenges related to working *as* department chairs, and we also discovered challenges related to working *with* department chairs. These included selecting and training the chair, working with ineffective chairs, and managing chairs' impressions of departmental faculty members.

CHAIR SELECTION. We found that the process described above for selecting chairs wasn't always followed. In the small departments of LACs, senior members had often already served as chair or were committed to other service responsibilities. This meant that pretenure, and sometimes even NTT faculty members, were asked (in effect, told) to lead their colleagues, including those who had a formal or informal say in their promotion and tenure. This resulted in faculty members who were newer to their departments than most of their colleagues, and who did not have the protection of tenure, being placed in formal leadership roles over colleagues who had little incentive to recognize their authority. In fact, some of those senior colleagues took advantage of their own informal authority and ignored or interfered with the efforts of the chair to provide departmental leadership.

CHAIR TRAINING. Some current and recent department chairs expressed concerns about the support and training they received from their institutions. Their desire for more effective training and support were easy to understand. One person talked about his efforts to obtain support for his work as chair: "There are no tools that I'm given, no training on how to deal with conflict or how to make it [the department] a better place. I've tried everything I can think of, and we're still dysfunctional. It's taken a toll on me."

INEFFECTIVE CHAIRS. Ineffective chairs are a source of conflict or poor departmental management. They are too timid when it comes to advocating for the department within the institution and allow negative or harmful behavior from department members toward other department members, themselves, or students. Because of the central role chairs play in managing and leading the work of their department, an ineffective chair can be a barrier to success at all other levels in the department. One person recalled: "We had a bit of a meltdown with the chair, who wasn't communicating too well, and we sought help from the dean's office. The entire department agreed that we need to get some help for this person from the dean's office and we just got silence." Of course, most chairs are not completely effective or ineffective. The range of responsibilities of academics who serve in these roles covers everything from financial management to conflict management.

IMPRESSION MANAGEMENT. LAC faculty members generally agreed that their chairs promoted equitable and inclusive departmental climates, but they were less likely to report feeling comfortable seeking career advice from their chairs. In fact, on average, faculty members were more likely to seek advice from other colleagues in their departments, including near peers and senior members, than from the chair. This may be partially explained by the fact that they want to manage the impression the chair has of them. Faculty members may be likely to mask concerns from their chairs or may seek advice from faculty peers about "managing up" in regard to their chairs, in an effort to positively influence their chairs' perceptions of them. Given the chair's role in hiring, assigning courses and teaching schedules, allocating resources, and reviewing and promoting faculty members, such behavior is unsurprising. The importance of, and potential tensions related to, the work of department chairs points to the need for alignment between the goals and behaviors of faculty members and those of department chairs—who serve as the first among equals.

We learned a great deal about the ways in which LAC faculty members fulfill their professional responsibilities in their department, as well as the crucial role that people skills such as colleagueship, communication, leadership, and management play in both departmental effectiveness and faculty experiences. These lessons raise vital questions about how to ensure that LAC faculty members are receiving the knowledge, resources, and support they need to perform successfully in their departmental roles.

What Can I Do? Advancing the Academic Department

"We have top-down initiatives, and one is global engagement. I wonder if I worked in an area that didn't have a lot to do with global engagement, if I or that department, would have some of the same opportunities. I see [senior administrators] setting the agenda of the institution. And in some ways that's good. But I think it's coming at the expense of supporting and valuing the work faculty are doing that might not connect to that."

–An associate professor in the humanities

The key focus of this chapter is on how departments shape faculty work in LACs. We identified challenges related to the department, which prompts us to consider how faculty development programming and practices might strengthen the alignment of purposes, strategies, and resource allocations between academic departments and the broader institutional contexts within which they are embedded. This leads us to the alignment framework for faculty development in liberal arts colleges (see chapter 7), which views the department as an essential provider of faculty support and development.

Effective policies and cultures of collaboration can help department members feel valued and connected to the institution. Departmental effectiveness can also be facilitated by making evidence-based and data-driven decisions. For example, a department might decide to rely on evidence to communicate departmental successes and needs to college administrators and others who influence resource allocation and the department's positive image. It is important to be realistic and strategic about the administrative and organizational realities of a college and its effects—and opportunities—within the department. Finally, academics would benefit from avoiding a "myopic, fortress-like" view and looking "up to what was happening at the top of the organization—and out—to see what was happening in their industry, their profession, their neighborhood, and the world" (Gratton and Truss 2003, 82).

In this section, we offer recommendations for what LAC faculty members and administrators can do to improve their careers, departments, and colleges in response to the challenges described in this chapter. Through such actions, they can use the department as a site for institutional thriving, individual thriving, and faculty development.

Strategies for Nontenure and Pretenure Faculty Members

Like Rachel in the opening vignette of this chapter, faculty members who are new to the LAC environment may be concerned about navigating their departmental environments. It is imperative for new hires or pretenure faculty members to demonstrate their commitment to the department and its students. It is equally important for them to be proactive in acquiring the resources and relationships needed for success and satisfaction. Although administrators and seasoned faculty members must support their junior colleagues, the culture of the academy has long been rooted in autonomous and independent work, often in competitive or demanding environments. For these reasons, we offer ideas to support NTT and pretenure faculty members in their professional development. Below are a few key questions and strategies.

QUESTIONS FOR CONSIDERATION

1. What actions are important for establishing effective support for recently hired NTT and pretenure faculty members?

We recommend that informal and formal leaders and mentors within departments take advantage of orientation programming, faculty development offices, and internal grant programs to help this population make quick and helpful connections to campus resources.

We also recommend that department members create opportunities for collaboration, advice, and support and thus early on communicate to new faculty members that the department is a collegial place that features rich relationships in the day-to-day environment of academic work. The norms and expectations of an institution are communicated to faculty members through their peer relationships within departments (Fries-Britt 2000).

2. What actions are important for recently hired NTT and pretenure faculty members as they become established in their departments?

Faculty members in this population might consider establishing a strategy for providing their departmental colleagues with information to help those colleagues form evidence-based conclusions about the value they add to the unit. This can include saying yes to invitations to departmental events, sharing successes in the classroom with colleagues, and keeping the chair and dean informed of accolades and accomplishments. Caution is warranted, however, as it is important to avoid seeming to engage in impression management instead of being authentic with departmental leaders about any challenges or concerns.

We further recommend that faculty members in this population consider how they might establish effective communication networks to help advance the department. They have a critical role in informing departmental leaders about the realities of departmental work and its challenges and limitations. The data required to inform and motivate change at the department level starts at the individual level. Newcomers, adjunct instructors, and NTT faculty members are likely to have insights that people who have been in the department for a long time might not have. Informing the department chair or others about any experiences with lack of collegiality is also key, not only for everyone's well-being and safety, but also to allow those with the formal authority to take action for positive change.

3. What long-term strategies may help NTT and pretenure faculty members receive support and develop in their departments?

We recommend that faculty members in this population reflect on their goals for advancing their departments, their need for support and development from within the department, and their needs that extend beyond the department. They should engage in networking and practice colleagueship within the college, the local community, and the disciplinary community. This can help mitigate the possible challenge of isolation.

Members of this population should be careful not to fall into the trap of comparing themselves to their advisors or peers working in research universities when trying to make sense of life in an LAC. Yet there are benefits to conducting reality checks with others, such as reminders about the many rewarding aspects of faculty work in LACs and seeing that the challenges of department life occur at all types of institutions.

Collaborations with community-based and academic colleagues outside of the department are as likely to strengthen the department as much as the faculty member, through reputation building, marketing, and the development of a stronger skill set that will benefit peers and students.

Strategies for Tenured and Senior Faculty Members

The role of mentorship, support, and collaboration within departments cannot be overstated. As Gappa, Austin, and Trice noted, senior faculty members play an important role in formally collaborating with department chairs and mentoring junior colleagues, as well as informally setting the tone of departmental environments as workplaces. The authors described the role of senior members in faculty hiring, mentoring, and evaluating as "critical to the overall quality of an institution's faculty" (2007, 164). Newly tenured faculty members have a chance to demonstrate their commitment to the department and their junior colleagues as they settle into their identities as tenured academics. Full professors and long-standing members of departments will experience an ongoing renewal of their reputations as they form relationships with newly hired colleagues and administrators over the years.

Senior faculty members will also have new goals and challenges unique to their career stages. It is important to educate them about their roles in the welfare and success of their departments and to empower them for success. For this group of faculty members, effective strategies for managing challenges and achieving vertical integration for their departments may include asking the following key questions and using the recommended approaches:

QUESTIONS FOR CONSIDERATION

1. What actions are important for establishing departmental policies and cultures that support tenured and senior faculty members?

We recommend that departmental leaders help tenured and senior faculty members feel valued and connected to the department and college. This may include drawing on their knowledge, successes, and networks to achieve the department's goals and communicating the value of their contributions. Requests for actions such as providing strong mentoring for a junior colleague having a bad day, helping a student find an alternative for a canceled class, or making progress on a departmental task in a committee meeting are just a few ways to engage senior departmental colleagues. These requests may help reduce feelings of fatigue and stress that faculty members could experience in LAC departments by providing day-to-day reminders of their value and contributions.

Departmental leaders might also ask what particular challenges and needs their tenured colleagues experience. Acquiring that information is the first step in advocating for this population in college-level conversations about faculty development and support, including drawing attention to this sometimes overlooked group of colleagues when it comes to matters of faculty development. Such information is also necessary for using one's authority to ensure departmental policies, resource allocations, and cultures demonstrate the continued investment in and support of tenured faculty members. The constant learning and growth opportunities are among the hallmark attractions of the academic profession. O'Meara, Terosky, and Neumann (2008) stress that this ongoing learning is influenced, and ideally supported, by collegial relationships.

2. What department-focused actions are important for tenured and senior faculty members?

It is important to conceptualize, and then commit to taking action related to, the ways that tenured faculty members can advance the work of the department. In their governance and service roles as search committee chairs and faculty mentors, this group can be instrumental in shaping the department's effectiveness and reputation and in connecting the college's strategic plan to that of the department. Creating positive experiences for potential and new colleagues is an important task. Senior faculty members also have power to use their voices to educate departmental and college leaders about the collective effectiveness of the department as well as its growth needs. Here, too, senior department members have a responsibility to communicate with leaders when they observe and can show evidence of a misalignment between college-level priorities and departmental realities. Unfortunately, we did not find consistent evidence of all faculty members being aware of, or protected by, informal commitments to collegiality or formal departmental policies related to faculty responsibilities, standards of conduct, or discipline or grievance procedures (Gappa, Austin, and Trice

2007). This group plays a valuable role in preventing or addressing challenges that come from the policy underdevelopment and inconsistency described above in this chapter.

Strategies for Department Chairs

No one person has a stronger effect on a department's success and reputation, and thus the experiences of its faculty members and students, than the department chair. Julie Carpenter-Hubin and Lydia Snover write: "The best chairs develop good relationships with their colleagues and make decisions through consensus-building. The wise chair keeps in mind that the next department chair will surely be chosen from among the colleagues affected by his or her decisions, and sets fairness and the good of the department as a whole as the standard" (2013, 36). It is worth considering how departmental effectiveness and department-based faculty development and support might be achieved through the work of the chair.

QUESTIONS FOR CONSIDERATION

1. What actions can a department chair take to foster collegiality, effectiveness, and faculty development and success within the unit?

    We recommend that the chair create a vision for how he or she will use the role to advance the department through the cultivation of an effective and positive organizational culture. One example is the lesson learned by a chair we spoke with: "I didn't realize in the beginning how important it was to have small conversations. . . . One of my goals is to have a fifteen-minute conversation with everyone in the department every week. . . . That just really allowed me to get that touch that I need with colleagues, and some feedback and support." Transparency also contributes to this goal. Conversations about service at the departmental level might center on transparency about service expectations and how those expectations are factored into faculty evaluations and workload decisions. We found transparency to be the one component of departmental activity that seemed to escape the streamlining and reduction mandates that have affected educational institutions in recent years. Other skills for department-level professional development include creative problem solving, advocacy, and diplomacy.

    Chairs must request additional support, if needed, to effectively advance the department through policies, budgets, and other administrative tasks. Department chairs have budgetary responsibilities and a seat at the table when it comes to departmental allocations of resources such as money for salary increases, instructional resources, and capital improvement. Effective fiscal management helps department chairs best use their resources to support faculty work. Just as a college president serves as the conduit between faculty, trustees, and external stakeholders, the chair plays a crucial role in achieving vertical alignment between the department and the college. Examples of effective strategies include integrating institutional priorities into departmental resource allocations, communicating with administrators when college-level priorities seem to be misaligned with departmental realities, and encouraging department-level conversations about proposed institutional policies and goals. Transparency and cross-training of all departmental colleagues as part of faculty development efforts about departmental administration may help create departmental cultures that include and welcome this aspect of decision making.

Furthermore, we recommend that chairs determine when and from where to obtain extradepartmental support, mentoring, colleagueship, and humor to advance their work and provide perspective, encouragement, and development. One of the most important resources for department chairs is other chairs, including former chairs of their own departments, other chairs across campus, and chairs at institutions affiliated with their own—such as in the same consortium. Consulting with others who can relate to the challenges of being chair is a key strategy. Chairs might also benefit from tapping into their support networks to envision goals they might set for themselves after stepping back into the ranks of the faculty and to learn from others who have managed the transitions into and out of the chair role.

Strategies for Academic Deans and Other Campus Administrators

The academic department provides a crucial opportunity for providing support for faculty members in all ranks and appointment types. While there are many ways to work toward vertical alignment between departments and their college, deans, faculty developers, and other administrators may be best positioned to alleviate the challenges experienced by faculty members in the departmental contexts of LACs. There are many ways administrators can foster effectiveness in departments. Here are a few relevant questions and recommendations:

QUESTION FOR CONSIDERATION

1. How can campus administrators invest in faculty success through support for academic departments?

It is important for LAC administrators to consider seriously how to leverage institutional resources and personnel to provide support for and reduce the challenges of faculty work. For example, faculty developers might help faculty members by providing training for group, peer, or virtual advising to help reduce the time needed to perform those roles effectively. Across all tasks, faculty members generally reported being underresourced, including the invaluable resource of time. As a result, concerns about heavy workloads are prevalent. How can the challenge of doing more with less inform faculty development? It may be an indirect relationship. Personnel and material resources were often mentioned in our interviews and surveys. If there are not enough faculty or staff members to do the work of the department successfully, there is little that professional development can do to solve the problem. This is where administrative action is needed.

We recommend that administrators identify which sources of information about academic departments would provide evidence of faculty members' commitments to college-level goals. Such an effort would aid the development and communication of faculty expectations and institutional goals that support strategic decision making, a critical step needed to align faculty development programming with institutional initiatives. As noted in chapter I, knowledge management systems can contribute to data-driven decisions, organizational knowledge, and transparency. Openness about why information is collected, how it is used, and what positive changes result from its use could do just that. Administrators have a vantage point from which to view their institutions systematically. Using data to make informed decisions about governance models and committee work, departmental resources, and teaching loads may help promote a culture of equity, transparency, and responsiveness to the stressors of a shortage of time and general fatigue experienced by those working to fulfill institutional missions.

We recommend that in their communications to internal and external stakeholders, administrators mention the centrality of faculty work and academic departments. For example, seeking out and celebrating departmental success stories is a way of communicating institutional values—including the value placed on supporting and recognizing faculty work. Campus leaders have many opportunities to share departmental successes externally to help communicate the ways in which academic departments and faculty members are fulfilling institutional missions and creating effective learning experiences for students.

Administrators would be wise to invest in strategies to effectively select, train, support, and compensate chairs. This is one of the most essential ways to support department- and individual-level faculty success and satisfaction. Other scholars have advocated for the importance of these tasks (for example, see Gappa, Austin, and Trice 2007). In the context of LACs, we saw examples of chairs being selected from among relatively small groups, which sometimes included people who did not want the task, did not have tenure or tenure-track appointments, or had shown no sign that they were prepared for the role or could be effective in it. Several chairs we spoke with noted a lack of training and development related to their assuming and continuing in the position of chair. Whether through informal mentoring lunches, programming from the provost's office, or the formal faculty development portfolio, faculty development that prepares and supports department chairs is necessary. Relevant topics include managing conflict, understanding and enforcing human resources policies and relevant state and federal laws, supporting individual faculty members' needs and goals, and building positive cultures and environments within departments.

Finally, we recommend that campus administrators be bold in providing support for department members who are managing challenges related to ineffective, or worse, behavior from their chairs. One faculty member told us that "there's absolutely zero support from the administration in trying to create a decent working environment at the departmental level, and there's no way for us to punish or reward people who behave poorly or well." It is up to administrators who oversee chairs to use their authority and institutional policies to respond to any problems with a chair's leadership and enable faculty members to be effective in their work for students and the college, and to provide a safe—maybe even enjoyable!—work environment.

Conclusion

In this chapter, we described the department as a core context for academic work in LACs. We presented an overview of trends in time spent on tasks and discussed the knowledge, resources, and support necessary to engage in faculty work successfully. Then we explored the alignment between departmental and institutional perspectives and actions and suggested ways to achieve faculty success and satisfaction in departmental environments.

This information helps paint a picture of how departmental contexts can be helpful to faculty members as they engage in their work and professional development. It is clear that faculty members in LACs are heavily invested in the work of their departments. This includes not only teaching and advising students, but also recruiting students into departmental majors; performing the department's administrative and managerial tasks; competing with other units for scarce resources; hiring, mentoring, and evaluating colleagues; and seeking external support from donors and funding agencies.

In line with findings from other studies, this chapter raises questions about the challenges of navigating the departmental and institutional contexts. Now that we know what happens in departments and institutions, we turn in chapter 3 to a more holistic look at the characteristics and work lives of LAC faculty members.

PART TWO

Understanding Faculty Members

What They Do and What They Need

3

A Holistic View of Faculty Work
Lives in Liberal Arts Colleges

James, an associate professor of English literature, was reflecting on the weekend as he hurriedly worked on getting out of the house and over to campus on a Monday morning. He was not as prepared as he would have liked to be for the workweek. He had cut short his routine Friday night dinner with his partner, also a faculty member at the college, so he could finish an overdue manuscript. At least, he thought, during their abbreviated date they had avoided arguing about working during the weekend.

Saturday afternoon found James on campus at the college football game with his children. It was senior week, and several of his advisees and students were members of the team. He reflected on how much the students had matured since they first arrived on campus. He came because they wanted him to meet their parents, and he genuinely enjoyed those fleeting celebratory moments. It also got the kids out of the house on a beautiful fall day and allowed his partner some time to work. Yet he also found himself preoccupied about the coming workweek—when would he find time to prepare for his lectures and finish grading those papers?

Sunday was typically reserved for time to recharge with the family, but instead he spent the morning driving an hour each way to the pediatric hospital emergency room with his daughter, who was having an asthma attack. James had wondered if he should cancel his Sunday dinner plans but worried about the signal a cancellation would send. He had long ago offered to host Kate, a junior colleague, and her husband, and had already rescheduled twice. James had met Kate during her on-campus interview, when he had assured her of the family-friendly environment at the college, despite a few inappropriate comments from the department chair and the lack of a formal policy for maternity or paternity leaves at the college. James wanted to continue to support Kate. Plus, he genuinely liked her and her husband. Although he was exhausted, he was grateful for their time together, and their conversation lasted well into the night.

As he packed lunches Monday morning, James focused on the positives of the weekend—the time with his partner and kids, the football victory, and the much-needed social time with friends. He knew the week ahead would be another busy one and was already daydreaming of the quiet Sunday afternoon the following weekend might (but probably wouldn't) bring.

Substitute a child's medical emergency for some other family-related issue, and James's weekend would probably be familiar to readers with a career in a liberal arts college (LAC). The work does not fit neatly into a 9-to-5 schedule, and the challenge is to be fully and equally committed to one's campus, scholarship, students, family, and self. Throughout their careers, faculty members are faced with the tension between immediate demands and long-term priorities in both their personal and their work lives.

In this chapter, we explore faculty work by offering a holistic view of life in LACs and faculty perspectives on their work environments. We then extend that view to consider how faculty members' personal characteristics, backgrounds, identities, and professional needs and goals interact with the environments of LACs. This perspective provides a structure for understanding faculty work and, thus, professional development needs. We propose strategies to better support faculty members in the myriad roles they hold. We suggest improved horizontal alignment through the development, implementation, and communication of effective policies to improve individual and institutional outcomes. In terms of the alignment framework for faculty development in liberal arts colleges (AFFD-LAC; see chapter 7), this chapter focuses on how departmental and institutional efforts toward faculty support and development must align with faculty members' goals and characteristics. We first review how strong horizontal alignment may enable administrators to use policies as one tactic for supporting faculty work.

Achieving Strong Horizontal Alignment

Scholars have noted the tensions in academic development work that arise from the conflict between the needs of individual faculty members and those of the institution (for example, see Macdonald 2009; Nilson, Nuhfer, and Mullinix 2011). In this chapter, we are concerned with understanding faculty experiences at LACs and how colleges are relying on development and human resource policies to support academic work.

The concept of horizontal alignment directs attention toward coherent and consistent approaches to managing people at the policy level, as opposed to the practice level (Gratton and Truss 2003). We discuss improving people strategies with strong vertical alignment in chapters 2, 5, and 6. Here, we provide an overview of what we learned about faculty experiences in LACs and then consider whether faculty experiences are both considered and understood by institutional administrators and faculty developers. Horizontal alignment is present when a college can demonstrate its commitment to supporting faculty members and their development through clear, consistent, and mutually reinforcing policies. Such policies are shown to be meaningful through their development and reliable use, and thus their integration into institutional cultures and practices.

We encourage readers to consider the following three key questions as they review the stories in this chapter about faculty life in LACs, and particularly to think about what institutions can do to support faculty work across life and career stages. First, how can LACs achieve the right balance of policies and practices for faculty development to send a consistent message about valuing faculty members' work and provide diverse supports needed to enable them to conduct that work? Second, how can colleges foster creative dialogue within and between two groups of people—those who engage in academic work in LACs and those who have the resources and decision-making authority to support them? Third, how can such balance and dialogue produce systematic thinking that goes beyond listing a series of initiatives to the development of a comprehensive set of policies that collectively provide holistic support for holistic work lives (Blackburn and Lawrence 1995; Gappa, Austin, and Trice 2007; Gratton and Truss 2003)? These questions inform the stories told in this chapter about faculty members' lives in LACs and the consideration of the important relationship between those lives and institutional policies.

Faculty Perceptions of LACs as Work Environments

"One of the strategies to be in a liberal arts context is, how do you do this and still do research? How do you find that balance? How do you negotiate certain things? I'm still groping my way along and asking a lot of advice from people. Typically, the people I know are all at major research universities. So their advice—I begin my question, and their first response is 'Wait, stop, you're teaching how many courses?' and we can't get past that. So it is not helpful."

—An assistant professor in the social sciences

What do faculty members—who have unique, complex, and evolving personal and professional needs and characteristics—think of their work lives in the equally unique, complex, and evolving contexts of their colleges? How can we learn from their experiences to create effective and equitable policies that support their work? Robert Blackburn and Janet Lawrence (1995) described the importance of the environmental conditions of faculty work in shaping experiences and outcomes. We were interested to learn more about LACs as environments of academic work, faculty perceptions of and experiences within those environments, and their related faculty development choices and needs.

Choosing to Work in LACs

During our interviews, we asked the faculty members why they were working in LACs and what had motivated them to accept those positions. Some faculty members had been relieved to receive a job offer at all, while others had had several offers and had deliberately chosen the LAC. Some had been discouraged by mentors and doctoral committees from considering employment in LACs, while others had been told that they would be able to make strong contributions at such institutions. Many faculty members had firsthand experience with the liberal arts model as undergraduates and were eager to return to that environment, but some were unfamiliar with the LAC as an institution type.

As these faculty members reflected on their experiences over the years—their careers at LACs ranged from several months to over fifty years—we learned more about their perceptions of LACs as work environments. Faculty members experienced the LAC environment quite differently. As one person succinctly put it, "people rank their priorities differently. Some people are overjoyed to be at a place like this, and some people last a year and can't wait to get out." There were some general themes, however, in their descriptions of LACs as work environments. These themes helped us understand the environments and specific challenges that arose within them.

Below we discuss the challenges, however, we wish to note the general enthusiasm from the faculty members as a group about their choice to work in a LAC. Many of them were extremely satisfied with their experiences and pleased to be a part of their institution. When asked to indicate their overall satisfaction with their institution as a workplace and their job overall, faculty members provided mean responses of 5.09 and 5.43, respectively, with 7.0 being the highest possible level of satisfaction. One person stated: "I am exceptionally happy. This is a great school, great students, great colleagues, great job."

Challenges Related to Working in LACs

We observed several related challenges in the ways faculty members spoke about their experiences with the general culture of LACs, including expectations for engagement, a lack of institutional vision, and an overreliance on the faculty role.

EXPECTATIONS FOR ENGAGEMENT. As we have described in other chapters, faculty members in LACs are expected to be engaged across all aspects of the institution. First and foremost among these expectations is that they be engaged in teaching and advising students. When we asked faculty members to name their most important role, they consistently replied that it was supporting and educating students.

Across the disciplines, faculty members were also committed to their research activity and creative scholarship. We heard concerns related to faculty service and "uncounted time" in the LAC environment, where service to the institution is a part of the typical conceptualization of faculty engagement. One associate professor of history explained a potential consequence of that expectation: "I'm well aware that I'm complaining about one of the better jobs in academia, but I do think there's a burnout problem. You use these faculty in the couple of years posttenure, but then you burn them out and for the rest of their tenure, they're not there any more. You know, it's interesting. When I got here, I heard that and I thought, 'Oh my God, how lazy.' And now, within a decade of being here, I'm facing it too. You know, 'Please. Let me fade back into the woodwork and stop talking to me.'"

Faculty members spoke of the challenge of institutional culture as it applied to recruiting new colleagues. There were differing perceptions of what was expected from junior faculty members by their peers and administrators, and what junior faculty members expected from their colleagues and institutions in turn. In short, many pretenure colleagues were heavily invested in their research and scholarly activity, while their senior faculty members saw that as secondary to teaching, advising, service, and institutional engagement.

LACK OF INSTITUTIONAL VISION. Across all ranks, faculty members expressed frustration about the conflicting messages they received about what their institutions actually desired, supported, and rewarded. A professor in the humanities said: "[The college] is trying to be all things to all people. We have no priorities, and we have no identity. And I find that incredibly frustrating, because I need to make choices about what I should and shouldn't do. And what we're trying to do, to be everything to everybody—I end up not even being able to breathe. I'm trying to do so much. Everything is equally important and just viscerally important. I'm exhausted. I'm just bloody exhausted because I need some things to go away, and the university isn't making priorities [clear]." Another faculty member shared his concern about his college's ability to retain a large group of recently hired junior faculty members, who are asked "to teach, engage in all the meetings related to service, do research and somehow do all the other work we are asked to do because of budget restrictions. I worry that we are going to overwork them and they will leave."

OVERRELIANCE ON THE FACULTY ROLE. We heard concerns from faculty members about the expectations placed on them and their peers to fill the many roles they are called to play in LACs. One of our informants commented: "Something's gotta give. The knob can't keep only going in one direction on all fronts." One reason for the increasing stress on the faculty was insufficient investment in student support services. Another informant listed several examples: "We don't have any health or wellness people, no support for managing alcohol and other drugs, no victim advocacy, no judicial system, no multicultural center that's dedicated to any kind of diversity inclusion or equity programming. We don't have a dedicated leadership program. We don't have anything like that, so a lot of that stuff falls onto the faculty to help students."

Faculty members also shared with us how institutional cultures promoted expectations of faculty work and time. According to one person, "there is an expectation that you're on campus 9:00 to 5:00, Monday through Friday—in addition, oftentimes, to evening and weekend commitments." Someone from another campus explained her struggle with work-life balance and with giving too much of her time to the college this way: "I think some of that maybe is cultural. Everyone just expects you to work all the time."

Related to this culture and working environment, people expressed challenges such as finding a work-life balance; achieving their rank-specific career goals; and responding to institutional challenges and inefficiencies, such as time wasted in meetings and a lack of accountability for poor performance or bad behavior. These challenges are related to some of the institutional aspects of faculty careers in LACs. We found that two other topics were also relevant—the locations of those colleges and the identities and characteristics of faculty members.

Faculty Life

"I think in our institutional culture, my most important role is my relationship with students. I take that seriously. I'm involved in a ton of stuff on the faculty, and also with the football team. I take my family to many women's soccer games, and I do lots of stuff with students. That's really what's most important here."

–An assistant professor in the social sciences

To understand faculty members' perceptions of their careers, one must first understand life in the LAC from the perspective of the faculty members. The themes of faculty life in small towns and faculty members' personal characteristics and identities characterized faculty lives in LACs.

Living and Working in Small Towns

One of the defining characteristics of many LACs is their location in small towns or rural settings. We observed three types of faculty members when it comes to the small-town environments of these colleges: those who are attracted to those environments and seem to have the DNA of the LAC in them; those who would prefer to be elsewhere, but the only opportunity they had for academic work was at the LAC; and those who worked in an LAC but, because of career opportunities for a spouse or partner or for other reasons, chose to live elsewhere and commute to campus. Some faculty members we spoke with viewed the geographic aspect of their work lives as a strength, while others viewed it as a challenge.

THE UPSIDE OF LIFE IN SMALL TOWNS. Some faculty members perceived small towns as an ideal setting for their lives, and felt that their life there was made possible by their career. One person explained her choice to work in an LAC this way: "In part I was looking for a school like [this] with a blend of teaching and scholarship in a rural area. I'm not a city person. I wanted to live in the countryside. I have a little farm outside of town, so it satisfies that angle. I can step off my porch and go cross-county skiing, or go kayaking, or whatever. It's not the hectic pace of an urban university."

Faculty members described enjoying needing only a short walk, bike ride, or drive to reach their office. They enjoyed the campus environment and college events such as speeches, film showings, athletics, the wellness center, and parks. One faculty member had worked at his college for twenty years. He said of himself and his family, "we really enjoy being here in this small town, and that's why we've never left." Another described the "quality of life" that came with being in a small town as "almost perfect" and an advantage to working at an LAC: "There's a farmers' market. We go down there and get actual real organic food without needing to drive twenty miles. I leave my house at 7:00 for a 7:00 movie and get to the theater when the previews are ending."

The connection between the LAC and the town was meaningful to many faculty members, as a way to make life better for their community through their faculty status. Connections with the campus community extended into the town, for both cooperation in response to challenges and opportunities for enrichment and enjoyment. Faculty members talked about spending time at a favorite café and enjoying conversations with community members and scholars from across the college. One person reflected on the challenging but rewarding aspect of life in his town, citing his experiences with the local school district and town government as one example: "Because we're in a small town with an awful lot of poverty, there's an awful lot of opportunities for community engagement." He explained how that aspect of his work may be unique to his role at an LAC, noting that "I've had all sorts of opportunities that are only really possible because the expectations for publication are less than they would be at a research university." Another faculty member described how the college's relationship with the community had influenced his work and provided an opportunity for "understanding the community that we're in, since one of the stated goals of the college is to have this high level of social action with the local community." He explained the relationship between the college and the community:

> If you went downtown, you saw [our] students. It was just a defining feature of the town. And so there was a lot of youth and vigor and . . . [the college] had this kind of influence on the town. It brought a very diverse continually rotating population in and out of the community, and those students often did co-op [work exchange experience] with businesses or with organizations that were in the town, so they developed close relationships with individuals who lived in the community. And for the students, developing relationships with a lot of very unique individuals that live in the community and have a lot to offer the students [is important].

These perspectives suggest that the environments of LACs can easily extend into their nearby communities in ways that affect faculty experiences and might be supported through faculty development and institutional practices.

THE DOWNSIDE OF LIFE IN SMALL TOWNS. Not everyone viewed life in a small town favorably. We heard concerns from a healthy portion of participants about "isolation" and "living in the middle of nowhere." One faculty member expressed the problem concisely: "If you live here, you can't go to the local chamber orchestra. Because there isn't one." Another said that "it can be challenging finding ways of occupying yourself that are not associated with the college." Still another faculty member, when asked to describe the challenges of working in an LAC, replied, "I mean, we're a town of 15,000 surrounded by corn and soybean fields." It is likely that many faculty members have relocated to a small town to pursue their educations and careers, and they may also have had experiences related to culture, travel, and diverse metropolitan areas. The location of their LAC shaped their experiences, and that factor should be considered by those seeking to understand and support faculty members' experiences.

One response to the realities of life in small colleges in small towns was for faculty members to create their own social opportunities. Faculty members described "the small-town vibe" and a feeling of community where "people are close." Several spoke of really enjoying their community of friends, including institutional colleagues. A professor in the humanities stated: "There's nothing else to do in [this town], so you get together with friends and make a nice meal and talk to each other. So we have really nice friends here." As we will discuss below in this chapter, this response was not always available to faculty members who felt that they had no time for social engagements or no group of colleagues with whom they wanted to spend their time in that way.

Another challenge related to the locations of LACs was that of the "trailing spouse" or dual-career couples. LACs had fewer opportunities to hire candidates or faculty members' partners than larger institutions did, and fewer nonacademic hiring alternatives than did institutions located in larger metropolitan areas. For some faculty members, this meant long commutes from the nearest city, where their partner was employed. For others, it meant living away from a partner and sometimes also children, and commuting home to them on weekends and over breaks. One person explained how this expanded beyond a faculty work-life issue to affect the institution as a whole:

> Not all of our faculty live in town. We have some that live toward [the nearest city]. We have some that actually live in other states and commute here and live here for a couple of days and then go back again. I mean, there's no way of getting around that. Where we are located has limited opportunities for spousal hires, and that actually is one of the issues with retention. I suspect if we were in—I don't know, just outside of Boston or something like that where people wanted to live, we would have much less trouble retaining faculty than we do. But you've got the dual-career issue and all the rest of it, and I think the institution does the best job that it can, but there's a limited number [of opportunities]. We can't hire every spouse.

Despite the limitations of being unable to hire every candidate's partner, there seemed to be an awareness on the part of the faculty that this was a small but important aspect of faculty development and career success in LACs, and that "being more proactive in that area could potentially be really helpful." One professor commented: "It's not like we can move [the college] somewhere else, you know? I would say that, with retaining faculty members, something that has sometimes been done that has helped retain people is making partner hires." Faculty members acknowledged that while the LAC's location was not something that could be controlled, it was imperative to be realistic and creative about how the location factored into building a strong faculty.

Related to the spousal hire issue, faculty members were mindful of the fact that their colleges' locations might not be appealing to all candidates, and that it was an important aspect of faculty recruitment and hiring. Another person we spoke with said: "We've had some cases where we attract really top-notch faculty, but they really don't resonate with the town or the region. And so that's a challenge, and from the college's point of view, we can't sell them something they won't actually get when they get here. So we need to be really transparent and up front about what it's like to live and work in this community. Many people really like it. I really like it; my family has done very well here. But I can see some of the aspects where people would have a challenge."

That person expressed the view that as a counterweight to the location-based challenges, the college should offer very competitive packages to faculty candidates, such as strong salaries, start-up funds, effective orientation, and assistance with spousal hiring or flexible scheduling in positions when possible. She also explained that location is a relevant factor not just for the individual faculty member but also for the institution when it comes to building a strong faculty, in sometimes complicated ways: "Considering stuff like that doesn't seem fair, but on the other hand, it seems best for everybody. . . . [It's] just an overall dynamic of getting the right match and the right fit for an area, or for the college." Another person spoke of the importance of having summers off in terms of factors that supported his happiness in a small college and town: he lived somewhere else in the summer months. As he said, "when I'm here, I enjoy being here. And when I'm away, I enjoy being away." The issue of how small colleges, particularly those with limited financial resources, respond to this reality of faculty recruitment and retention is a complex one. Many of the faculty members we spoke with mentioned lower-than-average compensation as a challenge of working in LACs. This suggests that it might not be possible to use higher salaries to balance issues of spousal or partner employment needs and other geographic-based challenges.

Finally, location was relevant for faculty lives and faculty support when it took the form of academic isolation. One person in a science, technology, engineering, and mathematics (STEM) field said: "What's difficult about being at a small college is being isolated research-wise. Most of my natural colleagues are not at small colleges in the Midwest. How do we support individual research efforts for faculty that may not be linked with faculty locally?"

Another faculty member shared this concern: "People in small colleges in rural settings are academically isolated. It takes a good deal of effort to make the journey to collaborate with someone." However, others found a greater sense of community at LACs than they had had at other institution types. One person said: "I know lots of people outside my department. I'm interacting with a broader cross-section of faculty, and that relates to the kind of work that I do and how I teach. So that's another advantage of being at a liberal arts college." This reinforces the finding that the realities of living and working in LACs, while having some general themes, depend on the characteristics of individual faculty members (both personal and professional) and the institutional characteristics of the college. Thus, we emphasize that an understanding of both is necessary for effective faculty support and development in LACs.

Personal Characteristics and Identities

Effective faculty development and awareness of faculty experiences in LACs involve more than the rational, task-based functions of academic work and require a consideration of the informal structures and characteristics that influence those experiences. As W. Richard Scott and Gerald Davis wrote, people "bring along their heads and hearts: they enter the organization with individually shaped ideas, expectations, and agendas, and they bring with them distinctive values, interests, sentiments, and abilities" (2007, 63). When faculty members experience effective development, they report practical gains related to institutional expectations and the promotion and tenure process. They also report "greater job satisfaction, feeling more connected to their work environments, reduced role strain, and more happiness" (Hyers, Syphan, Cochran, and Brown 2012, 23). Researchers have challenged the view that faculty development is something that must be done to regulate faculty behavior and called for new approaches to supporting faculty members. KerryAnn O'Meara, Aimee Terosky, and Anna Neumann referred to faculty growth as "having the potential to be self-directed, to unfold and deepen throughout the academic life, building on individual goals and talents" (2008, 18). Yet identity-based disparities in mentoring and professional development can separate faculty members from these desired outcomes (Gappa, Austin, and Trice 2007; Hyers et al. 2012; O'Meara, Terosky, and Neumann 2008).

Scholars have demonstrated that individual characteristics matter when it comes to the day-to-day and long-term experiences of postsecondary faculty members (Blackburn and Lawrence 1995; Gappa, Austin, and Trice 2007). To name just a few examples, Lauri Hyers and colleagues (2012) found that faculty members from underrepresented ethnic or gender groups reported far fewer development-based interactions with departmental colleagues than their majority-group peers. Meghan Pifer (forthcoming) found that faculty members may have different expectations for women's and men's roles—both formal and informal—in departments. And Caroline Turner, Juan González, and Kathleen Wong (2011) found that female faculty members of color experienced marginalization, discrimination, tokenism, racism, sexism, and other negative outcomes in their institutional and individual interactions on campus. However, these studies, like most about academic work about higher education, explored research universities. The questions of what faculty members experience based on their identities in the unique environments of LACs, and how these institutions should respond to mitigate negative experiences, have gone unanswered. Regardless of institution type, scholars of the academic career have consistently pointed to the importance both of understanding how individual characteristics affect faculty work and experiences and of having policies that support equity, satisfaction, and success.

Before considering the identity-based experiences of the faculty members we surveyed and spoke with, a few observations must be made about the sample. As shown in table 3.1, we had equal representation from male and female respondents (8 percent of respondents chose not to disclose their gender identity), which is in line with the current gender-based faculty composition in the Great Lakes Colleges Association (GLCA) (US Department of Education 2016). In addition, we conducted interviews with thirty-five male and forty-seven female respondents. Seventy-seven percent of our faculty respondents were white, which is similar to race-based faculty composition across the institutions in the GLCA; the percentage of white faculty members at those institutions is 77–87 percent (US Department of Education 2016).

RACE AND ETHNICITY. The limited number of survey respondents who were nonwhite faculty members restricts our ability to understand the experience of such faculty members in LACs. Yet we can draw some conclusions. One faculty member told us that her socioeconomic class and ethnicity shaped her experiences: "Sometimes I have doubts, personally, if I am in the right place. Do the students I teach reflect who I am? What is my inner self trying to tell me when I take sabbaticals away from campus to work with students who are disadvantaged?"

Several respondents described concerns about the experiences of their nonwhite peers, and their colleges' policy-based responses to recruiting and retaining faculty members of color. These observations and secondhand accounts of diversity-related challenges in LACs helped us identify opportunities for institutions to be proactive in supporting faculty members. An associate professor in the social sciences noted: "This is still a predominantly white institution. That's true among the students. It's true among the faculty. It's certainly true among the staff. I think we're continuing to work toward changing that. It's a long process." A professor in a STEM field observed:

> We have trouble retaining faculty of color. We also have trouble retaining gay faculty. And that's in part where we're located, but I think it's a cop-out to say every time it's because we live in a conservative small town, because that's not the only reason. And I think we need to ramp up our efforts to support those categories of faculty that we're losing because we

TABLE 3.1
Individual Characteristics of Survey Participants

Characteristic	Number and percent
Race/ethnicity	
American Indian or Alaskan Native	1 (0%)
Asian	9 (2%)
Asian American	2 (0%)
Black or African American	6 (1%)
Caribbean or West Indian	1 (0%)
Indian (subcontinent)	3 (1%)
Latina/o or Hispanic	7 (2%)
Middle Eastern	2 (0%)
Native Hawaiian or Pacific Islander	0 (0%)
White	317 (77%)
Other	13 (3%)
Prefer not to respond	52 (13%)
Sex	
Male	192 (46%)
Female	186 (45%)
Prefer not to respond	33 (8%)
Documented disabilities	15 (4%)
Identified as lesbian, gay, bisexual, transgender, or queer	34 (8%)
International faculty	35 (8%)
Years at institution	
0–5	96 (23%)
6–10	78 (19%)
11–20	106 (26%)
21–30	69 (17%)
31–40	23 (6%)
41–50	2 (0%)
Prefer not to respond	41 (10%)

Notes: Percentages may not sum to 100 because of rounding. Race/ethnicity includes US-born descendants of people who were born outside of the United States.

really, really want them here. . . . I think that's a place we really need to provide support. Not to me. I'm white, I'm senior, I'm straight. I'm not where the focus needs to lie.

This concern was shared by other LAC faculty members who were very interested in "redoubling our efforts" to attract and retain faculty members of color. They spoke of problems faced by those colleagues—such as overrepresentation on committees and in service, isolation, and tokenism—but were often at a loss as to what the colleges could do to improve in this regard. One female faculty member lamented the challenges experienced by some of her peers, which were inadvertently perpetuated by the college: "I'm watching all these people who got tenure last year being inundated with committee work . . . and especially women of color. God, the women of color get tapped for everything." She was unsure of possible solutions, however: "How do you recognize that you don't want to exhaust the resources of your associate professors who make tenure?" Some respondents to our survey about faculty work and experiences reported that there were barriers to success for underrepresented and underserved faculty members, but overall our respondents were more likely to report that their colleagues perceived such barriers than to report that they personally believed such barriers existed. That difference points to the complexity of culture and collegial relationships as they are experienced by individual faculty members, and thus the imperative for equitable and effective policies that support all faculty members across personal needs and individual characteristics.

FEMALE FACULTY MEMBERS' EXPERIENCES. One main way in which participants spoke about their identities was through the lens of gender, sometimes on its own and sometimes as a function of gender-related experiences such as pregnancy, maternity leave, child care and other caregiving responsibilities, domestic roles, and partnerships. None of the male faculty members we spoke with referred to their gender identities when discussing their experiences, but some attributed meaning to that aspect of their female colleagues' identities as it related to their institutional experiences and careers. Thus, there may be policy implications for supporting female faculty members in LACs in ways that are less salient for male faculty members.

Female faculty members shared stories of being the first or only woman in their department, experiencing sexism and inequity in service roles and informally supporting students, and a lack of mentoring. One told us about being sexually harassed by a senior colleague. Women also spoke of perceived inequities in the ways in which their scholarship was evaluated and their careers developed. One interviewee recalled a perceived disparity in tenure processes and said: "I've seen a situation where a woman had excellent teaching evaluations and current research. Her department supported her unanimously. And [the college committee] fired her at her third-year review. That same year, a guy who had not done one bit of research got tenure. I mean—explain that one to me! And you know, things like that happen. And I honestly think it's because he was in the poker group with the provost and some of the old boys who mattered."

A professor in the social sciences commented that institutional systems to support female faculty members mattered, but that women had mobilized to form their own support network on her campus: "There's a group of women faculty that gets together about monthly to discuss a whole range of stuff. Sometimes it's teaching, sometimes it's, 'Okay students are being sexist in this way, how do I deal with it?'" That particular group included both senior and junior faculty members from across the ranks, disciplines, and number of years at the institution. Some senior faculty members noted that there had been substantial changes in campus climates and policies related to women since they had arrived at the colleges, but others lamented that change had been insufficient. A woman in a STEM field said: "Most of us are dealing with, you know, thirty-year-old problems, to be honest. We're dealing with lack of recognition. We're dealing with getting paid less. We're dealing with all these things that you think we're not dealing with anymore."

Some male faculty members pointed to the experiences of their female peers when describing life in LACs or noted how their experiences would be different if they were women. One did so at length:

> If I were a female faculty member with kids, I would have less flexibility. The fact is my female colleagues who have younger kids have a harder time than my male colleagues who have young kids. It's just a cultural reality. And if something like early childhood centers made things more available, I think that could help them [the women] because that has implications for how much research they can get done and how much service they can get done. That has influence on promotion and tenure. And so that's the way in which I think institutions could help everyone and also maybe make the playing field a little more level. . . . If a woman has young kids and she sits there for three or four more years or even two more years, then that means she's years later [in achieving tenure]. And then, the next level, to go up to full professor, she's at least two years behind on that, too. And you're talking thousands of dollars a year. And then the percentage of that which goes into her retirement—and then you have compounding interest, and you're into tens of thousands of dollars' difference over the course of a career.

Of course, there were men who relied on family policies as well, such as paternity leave and childcare benefits. Challenges related to family, child care, and partnership responsibilities affected the work lives of all faculty members in LACs, as we discuss next.

FAMILY, CHILD CARE, AND PARTNERSHIP RESPONSIBILITIES. In addition to understanding how faculty members' individual characteristics influence their work experiences in LACs, it is helpful to consider how their relational identities, or their sense of self rooted in their personal relationships with others, influence their careers and related experiences and needs (Pifer and Baker 2016). As one person said, "The number one challenge that lots of people feel particularly at a liberal arts school is just the balancing of your teaching life, your research life, and your home life, which is not easy." Table 3.2 provides an overview of this aspect of the lives of the faculty members we surveyed

Almost three-quarters of our survey respondents were married or had a partner. Forty-six percent had at least one child who was school age or younger. Furthermore, almost one in ten reported having additional caregiving responsibilities.

An associate professor in the humanities summed up how life in an LAC posed challenges related to family needs that the institutions could do a better job of addressing: "There's the question of really having to negotiate childrearing, for instance, and I'm sure that would be the case for people who take care of their elderly parents as well." As with other issues, some senior faculty members with many years invested in their colleges noted progress related to this aspect of faculty work lives: "We've increasingly got female and male faculty who are having children before tenure, and it doesn't seem to—it delays them, but it doesn't seem to impede them. Uh, so I mean I think that's positive." For many, however, progress was insufficient. Faculty members who had no children or no young children in their homes often pointed to that fact as a reason for their ability to be focused and successful in the demanding LAC environments. We note, however, that there were some concerns from that group of faculty members about how to legitimize their desires for work-life balance. For example, one person told us: "Around here, children are an easy excuse for why you can't do something after hours. And so if you don't have children, you're the one who's expected to always accommodate [others]. I'm really respectful of the fact that it takes a village to raise a child, and I really want everybody to be able to have children, but I also really resent the fact that I don't seem to have a right to a personal life because I don't have children." Those who had—or hoped to have—children expressed concern about their ability to be successful across all fronts. A senior faculty member who had been involved in hiring new colleagues observed: "One issue the faculty is encountering is the point when they decide that it's time to have a family. We still don't have much in terms of child care." Similarly, another recalled: "It was hard that we didn't have day care on campus. I wish that we could have described a better maternity leave policy."

TABLE 3.2
Family Characteristics of Survey Respondents

Characteristic	Number and percent
Partnership status	
Married or in a domestic partnership	307 (74%)
Divorced	18 (4%)
Widowed	3 (1%)
Single	42 (10%)
Prefer not to respond	43 (10%)
Parenting status	
No children	113 (27%)
Pregnant	5 (1%)
Preschool-age child(ren)	60 (15%)
School-age child(ren)	123 (30%)
Adult child(ren)	105 (25%)
Single parent	3 (1%)
Coparent with current partner or spouse	7 (2%)
Coparent with former partner or spouse	7 (2%)
Other	7 (2%)
Prefer not to respond	32 (8%)
Caregiving responsibilities	
Parent(s)	23 (6%)
Grandparent(s)	3 (1%)
Sibling(s)	4 (1%)
Other	4 (1%)
Prefer not to respond	74 (18%)

Notes: Percentages may not sum to 100 because of rounding. School-age children includes those through high school. Adult children include those of college age. "Other parenting status" includes children in different age groups, foster child(ren), and pregnant partner. "Other caregiving responsibilities" include those for a disabled spouse or ailing parent.

Some study participants talked about their strategies for being effective in their faculty roles while still fulfilling caregiving obligations. An associate professor in the social sciences said: "I'm really fast. I do not work at home. I finish everything at work, and then I go home and I'm with my kids. And ever since I've been here, I've gone home at 3:00 every day, because my kids are important to me. And I used to do the 3-to-6 shift at home, and then at 6:00 I would start working again at home. I don't do that anymore. But my productivity at research has gone way down." Support from partners who provided full-time or primary child care was also fairly common. One woman said: "Well, honestly, what's helped me the most is the fact that my husband has chosen to be a stay-at-home father. If he weren't, then life would be much, much harder."

The challenges of building lives and careers in small colleges extended to partnerships for some people. It was taxing for some faculty members to incorporate the professional and interpersonal needs of their partners into the lives they were creating in those environments.

For example, a professor in the social sciences commented: "I think it's hard because my husband works from home—because he didn't want an hour-and-a-half commute. And that makes it a little bit difficult, because he doesn't have as big a circle of friends as he would if he had a workplace. So that puts more pressure on me at home, to be there for him. When I came here fifteen years ago, it was really unusual to have a female faculty member with a stay-at-home male spouse. And he felt pretty alienated from the beginning."

Faculty members struggled to negotiate what their career choices meant for their partners, as we began to discuss above in our consideration of life in small towns. We saw a range of choices to accommodate the "two-body problem," including partners' giving up their careers, assuming primary responsibility for child care, working from home and starting their own businesses, and maintaining two residences or living apart. One person had a very long commute between the city where her partner worked and the campus where she worked. A few faculty members were fortunate enough to have partners with academic or administrative appointments at their colleges or relatively close institutions. Some people described eventual compromises or other solutions to these challenges and told us how these resolutions had affected their personal lives. A professor in the social sciences said of her spouse: "It was a real struggle [in] the first few years for him to figure out what he was gonna do. . . . I mean, it's been hard. And it wasn't easy on our marriage, especially in the beginning." In fact, we heard repeatedly of faculty attrition or failure to hire the preferred candidate when a spousal accommodation wasn't possible.

We have discussed the two-body problem and the challenges of raising a family and focusing on a partnership in LACs; we also heard of challenges experienced by single people. As one faculty member put it, "I think for single people it's very hard to be here because there's not really a good way to meet people. I don't know what they can do about it, but I do think it's a big reason that we lose people."

SEXUAL IDENTITY. For some faculty members, family and partnership issues intersected with experiences related to their sexual identities. One person explained that she, her partner, and their children felt that they fit on campus, but there were also challenges related to their partnership:

> We are very comfortable here as a family. I think it is a lot harder for gay men in this environment, particularly in town. You know, [this] is a relatively conservative community, even though the college is a much more liberal kind of space. There is some support. There are domestic partner benefits for same-sex couples—for those of us who were not able to be legally married. However, and this is true nationally, we had to pay taxes on all of the contributions that the college made to our partner's insurance. And so even though she is able to be insured through the college, we estimated that we pay about $3,000 a year in taxes that our heterosexual married colleagues don't have to pay.

Sexual identities also affected faculty experiences in LACs in other ways, including what one person identified as "direct homophobia but also more indirect experiences" related to "not only the informal work of counseling students and things like that, but also a sense of a lot of committee work to represent diversity on the faculty." These unofficial and identity-based demands on faculty time resulted in what this person identified as "a lot of extra work on our plates [compared to] faculty who aren't part of a minority group on campus."

ADDITIONAL IDENTITY-BASED CHALLENGES. Individual characteristics and lived experiences go beyond race, gender, family structures, and sexual identity. The accounts shared here are limited as a reflection of the faculty members who were willing to participate in our study; they do not reflect the breadth or depth of experiences of all those who hold, or will hold, faculty appointments in LACS. For example, we heard from faculty members who were concerned about the diversity-related challenges of living and working in LACs in general. One person made the connection between the lived experiences of "minority faculty," institutional policy, resource allocation, and her own workload: "Going back to the point that I made earlier about minority faculty being overburdened with areas that are really outside of our purview, I think making sure that there are staff in the counseling center and in other areas of campus that are trained on issues of diversity is important. I think diversity becomes, in some ways, a really empty word, but I think that we need to have people that are trained in the kinds of issues that minority groups on our campuses face. And that would certainly help with my own workload." Another faculty member said: "I think probably one of the biggest challenges is the issue of ability and disability. I think [the college] has been mostly behind on that, both in terms of physical access and also in terms of faculty resources. It's very much individuals who go to the dean and make a case for something. They have issues that make it difficult to type, and then the dean gives them money to buy voice-activated software. There should be policies that make that accessible. People shouldn't need to go with their hand out to the dean." These concerns and experiences suggest the need for a closer look at the policies that support faculty members' work in LACs.

Challenges by Rank and Appointment Type

"The reality here is that after tenure you basically go into service mode, and then hopefully you find time within the next seven to ten years to do enough research to apply for promotion to full professor. We do have a lot of folks who take many, many years to get to full [professor], and a lot of that has to do with the service responsibility they take on."

–An associate professor in the social sciences

In this chapter, we have discussed the institutional, geographic, and individual characteristics that shape faculty members' work lives in LACs. Faculty experiences across career stages is a principal consideration in this book. Thus, we now examine how career stage influences a holistic view of faculty life. Across ranks and appointment types, we found that faculty members may experience challenges in their work lives, some of which are connected to those we have discussed in other chapters. These challenges include managing the workload and role expectations in environments that may not offer sufficient resources or clarity in vision or strategic priorities; balancing personal and professional responsibilities, including the management of partnerships and caregiving roles; and responding to sexism, racism, homophobia, unwelcoming environments, lack of diversity, and other sources of inequity or oppression. Yet, as we note in other chapters, professors, associate professors, assistant professors, and those without tenure-track appointments experienced these challenges in distinct ways.

Full Professors

In some ways, full professors experienced fewer challenges than their peers when it came to developing their careers and lives. If they had children, they likely already raised them and may have been enjoying time with their grandchildren. They generally felt confident about and satisfied with their careers. Yet work-life balance was still a priority, as they focused on their partnerships and anticipated potential challenges in the future related to personal health, retirement, and elder care. As one STEM professor said: "My parents are alive and well, in good health. Three years from now, three days from now, who knows? But right now, I'm not worried about that." Although some worried about achieving balance from day to day, others expressed concern about their quest for balance during the summer months, sometimes misunderstood to be a time not covered by faculty members' contracts and therefore when they are disengaged from their work.

Professors also expressed challenges stemming from their overinvolvement in administrative or service responsibilities, and sometimes in teaching responsibilities. These challenges were often mentioned in general terms, but they also arose specifically in response to the institutional goal of freeing up time for assistant professors to excel in research and scholarship. Some senior faculty members expressed feelings of not being recognized for their loyalty and contributions to their colleges, and of being taxed to support the new crop of faculty colleagues.

Associate Professors

Work-life balance was a stressor for associate professors, who had earned tenure but were still engaged in continuing or reestablishing their research agendas while also fulfilling their increased service and administrative responsibilities, reinvigorating their teaching, and investing in their family lives. Although most did not have young children, some did. All had familial, health-related, and interpersonal responsibilities and goals that interacted with their careers. For example, one associate professor in the humanities named work-life balance as the greatest challenge he experienced. His schedule was a familiar one: "Friday is my day off. I teach a four-day schedule; I shouldn't be here talking to you. I shouldn't have been at the meeting that I was at; I shouldn't be at the meeting that I'm gonna be at this afternoon, but the reality is there's only so many hours in the week, and Friday becomes the day that I catch up. So the research day in the week becomes a day for doing things that I didn't have time to do the rest of the week. And I try not to take work home, but I do." He attributed this challenge in part to years of academic socialization: "I have actually talked to my therapist about my inability to say no. I think part of it's ego, a sense of indispensability. Academics often tend to be quite insecure; it's bred into us in graduate school." We talked with many associate professors who experienced the posttenure letdown of burnout or the "mid-career slump." Another associate professor summarized these challenges aptly: "I think the biggest challenge is remaining viable in a scholarly fashion. I find that to be a huge challenge at a liberal arts college. . . . There's a lot of things that grab for your time. Because the teaching and the administrative and the community service kinds of things can really absorb you and consume you. Not to mention our families."

Assistant Professors

Of course, not only assistant professors were raising children—faculty members across all appointment types had young children. But assistant professors in particular told us about challenges related to child care; maternity and paternity leave concerns; negotiating responsibilities related to children and home with their partners; and negotiating their professional tasks, such as arranging teaching or meeting times with colleagues to accommodate parenting duties. Those without children or who had already raised their children noted that while they did not need these resources personally, their institutions should make them available to those colleagues who did need them, for the good of the group as much as the individuals.

Assistant professors also struggled to find a sense of fit in their new towns, colleges, and departments, and to achieve excellence across all roles on the path toward tenure. A lack of professional development resources such as clear policies, mentoring, financial support, and similarly engaged colleagues made that path an uphill one for some.

Non-Tenure-Track Faculty Members

The faculty members we spoke with who did not have tenure-track appointments were in a range of positions: some were administrators or athletics staff members with faculty appointments, and others were full-time instructors. The members of this group, too, were affected by the challenges we describe in this chapter. First, like all contingent faculty, this population depended on institutional budgets and personnel policies for support such as health care benefits, financial resources for professional development such as research supplies or conference attendance, and retirement options. While administrators with faculty appointments had more benefits and security than their non-tenure-track (NTT) instructional colleagues, both groups were uncertain about the degree to which faculty development support at their colleges applied to them.

Those who were early in their careers and had relocated to accept their NTT positions were reluctant to become invested in the town and college communities, given their lack of job security. This, coupled with the lack of job prospects for partners and spouses, made it especially challenging for this group to see themselves as fully part of the college community.

Finally, faculty members in this group expressed frustration at the amount of work they contributed to the colleges, with insufficient compensation or recognition. Administrators with teaching responsibilities spoke of "basically working two full-time jobs," and NTT full-time instructors were challenged by the degree to which departments relied on them for advising, supervising undergraduate research, and mentoring students without commensurate compensation for the hours invested in their roles outside of the classroom.

What Can I Do? Policy Generation and Implementation to Support Holistic Faculty Work Lives

"I have been thinking about this a lot lately. I feel that I need to wait until I receive tenure to start having a family. I want a family. There are no policies about maternity leave or taking time off related to tenure and supporting a family. The values are clearly there to support balance, but the policies aren't there."

—An assistant professor in a STEM discipline

This chapter highlighted the experiences, including the challenges, of faculty work lives in LACs. Let's consider what institutions, administrators, and faculty members can do to achieve strong horizontal alignment through the generation of effective policies that support all aspects of faculty experiences.

One observation emerging from these stories is that faculty members were not always able to identify institution-level solutions to the challenges and problems discussed here. In fact, when we asked hundreds of faculty members in LACs what their institutions could do to mitigate challenges or what policies were in place to support them, one of the most common responses was, "I don't know." Faculty members have the ability to shape their local departmental contexts, manage their own behavior, support their friends and colleagues, and contribute to cultures of collegiality, social interaction, and mentoring, as we describe in chapters 2 and 5. However, they are not responsible for or knowledgeable about college-level policies that may mitigate problems and improve faculty experiences—that is not what they were trained or hired to do. The issue reminds us of a passionate call to action from a frustrated faculty member on the topic of gender equity. She said: "You can do all the training you want. It's not about us. We're doing a good a job. We know all this stuff. What we're trying to do is engage the administration. And part of what *they* need to do is they need to do the work." Her perspective is a reminder of the key components of horizontal alignment, and the need for collaboration between and action from both faculty members and administrators.

For these reasons, LACs must rely on policies and consistent strategies when supporting holistic faculty work lives, not anecdotal evidence and individual behaviors. Horizontal alignment highlights the importance of policy-driven responses as much as informal or formal practices to support faculty work and development across their lives and careers. Policies are imperative for achieving horizontal alignment and shaping institutional practices. We draw on the AFFD-LAC (see chapter 7) to offer the following questions to consider, recommendations for advancing institutional policies that achieve those goals, and practical examples of how policies might better support faculty work and lives in LACs.

QUESTIONS FOR CONSIDERATION

1. How can institutional policies best acknowledge and respond to the holistic needs of faculty members as they engage in their work over time?

    We recommend that colleges avoid the "spaghetti-on-the-wall approach" (that is, offering a slew of programs that are neither strategic or focused yet hoping something will stick) to faculty members' professional development, which includes seemingly random programming based on common practices (often mislabeled as "best practices"). Such an approach can deplete institutional resources quickly, without any measured result or systematic reflection of institutional priorities. Instead, we encourage campus administrators to use the data presented here and in other scholarly work to learn what is truly needed to support faculty members' development across career stages and appointment types and invest resources accordingly. We found that faculty members overwhelming referred to policies for sabbatical or research leave and funding for their participation in professional associations and disciplinary conferences as among the most important sources of support for their work. This makes sense, given the stress they reported feeling as they routinely focused on teaching, advising, and institutional engagement and had little time left for scholarly activity and connections with disciplinary peers.

2. How can institutions obtain accurate information about faculty needs to inform policy creation, implementation, and evaluation?

    We recommend listening sessions, surveys about faculty needs, and strategic meetings with faculty members and administrators to strengthen horizontal alignment through policies that meet the particular needs of LAC faculty members. Although the director of human resources should be the expert on employment law, hiring practices, and maternity and paternity policies, for example, it is the faculty members who are the experts on how their goals and challenges influence their experiences and consequently their workplace success and satisfaction. Policies for documenting and disclosing needs-based decision making related to budget lines and resources for faculty and staff hiring—as well as campuswide communication about such decisions—can help achieve effective policy-based communication. Public dialogue may be most valuable in response to the challenges we have reported, which are connected to faculty members' identities and personal characteristics. We advocate for a dialogue between faculty and administrative stakeholders that spans policy and practice and demonstrates an institutional commitment to workplace equity, safe work environments, and cultures of inclusivity and nondiscrimination. Feedback tools that initiate creative dialogue may also be helpful in addressing faculty members' understanding of institutional priorities and goals.

3. How can campus leaders provide guidance for, and a commitment to, effective policies?

We recommend systematic reviews of institutional policies and their implications for staffing, resource allocation, and mission fulfillment. This will bring such policies from an individual level to an institutional level, which in turn will further customize effective policies for faculty development in LACs. A systematic approach may be most helpful in offering holistic approaches to faculty support. Systematic thinking about faculty work brings to light the challenges we described in this chapter, such as the need for clearly and consistently articulated policies about maternity and paternity leave and the desire for on-campus child care. In addition, the stories we heard about life in small towns highlight the challenges related to feelings of isolation and spousal or partner employment needs. While not all campuses may be able to afford to provide every possible option related to spousal or partner hiring, faculty members' needs must be recognized on this front, and responsiveness must be demonstrated through policy development and implementation. Systematic thinking may also help institutions make sense of the alignment between formal and informal messages, promotion and reward systems, and compensation (for example, faculty development funds) related to faculty work. We found that faculty members' efforts were not always rewarded through the tenure system or compensation model of their college, though these efforts seemed to be required to meet institutional priorities. The unsurprising result was frustration.

Conclusion

This chapter provided a complex portrait of faculty engagement in LACs, including both sources of professional fulfillment and development and sources of frustration and inhibitors to success and satisfaction. Participants in our study relied on their own characteristics, needs, goals, and life circumstances to make sense of their experiences, as well as the organizational environments of their classrooms, departments, and institutions. Our findings also illuminate potential relationships between faculty characteristics and their behaviors and attitudes about their careers in LACs. Hyers and colleagues (2012) emphasized that when faculty members receive effective professional development and mentoring, there are positive outcomes for institutions as well as for faculty members.

This chapter reinforces a key theme: relationships matter. A culture of collegiality, mentoring, and informal support is as necessary as institutional policies for faculty success and development. Policies alone cannot provide every needed support for faculty work in the unique environments of LACs. Nonetheless, policies are important. It is imperative for LACs to be mindful of the human side of the faculty labor force and to be proactive in developing and implementing consistent and coherent policies that support faculty members across their holistic identities as valued members of the institutions.

4

∘∘∘

Aligning Faculty Needs
with Institutional Priorities

It is a typical Wednesday on campus. The sidewalks are bustling with students leaving classes as faculty members head to an all-staff meeting at which the college president will discuss the new strategic planning process. The Leadership Council and Strategic Planning Committee members hope to receive faculty feedback about the college's priorities for the next five years. At the meeting, discussions about priorities ensue. Leadership Council members talk about the need for improved athletic facilities, a more deliberate strategy to recruit out-of-state students, and greater alumni support for campus initiatives such as fund-raising. The president says that the Admissions Office will add two staff members to support the student recruiting efforts, and the Development Office will add three to five staff positions in coming years.

The discussion then turns to student needs, including improved facilities, national recruitment strategies, and increased alumni engagement and support. Every speaker agrees that the overarching goal is to increase the college's national visibility. After the meeting, faculty members exchange comments in low voices on the way out. A biologist observes, "Another strategic plan with no explicit initiatives related to faculty members. Sad, but not surprising." A full professor from the humanities declares, "Administrators don't listen," and her junior colleague replies, "Well, faculty members don't articulate what they need." Discouragement spreads along with the faculty, as its members disperse across the campus back to their offices.

Does this story sound familiar? On your campus, how often do faculty members and campus leaders talk about college priorities, strategic initiatives, and personnel policies as interrelated? If they do have these conversations, do they act on them in visible, meaningful ways to achieve the desired ends?

The story above is just one of many we heard from faculty members. The scenario highlights many faculty members' perceptions of a disconnect between institutional priorities and faculty members' needs.

The challenge for leaders is how to frame and meet faculty members' needs in ways that also support and reflect organizational priorities and initiatives. This chapter focuses on the horizontal dimension of the alignment framework for faculty development in liberal arts colleges (AFFD-LAC; see chapter 7) as a way to facilitate dialogue within and among two groups—faculty members and administrators—that will lead to action.

Disconnects in Faculty Professional Development: Faculty Members' Perceptions and Needs

Academic deans and provosts in the Great Lakes Colleges Association (GLCA) do focus on their human capital, the faculty members, to sustain and innovate their respective institutions. These leaders realize that faculty members are at the heart of their institution's work and mission. Faculty members teach, serve as mentors to undergraduate student researchers, experiment with new pedagogies in their classrooms, and interact directly and daily with students. Indeed, an acknowledgment of the importance of one's human resources is not unique to liberal arts colleges (LACs).

Yet researchers have found that this realization does not always translate into organizational policies. There appears to be a disconnect in the appreciation administrators have for their human capital and the policies that support those individuals. As Jay Barney and Patrick Wright asked, "Why do many organizational decisions not evidence this stated commitment to people or a respect for the HR function?" (1997, 3). This gap was recognized by the campus leaders in the LACs in our study. They were concerned that faculty development programming could be better, particularly for faculty members beyond the early-career stage, and that professional development efforts for all faculty members might not be supporting the organization's goals—at least, not as explicitly as they could or should be doing. Our findings add urgency to their well-founded concerns.

It seems obvious that faculty members move through a predictable progression in their career, yet our results suggest that needs specific to different career stages are relatively neglected in faculty development programming. Faculty members experience and manage career stage challenges as they advance through the professoriate. And while on the surface the needs of all faculty members may appear to be similar, they experience challenges quite differently and thus require supports specific to their career stage.

Full Professors

"I start every academic year at this stage in my career asking myself, 'Is this the year I become irrelevant?'"

—A full professor of biology

Full professors are often regarded as campus leaders by virtue of their greater institutional memories and experiences, and they hold an important place on their respective campuses. Full professors are typically within ten to twelve years to retirement (Austin 2010). They have weathered changes in administration and in student preferences and learning styles, as well as evolving internal and external expectations. The number of senior faculty members has increased over the past twenty years, leading to an expected steady stream of retirements in the coming decades (Austin 2010) and a loss of institutional knowledge and leaders. Ann Austin wrote, "This group of faculty members experiences specific challenges, issues, and concerns that faculty development programming can address" (2010, 366).

Full professors in our study described their unmet needs, which were influenced by workload, institutional culture, and career stage challenges. These deficiencies inhibit their ability to contribute to their respective campuses and departments at the level to which they aspire.

WORKLOAD: TOO MUCH TO DO, NOT ENOUGH TIME. Forty-two percent of the full professor survey respondents reported that their workload most affected their responsibilities. Two overarching themes influenced their ability to effectively engage in the myriad responsibilities with which they were tasked: not having enough time and having too heavy a workload. Not having enough time to effectively teach, advise, mentor, engage in scholarship, and serve in administrative capacities is related to having too many roles, both of which were detrimental to full professors' efforts in the areas they deemed critical to their presence on campus. For example, they discussed their desire to remain relevant in the classroom, which fueled their reinvention of themselves as teachers. They sought new ways to engage students and remain on the cutting edge in their respective fields by incorporating the latest technologies in the classroom. Yet as one full professor noted, "such reinvention takes time and persistence given the amount of relearning and giving up old ways of doing."

Across all the GLCA institutions, full professors had service responsibilities in addition to other duties, and those responsibilities became increasingly important in ways that were overwhelming for many faculty members. Full professors perform service in roles such as department chair, committee chair or member, faculty liaison, or representative of the campus to the community.

Several professors mentioned their feelings of obligation to "serve the institution" that has supported them throughout their careers as a means of ensuring a vibrant campus community, one steeped in faculty governance. Yet faculty members noted that service came at a cost. One observed that there was a focus on service as "a proliferation of administrative responsibilities," while others noted that "[service commitments] tend to be very time-consuming for the [limited] benefits accrued" and that there was a "long-established tendency for, or administrative expectation of, faculty to assume ever-increasing service workloads." Despite these challenges, full professors generally reported feeling compelled to continue taking on these service roles as a means of "protecting" their early-career colleagues as they worked to earn tenure.

Lastly, full professors also viewed mentorship as an important, often minimized, form of service that was time-consuming yet rewarding. While such mentorship, allows senior colleagues to draw on their years of experience as they support new colleagues, as Austin (2010) described, the changing institutional and disciplinary landscape creates challenges to delivering effective mentoring. Full professors cited changing institutional policies related to promotion and tenure (P&T). One faculty member commented, "I am happy to shepherd colleagues through that process, but the standards I was tenured and promoted under are not the same, and I find it challenging to be as helpful as possible as a result." Similar feelings related to relevance in the classroom also surfaced. Another full professor noted, "I start every academic year at this stage in my career asking myself, 'Is this the year I become irrelevant?' And when the answer is yes to that question, I'll know it's time to retire."

INSTITUTIONAL CULTURE: WHAT ABOUT ME? Twenty-nine percent of the full professor respondents thought an "early-career culture" dominated their respective campuses. That culture was a contributing factor in deciding what faculty development programming would be offered or created and how funding decisions were made. One full professor said, "I fully understand the need to fund and support my younger colleagues as they work toward P&T. But I sometimes think such a strategy is demotivating for us senior colleagues looking to stay engaged and active in our disciplines and scholarship." Another one shared a similar sentiment by noting that "there is some funding available institutionally, but applications are generally structured toward traditional areas of scholarship, laboratory research, student assistants, and publications with a real emphasis on early-career faculty." And a third full professor commented, "It is difficult to find ways even to suggest faculty development workshops, speakers, or events that focus on research matters at the more senior levels of the faculty."

These professors mentored their peers willingly and often enjoyed doing so. However, full professors also desired mentoring support for themselves but found limited institutional opportunities to connect with appropriate mentors (see chapter 5 for more on mentoring). A full professor summed it up in this way: "Of course we are happy to support our more junior colleagues, but the administration has failed to realize or consider that we [senior faculty] too would benefit from the mentorship of peers either in our own institutions or from others." The predominant opportunity for full professors to receive mentoring occurred at the level of the GLCA, as the association's staff members sought to connect faculty members across institutions through various funded programs and initiatives.

CAREER STAGE: NEARING RETIREMENT. Lastly, 21 percent of the full professors discussed their specific career stage as a challenge for which they could use support. The biggest challenge is related to deciding when to retire—or, as several said, to "pull the trigger" or "go gently into that good night." One full professor explained that at his institution "we have no guidelines or procedures for retirement; only individual arrangements to continue to teach a course or so after retirement." Currently, only three of the GLCA institutions have phased retirement programs.

Associate Professors

"I see no way toward full professorship."

–An associate professor in the humanities

Faculty members at the mid-career stage experience personal and professional demands that may derail or detain talented individuals if they do not have appropriate institutional supports. Associate professors have passed a probationary period as assistant professors (on average, six years) and have been awarded tenure if the institution has such a system (Austin 2010). All the GLCA institutions have a tenure system. (At the time we collected our data, there were no tenured professors at Antioch College. During the writing of this book, three professors earned tenure.) For our purposes, we categorize associate, or mid-career, faculty members as early-career associates (up to five years after being promoted to associate professor) and late-career associates (six or more years after promotion) (Mathews 2014) to respond to the varied needs of both newer and more senior associate professors. Mid-career faculty members in our study faced three main challenges, those related to their increased workloads, career stage, and professional aspirations. Associate professors experienced these challenges in different ways than their full professor colleagues did.

WORKLOAD: INCREASED SERVICE. Nearly half of the mid-career faculty participants who completed the survey discussed their increased service and leadership responsibilities and administrators' mounting expectations of them as "overwhelming" and "impossible to manage . . . effectively." These associate professors seemed unprepared for the expectation of increased service work that came with earning tenure. As early-career faculty members, they had felt protected to a large degree from such requirements. In the GLCA, it was uncommon for a nontenured faculty member to serve as department chair, although we did learn about a few exceptional cases in which such a person assumed a formal leadership or administrative role.

One faculty member noted, "My day is so full of chair responsibilities, committee work, immediate teaching responsibilities, and advising that I do not have time to engage in the development opportunities for faculty that I used to participate in with enjoyment." Faculty members consistently mentioned that administrative or more bureaucratic tasks took time away from responsibilities associated with serving as department chair, such as mentoring other faculty members.

In discussing their workload challenges, mid-career faculty members recognized that despite increased leadership and administrative roles, positions such as department or committee chair come with little or no actual authority, relegating their role to, as one participant put it, "being a pencil pusher." We heard comments such as: "there really is very little accountability for faculty, especially poor faculty behavior and, as department chair, the truth is there is very little I can do about it" and "unfortunately, I have realized, now that I am tenured, there are no rewards and no punishments for faculty behavior. Talk about breeding mediocrity!"

CAREER STAGE: DISILLUSIONMENT. Once tenure is earned, mid-career faculty members must assume increased leadership, administrative, and service responsibilities that require new skill sets. Learning these skills often comes at the cost of abandoning the research agendas and course development plans that were so energizing to these faculty members in the first place. Thirty-three percent of mid-career faculty member survey respondents cited this as a challenge. As mid-career faculty members prepared to welcome and mentor their early-career colleagues, they also sought to reinvigorate their own research and teaching agendas but found insufficient institutional supports to do so.

The late-career associate professors in our study were beginning to think about and prepare for the latter half of their careers. One said: "I'll soon be entering the late stage of my career, and I'm indecisive about how I want to approach my last 10–15 years. Should I just keep on doing the mix of teaching, scholarship, and service that I've been doing, or should I change the focus of my professional activities or the direction of my research? I feel a constant pull into service leadership roles, and at times this conflicts with my goals for teaching and scholarship."

Some of these late-career associates have clear plans on how to work toward promotion, while others do not. One participant commented, "I see no way toward full professorship. I spent so much time serving my institution and department to ensure my junior colleagues would earn tenure, and I feel so out of the loop with my discipline." Another said, "There is a dearth of programs for mid-career faculty who aren't part of the latest trends on campus, thus making it really hard to get the needed support to get over that 'I'll forever be an associate professor' slump."

PROFESSIONAL ASPIRATIONS: REINVENTION. "Reinvention" and "risk taking" were goals of 28 percent of the mid-career faculty members who participated in this study. The participants at this stage described feeling relieved about earning tenure—a feeling quickly followed by panicking and wondering, "What's next?" Added to that anxiety was the reality that very few institutional supports exist to help overcome it. One faculty participant noted, "I have just published a well-received monograph that was the culmination of fifteen years of work, and [I] am having a lot of trouble settling into a new research project." There were no institutional structures and supports, such as posttenure reviews, to encourage and support faculty members to "stay on track." None of our mid-career faculty members expressed the desire to remain at the associate rank until retirement, nor did they feel that they had already accomplished all they could. Rather, they had a desire to keep learning, improving, and evolving. One faculty member explained: "We urge, or rather require, our students to seek to be continually learning, and we create structures and experiences to support that. Ironic [that] we fail to do that for faculty members posttenure."

Assistant Professors

"Establishing myself as both a researcher and teacher so quickly after graduate school–it's overwhelming to say the least."

–An assistant professor of economics

New professors will replenish the leadership ranks. Research and practice that focuses on assistant professors—who are in the early stage of their careers—has dominated the literature (see Austin and Rice 1998; Sorcinelli 2000). New professors require a variety of supports in the traditional academic areas of teaching, scholarship, and advising (Solem, Foote, and Monk 2009). They also need support navigating campus and community politics, work-life balance, and the unwritten rules of the profession. The challenges these faculty members face are worsened by the lack of attention paid to the topic of the traditional academic roles in graduate school (Austin 2002; Golde and Dore 2001). Given the variety of roles professors are expected to engage in at an LAC, the assistant professors in our study probably experienced an even steeper learning curve, compared to their peers at research universities. Assistant professors in our study identified their top three challenges as related to their workload, career stage, and navigating the institutional culture.

WORKLOAD: BALANCING ACT. From the moment the assistant professors in our study stepped onto their respective campuses, they were expected to be fully engaged (or learn very quickly how to become so). As a result, 43 percent of them noted that their workload was a key challenge. The average course load for all the GLCA faculty members is six courses in an academic year (table 1.2, chapter 1). In addition, assistant professors were acutely aware that the "tenure clock is ticking," thus requiring them to be productive scholars as well as teachers. All the GLCA schools waived advising responsibilities for assistant professors in their first year, but only a few waived those duties in the second year. One assistant professor described his workload challenge as the need to "manage my time balancing between work and family. Establishing myself as both a researcher and teacher so quickly after graduate school—it's overwhelming to say the least." Another described her workload challenge this way: "Currently workload is a major issue. Learning how to balance my responsibilities across teaching-related activities, scholarship, and service with a life outside of work is an ongoing challenge. [The institution] wants you to excel in all of these areas, but there just aren't enough hours in the day, nor do they provide you with the necessary supports to excel in all of these areas." Many assistant professors realized that "getting it all done" was impossible, and therefore they needed to prioritize tasks and be more deliberate about their approach to fulfilling their academic roles.

CAREER STAGE: ALL ABOUT EARNING TENURE. The top career stage challenge reported by assistant professors was the P&T process—half of them mentioned it. "I have concern regarding the promotion and tenure process," one said. Another felt overwhelmed by "not knowing the details of what is expected of me as a new tenure-track faculty member," and a third said, "Now that I have a tenure-track position, [a challenge is] earning tenure with no real clarity around that process so far." These feelings are not unique to assistant professors in LACs. In fact, Austin (2010) classified this as the dominant challenge across institution types for faculty members employed where a tenure system exists.

INSTITUTIONAL CULTURE: MISMATCH? Institutional culture was a challenge facing both full professor and assistant professor survey respondents, with over 28 percent of the latter group mentioning it. However, these two populations defined institutional culture quite differently. While full professors felt that their institution's culture was biased toward early-career faculty members, the assistant professors felt ill served by the same culture. Assistant professors focused on a perceived or real mismatch between unspoken expectations from their school in terms of what they needed to achieve to earn P&T. This could include, for example, institutional policies and practices that support the academic performance for early-career faculty members designed to help them stay at that institution. One faculty member commented, "In one breath, the administration keeps talking about the importance of scholarship, yet the amount of funding available or the process by which you request and receive that funding is cumbersome and seemingly arbitrary, to say the least." Another told us: "As a first-year faculty, I'm still trying to figure out the institution more generally, and from my understanding and experience I am part of a dysfunctional department. The administration knows it yet does nothing about it."

Non-Tenure-Track Faculty Members

> "Colleagues just assign me the least popular courses and put me on the unfavorable campus committees."
>
> —A non-tenure-track faculty member in the fine arts

There is an increasing reliance on contingent (for example, adjunct and other part-time) faculty positions across higher education, and LACs are no exception to this trend. This faculty population is often neglected by their institutions and researchers. Indeed, we did not expect there to be many non-tenure-track (NTT) faculty respondents to our surveys because we incorrectly assumed that LACs might rely less than other institutions on temporary faculty positions. However, 10 percent of our respondents were not on the tenure track. According to a report titled "Background Facts on Contingent Faculty" (American Association of University Professors 2014a), NTT faculty members accounted for about half of all faculty appointments in US higher education at that time and could be divided into two categories: those who teach part time, and those who have full-time teaching responsibilities but are not on the tenure track. Since the report was published, "faculty work has become more fragmented, unsupported, and destabilized" (American Association of University Professors 2014b, 1). Researchers have noted that contingent faculty members account for more than 70 percent of all faculty members in the United States, or three out of four new faculty hires (Kezar and Gehrke 2014). The challenges faced by these faculty members that were mentioned most often in our study were job insecurity, lack of institutional supports, and feeling like second-class citizens.

JOB INSECURITY. Unsurprisingly, job insecurity was the number one challenge reported by 60 percent of the NTT faculty members who completed the survey. One NTT participant explained: "Teaching on short term NTT contracts is a challenge. At [my institution] adjunct employment reviews take place every three years and are as rigorous as a pretenure review but without any employment guarantees." Another NTT faculty member commented, "It's really challenging mentally and emotionally to not know if I have a job from semester to semester." The lack of job security not only affects these faculty members, but it also creates challenges at the department level when developing staffing and course plans.

LACK OF INSTITUTIONAL SUPPORTS. Over half of the NTT faculty members who responded to our survey mentioned the lack of institutional supports to assist their efforts as they engaged in "all the same roles tenured and tenure-track faculty do." NTT faculty members taught a full course load, and all NTT faculty members supervised student research projects, served on thesis committees, advised students on their academic plans, and served as advisors to student organizations. NTT faculty members felt extra pressure to excel in the areas of teaching, scholarship, and service in the hope that excellent performance would win them a permanent appointment at the institution where they were employed. But the pressure to excel and outperform others, or to "prove worth," required support. One noted: "Other than my appointment type, I am no different than my tenure-track early-career peers in terms of what I do on this campus. We [NTT faculty members] need more professional development funding to attend conferences and do research. And not everyone [of us] is even eligible to receive these funds."

SECOND-CLASS CITIZENS. Thirty-four percent of NTT faculty members expressed frustration over receiving less than ideal course assignments or service responsibilities. One said: "I feel like my departmental colleagues just assign me the least popular courses and put me on the unfavorable campus committees because they don't want to do it. I get [that] I am pretty much a second-class citizen, but talk about frustrating!" Such assignments create a disappointing experience for NTT faculty members and might contribute to poor teaching evaluations, making it more challenging for them to earn a tenure-track appointment. One commented, "Being assigned the classes no one else wants to teach at the worst times is a sure way to get the lowest teaching evaluations."

NTT faculty participants described wanting to feel part of the campus and surrounding community and feeling instead like "outsiders looking in." All of them were expected to participate in new faculty orientation and engage in the "welcome back" faculty retreats at the beginning of the academic year, but otherwise they felt excluded from campus activities and events. One said: "My voice is irrelevant on this campus. I teach a full load, engage in scholarship, and support students through advising and in research. Yet I have zero vote in faculty or departmental meetings." NTT faculty members expressed concerns about being fully participating community members in terms of teaching, scholarship, and service, yet not being recognized in faculty governance or being ineligible to receive some institutional supports.

Our results demonstrate the importance of explaining faculty needs by career stage and rank. For example, at first glance it appears that workload is a challenge for everyone, and institutional leaders might assume that this challenge could be solved uniformly across types of faculty members. Yet various groups experience faculty workload challenges quite differently, and thus a more thoughtful and strategic approach to faculty development that spans the career trajectory and different appointment types is needed. Now that faculty needs have been identified, we turn our attention to who is deciding how and in what ways those needs are addressed.

Who and What Informs Faculty Development?

Chapter I painted a picture of the institutional infrastructures that underpin faculty development in the GLCA by taking a broad view of structures, supports, and evaluations. In this chapter, we examine faculty perceptions about who is responsible for faculty development and why that support takes the form it does. In other words, who do faculty members believe is or is not in the driver's seat when it comes to faculty development?

Our faculty respondents believe that the primary drivers of faculty development at their college were either an appointed or selected committee of faculty members (30 percent), or an individual faculty member or administrator with faculty development responsibility (21 percent). These results support the details in chapter I outlining the specific faculty development structures across LACs. Furthermore, 32 percent of our faculty respondents believe that faculty interests determine what supports will be offered, while 27 percent believe that senior administrators make that determination.

The good news is that 59 percent of the faculty respondents who completed the survey perceive that someone on their respective campus is working to meet their developmental needs. The worrisome news is that 41 percent of them do not believe that either faculty members' interests or senior administrators are the primary drivers of programming (and subsequent practice). Instead, these respondents believe that the primary drivers are organizational issues, priorities of the director or dean responsible for faculty development, and priorities identified in the higher education literature. Many of the faculty members in these institutions are unlikely to even attend professional development events if they do not find activities of value. At a minimum, there is confusion among faculty members about what or who influences the content of faculty development programs. Our recommendations in chapter 1 and below in this chapter are offered as a means of clearing up this confusion. Faculty members in the LACs we studied appear to know what they need and want. Campus administrators can use that information to enhance and expand existing efforts while also developing new programming to support institutional goals and priorities.

Policy Considerations and Administrative Priorities

"As with everywhere, those who are willing to contribute and interested in contributing get asked to do more and more."

–A dean

The real question before academic leaders is how faculty members can be supported to develop the skills and knowledge needed by the institution. The AFFD-LAC framework provides a way to think about and to answer this question. Our research suggests that campus leaders want to develop faculty members, and that faculty members wish to be productive organizational citizens.

However, there appear to be numerous organizational policies that are at odds with a coherent development strategy. Unintended roadblocks can stifle faculty creativity and engagement and create more work on both sides. In this section, we identify organizational policies that may need to be reexamined as institutions seek to do more with less and to retain talented faculty members (see table 4.1).

Full Professors

"There is an apparent contradiction [between what the school says it values and what it actually does] for those of us that have been here for fifteen-plus years."

–A full professor of anthropology

Full professors in our study discussed policies or "ways of doing business" at their institution that hindered their progress in surmounting the challenges we

TABLE 4.1

Faculty Development Programming by Professorial Rank across the Great Lakes Colleges Association (GLCA) Institutions

Assistant professor	Associate professor	Full professor
New faculty orientation	Sabbatical	Sabbatical
New faculty mentoring program	Professional development funds	Professional development funds
Start-up funds	Faculty Retreat	Faculty retreat
Faculty retreat	—	Endowed professorships (predominantly in the sciences)
No or limited student advising in first 1–2 years	—	—
Professional development funds	—	—
Reduced course load after interim review	—	—

Note: Programs included in the table only recognize the career-stage-specific programs that are consistent across the GLCA.

enumerated above in this chapter. The problems with those policies were that full professors' service did not contribute toward their career advancement, there was a lack of knowledge management (that is, a structured way of maintaining records, processes, and institutional memory), and there was also a lack of accountability for poor or negative behavior at the institution.

SERVICE DOES NOT LEAD TO ADVANCEMENT. Despite having already been promoted to full professor, 33 percent of the full professor respondents to our survey still noted that "service to the institution" carried little to no weight in P&T decisions. There was a perception that even for early-career colleagues, if someone's teaching and scholarship were strong, a lack of service would not result in a negative P&T decision. One full professor stated that "university service is no longer counted as significantly in decisions about tenure, merit, and promotion, which is serving to undermine the faculty governance of our curriculum and personnel system." Another commented:

> There is an apparent contradiction [between what the school says it values and what it actually does] for those of us that have been here for fifteen-plus years. When we arrived on campus, sure we had to publish, but not to [meet] the same standards early-career faculty are expected to today. We have assumed leadership roles on campus, willingly to serve our institutions. Yet that service really amounts to nothing to earn advancement. Bottom line: the standards we were hired in under have changed, but supports have not kept up with that to support those of us who want to earn full [professor status]. I was one of the lucky ones, but I have colleagues who have been on every campus committee [and] who are excellent teachers, with no hope of promotion because they did not publish. Seems wrong, almost, for a liberal arts college.

This policy is directly related to the challenges of workload and career stage because full and associate professors are expected to assume increased leadership roles (both formal and informal) on their campus, yet when it comes to P&T, that service means little.

LACK OF KNOWLEDGE MANAGEMENT. A related problem was a perception by the faculty that policies such as those related to P&T or who and what was awarded internal grant funds were inconsistently applied, as a result of poorly executed attempts by LAC leaders to manage that information (see the discussion of knowledge management in chapter 1, "What Can I Do?"). There was a disconnect between expectations of faculty members' engagement on campus and how that engagement was recognized and rewarded, as 27 percent of our full professor respondents noted. They mentioned the apparent "inconsistency in how evaluation standards are interpreted or acted upon" or in "how resource allocations are decided." Given the turnover on faculty committees and among administrators, full professors argued that there was a need to create systems, checks and balances, and best practices within the administration that ensured consistency—particularly related to the major decisions about P&T, resource allocation, and approval or disapproval of faculty lines. Full professors strongly believed that these decisions were too often personality driven rather than institutionally enacted.

LACK OF ACCOUNTABILITY. Finally, 21 percent of the full professor respondents mentioned the growing problem of "zero accountability" on campus. This lack of accountability was described as "a one-size-fits-all approach to administration," "the way we've always done things," and "no consequences for bad behavior." However, they described it, the unintended consequence of this lack of accountability is a lowered standard of engagement and behavior for faculty and staff members and administrators. It also results in low morale and disappointment for those faculty members who are active and engaged on campus.

Associate Professors

"It's a little ironic that we talk about meeting students at their learning styles based on their needs and motivation. Where is that effort for faculty?"

—An associate professor of neuroscience

As noted above, associate professors identified their three primary challenges as workload, career stage, and professional aspirations. These mid-career professors cited three types of problematic institutional policies related to these challenges: a deficiency of professional development programming specific to their career stage, the "problem of the count," and a lack of family-friendly policies, which we turn to next.

MID-CAREER FACULTY DEVELOPMENT PROGRAMMING. Sixty-five percent of our associate professor respondents mentioned the lack of supports specific to different career stages. One reported the "lack of an institutionwide plan for faculty development beyond the first year." Others mentioned a focus on early-career supports and even characterized them as very important to their early-career experiences. However, they noted an abrupt end to any programming for them once they became associate professors and aged out of the beginner stage of being a faculty member. One said: "It's a little ironic that we talk about meeting students at their learning styles based on their needs and motivation. Where is that effort for faculty? It's almost as if you get promoted, now you are on your own. Good luck." Another commented: "There is a real lack of true understanding about the needs of faculty at the various stages of their careers. Perhaps worse, there appears to be no real interest to find out, either."

THE "PROBLEM OF THE COUNT." The phrase "the problem of the count" has been used in relationship to faculty mentoring of undergraduate research (Baker, Pifer, Lunsford, Greer, and Ihas 2015). But 43 percent of our mid-career faculty respondents used it to refer to the factors contributing to their workload challenges that were specific to their career stage. In addition to teaching the typical course load in a given academic year, these faculty members also supervised students' directed studies and tutorials, honors theses, independent research projects, and internships. In most cases across the GLCA, these additional responsibilities are not remunerated either monetarily or via course release. Such institutional requirements place even greater demands on faculty members.

FAMILY-FRIENDLY POLICIES. In discussing their workload, career stage, and professional challenges, 37 percent of our mid-career faculty respondents mentioned the tension they faced when trying to manage professional and personal responsibilities. Many of them had school-age children or other dependent care responsibilities, and others were hoping to start a family now that they had become associate professors. Mid-career faculty members referred to having to meet the institutional expectations for earning promotion, the increased service responsibilities and the other teaching work they did outside of the classroom (for example, supervising theses, directed studies, and internships) as problematic. They also discussed issues related to committee and campus meetings, campus speakers, and other campus-related events. Most of these occurred in the evenings or on weekends, which took their time away from home and family. Perhaps more alarming was the apparent or perceived rigidity of administrators about adjusting times or being open to a related discussion. A mid-career faculty member noted:

> We have several elected faculty committees on campus. But when thinking about whether to run for a given committee, we have to think about the time that committee meets. Rather than let the new committee members decide based on their schedules when they can meet in a given semester or academic year, we are just told the committee meets Mondays and Wednesdays from five to seven. When asked why, we hear "That's what time it's always met." Why are we not able to at least have a conversation about that to discuss the possibility of changing that time based on the needs and preferences of the committee members? Those of us with families at home aren't going to participate, which is unfortunate—because a lot of good people who would serve our institution well in that capacity opt out.

Many mid-career professors said they did not believe that such policies were intentional or meant to create challenges for them. Rather, the policies represented a failure by administrators to have an open discussion or examine instances in which such unintended consequences further worsened the problem of faculty participation.

Assistant Professors

"The funding available does not support the institutional expectations."

–An assistant professor of history

Assistant professors offered their insights on the institutional policies that hampered their progress in dealing with their professional challenges. Like associate professors, assistant professors discussed frustration about family-friendly policies and P&T, and they felt a real disconnect between available funding and expectations.

FAMILY-FRIENDLY POLICIES. Thirty-nine percent of our early-career faculty respondents noted that they had child-care responsibilities at home, echoing the sentiments of their associate professor colleagues regarding the problem of campus events, committee meetings, and other community events conflicting with personal responsibilities. One assistant professor said: "I really love my job, but I also really love my kids and spouse. I know the importance of being present and visible at these events, but my kids are only this age for a short time."

Early-career professors also felt uneasiness related to managing their personal and professional demands as they sought to engage in impression management at work. They understood that having children was a choice, and that not all of their peers had children. And while the assistant professors in our study sought to be thoughtful about internal equity related to fulfilling institutional or departmental responsibilities along with departmental colleagues, some of them thought that their more senior colleagues felt as if they were "picking up their [assistant professors'] slack."

PROMOTION AND TENURE. Forty-two percent of our early-career faculty respondents stated that P&T policies at their institution were unclear, and they wanted more transparency about the few institutional supports that existed. Respondents noted the importance of the interim tenure review, but once they were working toward tenure after that milestone, their goals seemed more "fuzzy." In addition, as one assistant professor noted, there were "inconsistencies between the institution's emphasis on excellence in teaching and a lack of a definition of what this is, how it will be assessed, or how much weight teaching will receive in faculty assessments in comparison to scholarship and service." Another interpreted the same problem in the following way: "The emphasis on teaching can hide the real need to publish and advance your research."

DISCONNECT BETWEEN AVAILABLE SUPPORTS AND EXPECTATIONS. Finally, 24 percent of our assistant professor respondents felt that expectations related to their primary roles of teaching, scholarship, and service were not aligned with the funding and supports available. We heard comments such as, "We are expected to take on research students during the summer but do not get paid for our time," and "The funding available does not support the institutional expectations or all of the ancillary parts of being a productive scholar of broader national and international communities." Early-career professors believed that an examination of this apparent disconnect was warranted.

Non-Tenure-Track Faculty Members

"I am teaching or will teach a total of ten courses this year."

–An NTT faculty member in theater studies

NTT faculty members experienced their share of unintended roadblocks as a result of the policies at their respective institutions—policies that exacerbated the challenges they faced. The most frequently cited of these policies included those pertaining to academic appointment type and to salary and benefits.

ACADEMIC APPOINTMENT TYPE. Holding an appointment off the tenure track presents challenges, as we discussed above. Depending on the type of position held (full-time visiting, part-time visiting, or adjunct professor or instructor), the NTT faculty member might be searching for a position year after year or always piecing together several part-time or adjunct positions. This institutional policy related to contingent faculty hiring was noted by nearly 60 percent of our NTT faculty respondents. One noted: "Every semester I update my CV [curriculum vitae] and submit it. My goal is to stay here, and I have been fortunate to be renewed, but that is never a guarantee." Another peer stated: "I am teaching or will teach a total of ten courses this year. Five at [this college] and five nearby, and sadly, I am not considered full time at either institution."

SALARY AND BENEFITS. The second most cited challenge (mentioned by 45 percent of our NTT faculty respondents) is related to salary and benefits. If a person was fortunate enough to be a full-time permanent faculty member teaching a full course load (on average, six courses across the GLCA institutions), he or she would be eligible for full salary and benefits. Since most NTT faculty are not full time—even though they may be teaching four or even five courses—they are paid per course. The average pay per course for the NTT professors in our study ranged from $3,500 to $4,250, or $21,250 per year (at the high end) as a salary with no benefits. Such meager pay often required NTT faculty members to seek opportunities at other institutions as well, creating a juggling act of institutions and responsibilities.

At the beginning of this chapter we posed the question, "How often do faculty members and campus leaders talk about college priorities, strategic initiatives, and personnel policies as interrelated?" Based on our research at the GLCA, we believe that these conversations happen, but that more often than not, they are disconnected. The institutional priorities observed by the faculty members we spoke with not only sometimes failed to address faculty members' needs at times, but even worsened them at other times. Administrators and faculty members should engage in a more strategic assessment of needs and the primary—and in some instances, secondary—policies that relate to those needs. This assessment would facilitate a closer examination of actual practice. It would also help answer another question we asked above, which is the focus of the next section: "If they do have these conversations, do they act on them in visible, meaningful ways to achieve desired ends?"

Faculty Professional Development: Campus Leaders' Aims

"We're interested in developing our faculty to grow as scholars and teachers while they're here. In turn, we hope that allows them to deliver a better educational experience to the students enrolled at the college."

—A provost

The insights into and willingness to support the work of faculty development offered by academic deans and provosts in our study is a testament to their interest in improving faculty development supports at their respective institutions. For example, they spoke openly about their institutions' strengths and weaknesses related to faculty development programming. Understanding faculty development and how to improve it includes understanding the views of campus leaders and administrators about institutional priorities related to faculty development. During our conversations with faculty administrators, we learned that they were concerned about department chair training, faculty mentoring, leadership development, and programming focused on mid-career faculty members.

Department Chair Training

Department chairs are the frontline managers of departments and play critical roles. Indeed, eleven of the thirteen academic deans or provosts interviewed for our study discussed the importance of the department chair role on their respective campuses. (It is important to note that Earlham College does not have the position of department chair. Instead, it has conveners. The occupant of this position brings people together but does not have the authority that a traditional department chair might. Antioch College also does not have department chairs, given its institutional structure.) Their hope was a chair would be able to fulfill all the "bureaucratic duties but also serve as a leader for the department, and mentor junior colleagues." However, they acknowledged the limited formal supports provided to rising or current chairs. One dean noted: "In the past, we've provided very little training for department chairs. So this year we put in place a program to send several new department chairs to the CIC [Council of Independent Colleges] workshop on serving as chair." A dean of faculty development also mentioned the weaknesses on campus and described the following efforts to address them:

> I really felt that our chair system was weak. Department chairs needed more supports and better training and to have a bit more authority in these positions. An initiative that I've started since I became dean is over the summer I began working with some former chairs and some current chairs . . . to develop a department chairs' manual. We're going to do a more extensive set of new chair orientation activities. We will have a meeting where chairs meet together as we seek to give more ownership over to chairs, rather than it being more of an administrative committee. We will have work to do, but I'm pleased with the direction it's going.

Other deans talked about bringing faculty members to the annual January meeting of the Association of American Colleges and Universities or assigning faculty members to a department chair mentor who had successfully served in that capacity. Deans also expressed the belief that more could and should be done to support the role of chair on their campuses.

Faculty Mentoring

As we discuss in chapters 1 and 5, all of the GLCA institutions offer a mentoring program for early-career faculty members. The deans and provosts were committed to providing and supporting mentoring to junior faculty members. However, most of these mentoring efforts did not extend beyond a professor's early career, and often not past the first one to two years of a faculty member's time on campus (the few exceptions include Hope and Kenyon Colleges). Several academic deans mentioned their desire to extend mentoring supports beyond the early-career stage, provide more in-depth training to mentors, and complete program assessments that were more formal than satisfaction ratings.

Deans faced challenges in recruiting mentors and providing the necessary incentives. In chapter 1, we noted that only two of the GLCA institutions provide a stipend to mentors. The GLCA schools varied in terms of how mentors were selected (in some cases, they volunteered; in other cases, they were invited to be mentors by a dean or provost). None of the deans discussed any formal training of mentors beyond hosting mentor-mentee lunches at which time mentors and mentees were introduced and informed about the expectations associated with the mentor program (for example, its goals and requirements). None of the deans described formal assessment processes of the mentorship program beyond satisfaction surveys, and even such assessments were not widespread. In several cases, mentoring programs were created as extensions of other campus initiatives.

Leadership Development

Nine of the academic deans interviewed talked about needing to provide more deliberate leadership development programming for their faculty members. One said, "We have some amazing faculty leaders on this campus, and we need to do a better job of fostering and developing these skills for future campus faculty leaders." However, such development is a challenge when supports specific to the mid-career stage are lacking overall.

Deans also explained the need to have leadership development support related to formal and informal leadership roles—such as department or committee chair roles—covering topics like how to manage conflict and run an effective meeting. But the deans and provosts who participated in our study also discussed the need to help faculty members feel comfortable being a leader through example in faculty meetings. A dean stated: "Faculty members, especially those in their later years, can and should be able to model leader behavior to those early-career faculty through the ways in which they interact with their peers, push back against ideas discussed in faculty meetings, and by being professional and collegial. We have some very well-respected, thoughtful faculty on this campus because they model these behaviors and we need to support and encourage others to follow suit."

Programming Focused on Mid-Career Faculty Members

All thirteen deans or provosts expressed their desire to expand and enhance their existing faculty development portfolio by creating supports specifically for mid-career faculty members. The most typical of these supports are the sabbatical and the endowed professorship (though such professorships are predominantly found in the sciences). The deans and provosts acknowledged that the career stage challenges and increased service expectations that mid-career faculty members experience created obstacles as these faculty members work toward promotion. One provost noted: "Our mid-career faculty members are called upon to do a lot for us, and we don't always provide the necessary training to support them in fulfilling those requests and roles. We need to do more, and we are working to do so on their behalf."

We note that these priorities are not static—indeed, the deans were making progress in these areas even as we collected data. For example, several of the GLCA institutions were beginning to create programming or associated policy adjustments aimed to help mid-career faculty members. Allegheny College faculty members approved updates to the P&T guidelines intended to more fully recognize the breadth of professional work that constitutes research (that is, scholarship; creative activity; and professional development, including work resulting in forms other than published or public works and presentations). The changes included more direct recognition of work undertaken with students and community members and work in the field of scholarship of teaching and learning (T&L). Hope College is also working to develop and deliver more supports specifically for mid-career faculty members. While most mid-career programming is on an ad hoc basis (such as a mentors' workshop luncheon facilitated by divisional deans), the associate dean for T&L at Hope College is cochairing a committee that is exploring a more formal program of faculty development for posttenure faculty. Albion College recently created an associate provost position. The holder of the position will be responsible for supporting institutional and departmental assessment initiatives and creating more training and development related to the advising role, to support faculty members' efforts in this area.

After reviewing administrators' communication of institutional priorities as compared to faculty challenges and needs, we saw some consistency in terms of programming and mentoring for mid-career faculty members. Administrators' interests in department chair training and leadership development were communicated as a priority by all deans and provosts with whom we spoke. Furthermore, we believe that meeting the needs of faculty members through related programming will support institutional priorities. Such consistency makes us think back to the questions we asked at the beginning of this chapter, which touch on administrators' failing to listen and faculty members' being unable to articulate their needs and wants. Clearly, both perceptions are inaccurate, at least at this level. However, these perceptions exist for a reason, so we turn our attention next to an examination of actual faculty development programming across the GLCA institutions to identify possible explanations for the perceived or real disconnect between institutional priorities and faculty members' needs.

Faculty Development Programming

While many of the GLCA institutions offer at least some of the unique career-stage faculty development programming highlighted throughout this book, here we focus on the programming that is consistent across institutions, by rank, as shown in table 4.1 (see also Baker, Lunsford, and Pifer 2015).

The good news is that the institutions have an appropriate focus on new and early-career faculty members. Austin (2010) noted the importance of providing sufficient resources to explain their responsibilities to these faculty members. Such information is communicated through orientation programming before the start of classes and throughout their first years on campus by means of workshops, brown-bag lunches, and other events. Participating in these types of events helps early-career faculty members feel a sense of community with their peers and provides opportunities for them to interact with colleagues outside of their own department (Austin 2010).

Additionally, early-career faculty members have access to funds that support their development in the areas of teaching, scholarship, and service. Such funds are essential to encourage faculty members' development in their primary campus roles as they seek to earn P&T. In addition to monetary supports, guidance can be provided through formal and informal mentoring programming. All GLCA institutions offer a formal mentoring program for early-career faculty members, which is a best practice for this population. Mentors serve as a resource for institutional policy and political insights and act as advocates for junior faculty members on campus.

Through our individual faculty interviews, focus groups, and survey responses, it became obvious to us that mid-career and senior colleagues greatly appreciate the sabbatical as a time to refresh, refocus, and complete those "never-ending projects" that get pushed to the side during the academic year. Endowed professorships provide financial and symbolic supports and recognize outstanding contributions. But we saw a dearth of programming at the associate and full professor levels, and a failure by the institutions to address the challenges described above.

The AFFD-LAC framework highlights areas of institutional strengths and needs that can inform short- and long-term initiatives. We applaud the GLCA institutions for their early-career programs and policies, and those efforts are an excellent foundation on which to build. We see many opportunities to better meet the needs of early-career faculty members and to support associate and full professors. Perhaps you realized that our discussion of common practices failed to acknowledge programming for NTT faculty. That is not an oversight: in fact, there are no faculty development supports available to NTT faculty members across the GLCA. We remind you that we included only those practices that are common among all of the thirteen institutions; some of them provide supports to NTT faculty members and those in other career stages.

Our examination of the challenges of and unintended roadblocks to faculty development as compared to administrators' priorities and existing institutional programming revealed opportunities to improve the lives of faculty members as they engage in academic work and to improve the institutions that employ them. The feedback from the deans and provosts about needed faculty development programming and priorities was aligned with that from the faculty members. We applaud the deans and provosts for recognizing the gaps in their current programming and for highlighting significant, related institutional priorities, yet implementation of high-priority actions and desired programming is still falling behind. As faculty members, we appreciate the frustration of knowing that a dean recognizes an issue—which many deans do in this case—but also seeing that it remains unaddressed. In the following section, we offer advice on how to address these issues by targeting horizontal alignment through recommendations specific to different career stages.

What Can I Do? Implementing Alignment

An alignment framework clarifies what institutions wish to do and what they are doing. Furthermore, the horizontal dimension of alignment can help leaders understand whether faculty development activities are a set of disjointed tactics or part of a coherent process. The goal of horizontal alignment is the development of a logical, consistent approach to people management (Gratton and Truss 2003)—one that moves away from one-size-fits-all policies to acknowledge the nuances of challenges specific to different career stages and appointment types. A focus on horizontal alignment can facilitate conversations between campus leaders and faculty members, thus focusing on institutional and faculty priorities and an identification of areas of commonality for short- and long-term planning. The point of this section of the chapter is to highlight how institutional leaders can use horizontal alignment to improve faculty development strategies to meet the needs and challenges of faculty members across career stages, appointment types, and ranks.

Below, we make two points about developing faculty members. First, leaders must reduce the number of tactics and examine their current efforts to ensure they are part of a coherent strategy of faculty development. Then, they must identify tracks or an area of focus that allows faculty members to develop successfully to meet a range of institutional needs—for example, becoming an excellent scholar, department chair, dean, or informal mentor or leader of new faculty members.

Developing Full Professors

The following recommendations are informed by the voices of the full professors who participated in our study. They also take into account the needs and desires that academic deans and provosts communicated to us.

MENTOR SUPPORT. We recommend greater mentor training to support full professors in their efforts to mentor their colleagues and to provide mentors for full professors as they seek guidance and support. While these supports are necessary across all career stages, we believe them to be particularly important for full professors. Mentoring is a function many professors provide on their respective campuses, but they acknowledged the challenges they face given the changing expectations and roles of newly hired faculty members. More thorough mentor training would also support institutional goals and administrators' priorities related to current practices. We provide more specific recommendations about mentoring supports and training in chapter 5. While full professors were happy to support their junior colleagues both early and in the middle of their careers, they too sought the support of a mentor. We suggest mentor assignments for full professors within and across the GLCA institutions.

QUESTIONS FOR CONSIDERATION

1. What role can, and should, a consortium play in developing and implementing cross-institutional mentoring supports?

FUNDING. Faculty members and academic deans and provosts discussed the importance of having internal funds to support the professional development of the faculty. However, there is a perception among mid-level and senior faculty members that early-career faculty members are given priority when such funds are allocated. We suggest having funds specific to full professors that support both their teaching and scholarship. Competitively awarded funds may encourage full professors to reengage in scholarship, pursue a new line of inquiry, support course development, and/or begin interdisciplinary collaborations with peers (either in teaching or research). This is an opportunity for faculty members to partner with development office staff members, as they seek to attract alumni donations or corporate sponsorship. Such a partnership will make development officers more aware of the needs and efforts of full professors at their school, while also creating opportunities for alumni to support their favorite former professors.

2. How might institutions create career development supports such as the one we describe, in which development officers and faculty members collaborate?

RETIREMENT SUPPORT. Full professors talked about the "great unknown" of retirement. We also heard retirement policies discussed by deans and provosts as an area in which they could "stand to develop more" related policy. Given that retirement planning is very individually and institutionally specific, we suggest adding phased retirement planning and programming as an agenda item to deans' meetings within the GLCA. Discussions at those meetings can identify best practices at both the institutional and consortium levels.

Developing Associate Professors

"Why Are Associate Professors So Unhappy?" (Wilson 2012), "I've Got Tenure. How Depressing," (Blanchard 2012), "Unhappy Associate Professors," (Jaschik 2012b), and "The Academic Therapist: Treating Post-Tenure Depression" (Douglas and George 2003) are just a few prominent news headlines in higher education. Austin noted that "far less [research] has been conducted on the experiences of faculty at mid-career than those at the early career period" (2010, 371). Kiernan Mathews (2014) described this as the associate professor "let-down" (2014, 1). Here, we recommend addressing this problem by creating professional development supports related to leadership development, cohort modeling, promotion support, and funding.

QUESTIONS FOR CONSIDERATION

1. How can leadership development achieve institutional and individual outcomes?

LEADERSHIP DEVELOPMENT. Through our own leadership development training program (www.leadmentordevelop.com), we support and encourage faculty members to create an individual leadership and development plan. As part of that plan, the faculty member is assigned a content expert or mentor to support his or her progression through the plan. For example, a faculty member might want to enhance his teaching and therefore partner with the director of T&L; another faculty member seeking external funding for her research might work with a staff member in development; and still another, who aspires to hold an administrative role, could engage in an administrative rotation through key institutional areas including institutional advancement, student affairs, and academic affairs. The plan serves as the foundation, determining the activities, resources, and supports necessary to achieve the goals in the plan. This, we argue, is a very personalized approach to leadership development that supports individual and institutional goals and outcomes.

2. What role can, and should, succession planning have in rotational leadership roles on campus?

In this area, we see a great need for department (and committee) chair training. At the time we conducted this study, many of the academic deans and provosts of the GLCA were working to enhance their training for department chairs. We believe that such training is vital to equipping both new and seasoned chairs with the tools and resources they need to fulfill the role more effectively. At a minimum, department chair training should include interpersonal skill development and communication (for example, managing up and laterally) and training in conflict resolution, budgeting, and knowledge management. We also suggest making incoming chair assignments at least one semester—preferably two semesters—in advance. This would allow for some succession planning and job shadowing, which would prepare the incoming chair and to expose him or her to the required tasks and responsibilities while under some guidance from the current chair. Compared to department chair training, we saw much less effort in terms of committee chair training, and we note that many of the same supports we have mentioned for department chairs is applicable to committee chairs, too.

3. How might institutions across the GLCA cooperate on leadership development initiatives?

COHORT MODELING. All of the development programming for early-career faculty members in the GLCA centered on a cohort model, in which all of those faculty members engaged in orientation activities, lunches, and other workshops as a group. Research shows the importance of such cohort models at the undergraduate levels (D'Abate and Eddy 2008), and these models are often used with early-career faculty members. We believe that administrators are missing an opportunity to create similar peer supports and mentorships by neglecting to create programming for mid-career faculty members that brings them all together as a cohort.

PROMOTION SUPPORT. Below we advocate for the importance of P&T supports for early-career faculty members, and similar supports are valuable for mid-career faculty members as well. These supports can include interim reviews and other developmental activities. One example is a performance review in the primary areas of evaluation to help the faculty member learn more about the promotion process and corresponding expectations and to gain mentoring in this area of need. Knowing what is involved, what the expectations are, and how to compare one's performance in relation to those expectations can go a long way in supporting associate professors on their path to promotion.

4. How might such efforts be supported divisionally—by a committee with rotating members, for example?

INTERNAL FUNDS FOR MID-CAREER FACULTY MEMBERS. Similar to our recommendation for full professors, we believe that making funds available specifically for mid-career faculty members to support their teaching and scholarship is a wise investment. Raising the funds could be added to the portfolio of development officers as they seek to engage alumni and donors in initiatives aimed at increasing funds that support on-campus faculty development efforts. Receiving these funds should be competitive; require a review process; and support teaching, scholarship, or service.

Developing Assistant Professors

As discussed above in this chapter, we are pleased with the programming already available to early-career professors at GLCA institutions. This programming provides a strong foundation in the early years of a newly hired professor's career. There are some opportunities to enhance available supports as well as the need to extend early-career programming beyond the first one or two years of employment. We recommend topic-specific workshops and more supports related to the P&T process.

TOPIC-SPECIFIC WORKSHOPS. Early-career faculty members face many challenges as they work toward P&T. Having to learn lessons on the job because they were not taught in graduate school makes the transition from student to professor challenging, to say the least. We believe topic-specific workshops are needed to support these faculty members in their teaching, scholarship, and service, as they work to establish their professional careers and identity. Sample topics might include creating a personal brand, managing a research agenda, directing a successful collaboration, or publishing one's first book. All of these are necessary skills to develop, yet they are often neglected in faculty development programming for early-career faculty members, which focuses on socializing them to their community and campus. The workshops we propose, however, support professional growth as well.

QUESTION FOR CONSIDERATION

1. How can cross-function or cross-departmental initiatives support faculty and staff development?

P&T SUPPORTS. The P&T process can be a challenging experience for faculty members in tenure-track positions. Even the most well-prepared early-career faculty member needs support and guidance to navigate these murky waters. We suggest that committee members responsible for personnel matters host P&T panels featuring faculty members who had recently completed their interim review or tenure review. They could show their P&T packet material as examples and offer strategies and tips for preparing P&T packets. We suggest organizing these panels on a divisional basis to account for the disciplinary differences in how faculty members are evaluated. We also suggest hosting a session in which administrators and faculty members (for example, members of the personnel review committee) discuss institutional expectations related to P&T (such as what is meant by teaching and the ways in which teaching occurs in and out of the classroom, and how scholarship is defined in the faculty handbook and viewed by the committee). We also strongly encourage this same group of faculty members and administrators to engage in an assessment of the supports available to faculty members in the areas of teaching, scholarship, and service to ensure that they are adequate to support faculty members' development in the three areas.

Developing Non-Tenure-Track Faculty Members

Lastly, given the rise of NTT faculty members in higher education generally and at the GLCA institutions in particular, this population needs and deserves supports specific to its members' career stages and appointment type. Taking into account faculty needs, we believe that granting these faculty members access to internal funds and workshops specific to their appointment type may be useful.

INTERNAL FUNDS. NTT faculty members are engaged in teaching, scholarship, and service at levels equal to those of assistant, associate, and full professors. Such engagement contributes to student learning, helps achieve institutional outcomes, and sustains departmental initiatives. Colleges should consider whether NTT faculty members should be eligible for internal funds to support teaching, scholarship, and service. This may be costly, but making such funds available, even on a scaled basis, is appropriate. If NTT faculty members are trusted in the classroom to deliver instruction that helps fulfill the institution's mission and goals, their contribution should be supported through internal funding.

NTT-SPECIFIC WORKSHOPS. NTT faculty members face challenges specific to their career stage, just as assistant, associate, and full professors do. We suggest creating opportunities to engage all NTT faculty members by bringing them together in topical workshops. Themes addressed might include managing the academic or nonacademic job search, preparing for an on-site interview, and highlighting one's research potential. Creating opportunities in which NTT faculty members can practice job talks or research presentations may be valuable to their professional development and costs the institution little.

Process Supports

While we suggest career stage-specific supports, we also offer some additional recommendations to address the unintended roadblocks we discussed above in this chapter. First, we suggest that LACs consider creating various paths to promotion to full professor. Doing so would recognize the work and contributions that faculty members make in the areas of teaching, scholarship, and service. For example, we suggest that promotion be granted to those faculty members who exhibit exemplary performance in two out of three areas (with satisfactory performance in the third) would acknowledge those faculty members who are excellent in service and as teachers, or strong in teaching and scholarship, while meeting only minimum service requirements perhaps because of family care responsibilities. The people who would take on such a task of reenvisioning the path to promotion are likely not to be administrators, but faculty members—who need to play leadership roles on their campuses in this regard.

Second, administrators and faculty members should regularly review and revise language in the faculty handbook. Collaboration will ensure that the language captures all the ways in which teaching, scholarship, and service are performed. It will also ensure that the language is based on current practice and institutional expectations. Some critical areas that are usually neglected in faculty handbooks and evaluation criteria language have to do with mentoring undergraduates in research, providing a broad definition of scholarship that accounts for disciplinary differences and institutional expectations, and teaching outside of the classroom.

Third, we urge all administrators, faculty members, and staff members to regularly review institutional work-life policies. This examination should include a review of policies related to committee meeting times and the number of weekend and evening events, for example. Such a review may identify policies or practices that may be unintentionally excluding faculty members or creating increased demands on family time. The review may also uncover a disconnect between the written policy and its implementation or the degree to which it is implemented inconsistently, thus identifying the need to update the policy.

Fourth, we suggest creating awards and other forms of recognition to acknowledge the variety of areas in which faculty members and staff excel. Most of the institutions in our study had awards or formal recognition beyond promotion and tenure for faculty members with strong teaching and scholarship. We also suggest creating mentoring awards, leadership awards, and community engagement awards for faculty members who demonstrate excellence in those areas.

Conclusion

In this chapter we sought to answer two critical questions: how often do faculty members and administrators talk about college priorities, strategic initiatives, and personnel policies as interrelated; and if they do have these conversations, do they act on them to achieve the desired ends? The answers to these questions revealed that the faculty members who perceive a mismatch between institutional and individual priorities are correct. However, administrators and faculty members alike recognize the inherent weaknesses in current faculty development programming and agree on what is needed and the priorities of those needs. Missing are continuing conversations among administrators, faculty members, and staff members about the development, implementation, and assessment of policies to ensure policy and practice are aligned.

PART THREE

Aligning Resources

Supporting Faculty Members and Academic Work

5

<hr/>

Mentoring and Key Relationships

"I love learning, and that's why I went to a liberal arts college," declared Steve, a successful mid-career faculty member. He had earned tenure and continued to develop his teaching. In fact, he had been named the state's professor of the year. Steve had also received a prestigious Fulbright scholarship and grants to enhance education in his field. He was well positioned to reflect on the mentoring that he and other professors he knew had received or might have needed. At this point in his career, he really felt a lack of mentoring both for new faculty members and for himself. Socialization for new faculty members is, in his words, "pretty haphazard." He had helped build a "network of faculty members" around his curriculum, but the climate in his department could have been better. At one meeting with the college president, he had noted that there was an opportunity to build a more supportive mentoring culture. Rather than inquiring about his needs or exchanging ideas, the president diminished his concerns by replying that all of his friends were gone on sabbatical, and he was simply missing them. Steve reflected that while it might sound as if he was discontented, he was not. He merely had a keen awareness of the lack of mentoring support in his department and institution, and he had ideas about how to improve the situation.

Mentoring is central to both faculty work and the mission of LACs. The literature about faculty-student mentoring highlights the benefits of mentoring relationships, which includes better grades, greater engagement, and increased retention in their field for students (see, for example, Bordes and Arredondo 2005; Hill and Reddy 2007; Lopatto and Tobias 2010). Indeed, mentoring students is a central activity that many faculty members described to us when they discussed their work. One faculty member illustrated this point well: "We're trying to mentor students through teaching and our relationship and guiding students. That's the most important thing."

Indeed, we would be remiss if we did not acknowledge the importance of faculty-student mentoring activities at LACs, including how they may benefit faculty members. Yet our primary focus is on mentoring experiences that promote and support faculty development. The overarching question that guides our focus in this chapter is, to what extent do faculty members feel supported to do great work at their institutions? A related question is, how do they learn to navigate their departmental, institutional, and professional cultures successfully?

This chapter highlights what we know about the mentoring experiences of faculty members. We first examine the vertical alignment of mentoring supports in LACs by examining institutional goals and how current mentoring policies and procedures fit with those goals. Next, we view the horizontal alignment of mentoring supports, or the extent to which mentoring-related policies have permeated all academic units. Then individual faculty members' experiences are shared by career stage, which provides insights into how mentoring strategies and policies are being implemented. Our data points to the characteristics of optimal mentoring relationships and their outcomes. The chapter concludes by using the alignment framework for faculty development in liberal arts colleges (AFFD-LAC; see chapter 7) to present recommendations and pose questions for consideration that may enhance mentoring in LACs.

Mentoring the Modern Faculty Member

"I will say one thing, my mentor at grad school gave me the appreciation that teaching was hard work."

–A professor of biology

The teacher as mentor is an iconic image of a faculty member's main contribution, especially in LACs. Indeed, Ernest Boyer noted the centrality of this role in his treatise *Scholarship Reconsidered*: "In the end, inspired teaching keeps the flame of scholarship alive. Almost all successful academics give credit to creative teachers—those mentors who defined their work so compellingly that it became, for them, a lifetime challenge. Without the teaching function, the continuity of knowledge will be broken and the store of human knowledge dangerously diminished" (1990, 24). Mentoring aids a faculty member in developing his or her teaching excellence and supporting students. Many faculty members talked about the role of mentoring in their teaching. Furthermore, their institutions often defined mentoring in the context of teaching and the evaluation of teaching by noting that a professor's mentor was expected to visit the professor's class. However, mentoring has a broader role than just preparing teachers or as an activity that faculty members engage in with students. Mentoring relationships, both informal and formal, can provide faculty members with critical professional development to help them fulfill their personal and professional aspirations, and it is needed to develop future academic leaders.

Mentoring in the Great Lakes Colleges Association (GLCA)

"They [the faculty] will be conscientious advisors and mentors."

—A GLCA institution's faculty handbook

What is the expectation about mentoring in faculty work? In speaking with faculty members and administrators, and in reviewing institutional websites and faculty handbooks across the GLCA institutions, we learned that mentoring is viewed as an important activity in these LACs, with faculty members both mentoring students and being mentored for their own development. For example, Allegheny College has a website devoted to faculty members' mentoring students in research, scholarship, and creative activities and a faculty-student mentoring program for women in science (Association for Women in Science n.d.). Similarly, Albion College's website has a page describing guidelines for faculty members who mentor undergraduates (Albion College 2017). We found many examples of activities in the GLCA where mentoring was expected.

Institutional Support of Mentoring

"Mentors in general do get a lot of guidance in terms of what's expected. Now what actually transpires . . ."

—A dean

FACULTY HANDBOOKS. Archival records and procedures provide one glimpse into institutionalized support for mentoring. To gain insights from an institutional perspective, we examined the faculty handbooks and promotion and tenure (P&T) and evaluation guidelines at each GLCA institution. Eight institutions specifically mentioned the term "mentor" in their faculty handbooks. However, some of the handbooks referred to mentoring as a faculty-student activity, while other handbooks addressed it as part of faculty development. Two handbooks did not use the term "mentor" but conveyed the expectation that faculty members should advise students, such as through teaching apprenticeships or in the course of teaching. Most colleges considered student advising as part of teaching; however, one college listed it as part of a service obligation, and another college noted that it could also be considered under research. All but three schools had some expectation that faculty members who desired promotion would engage in advising or mentoring of students.

Expectations for faculty mentoring by other faculty members as professional development were well developed at some colleges, especially for new faculty members. For example, one handbook noted: "At the beginning of their first year . . . all tenure-track faculty members are eligible for, but are not required to have, an institutional mentor, a tenured colleague from a department or program other than that of the new faculty member. A candidate post-multi-year review can also request an institutional mentor." Another school's handbook commented that a new faculty member's departmental experiences should include mentors: "Ideally, the pre-tenure experience in the department is one of mentorship." Such a mentorship would be accomplished through peer review of classroom teaching and annual "intentional conversations" about scholarship.

Some colleges formally identified the department chair or dean as responsible for mentoring faculty members. The mentor was to communicate institutional policies and support faculty members to fulfill expectations. One college's faculty handbook specifically outlined a mentor's duties: to "serve as mentors to the members of the school or department, particularly the newer members, informing them of development opportunities, facilitating peer teacher observations, communicating University and departmental expectations, and helping faculty members to meet those expectations." The best example of the importance of mentoring was the institution that saw mentoring as contributing to a collegial culture of mentoring. This college noted that faculty members "will be known for their role as mentors to their colleagues and for their service to the University." Colleges with stated policies such as those listed above seem to have strong horizontal alignment related to mentoring expectations across units. Yet strong horizontal alignment is only the first step. Strong implementation is also needed, as we discuss in our recommendations at the end of the chapter.

In contrast, five colleges did not have apparent mentoring support for faculty members, new or otherwise. Their documents made no mention of any mentoring for new or continuing faculty members, nor did their handbooks indicate any expectation that faculty members would mentor their colleagues. These institutions have weak horizontal alignment in their mentoring policies.

ADMINISTRATOR PERSPECTIVES. Because academic leaders' attitudes influence the allocation of resources for mentoring (Gehrke and Kezar 2015), we interviewed administrators to learn what they thought about mentoring. The presidents and provosts we talked to saw mentoring as an institutional activity that supported their institution's goals related to students. In fact, some leaders were quite involved in faculty mentoring programs, some of which were managed through the provost's office. For example, at one college the provost selected mentors for new faculty members and checked in with the new faculty members within the first week of the academic year. The aim was to see if faculty mentees had connected with their mentors and to learn how the new faculty members were doing. This intentional and formal involvement proved to be the exception rather than the norm, though. This college has strong vertical alignment because of the provost's commitment to faculty development as being in line with the school's institutional goals. However, the lack of formal processes and procedures mean that the institution has weak horizontal alignment. If this provost leaves, for example, what might happen to the mentoring support?

Most institutional leaders knew that mentoring took place, even when they acknowledged that it was likely informal or even invisible. Many leaders told us that guidance was provided to mentors, but that they didn't know how the mentoring relationships actually progressed. One provost said that in "the majority of our academic departments, the whole department just sort of serves as a general mentor for the . . . person they brought in." A dean of faculty development explained that the mentors and mentees were given suggestions about how often to meet and what they might do together, as well as given funding for meals together. However, the dyads were otherwise left to develop the relationship as they saw fit. In fact, one provost noted that the college's surveys of faculty members revealed that informal mentoring was perceived as more valuable than formal mentoring.

There was a recognition that all mentor-mentee relationships might not work equally well, even though mentors might receive considerable guidance about what is expected of them. One dean said, "There's a lot that's left to the mentor and mentee [to decide], and to be honest, not each and every pairing works perfectly." This person discussed occasions when a new faculty member might request a different mentor, but the onus was on the mentee to make such a request. Another provost observed, "You know, again, in the departments there may or there may not be good mentoring of, say, associate professors."

The administrators who spoke supportively about mentoring were unaware of training for mentors. When we asked about mentor training, we received replies such as this one from a college president: "That's a good question, and I honestly don't know if they have been trained to do this or not. I'm not aware that there is but again, there could be." A provost at one college directly said, "No, we really don't do that." This person went on to say, "I guess we kind of know who's going to be a good mentor and who's not." When we talked to individuals in charge of faculty development, they reflected that training was needed for mentors. But one person commented, "Now I probably should, but, no, we don't do any training for the mentors."

A few administrators sought to further institutionalize mentoring efforts or strengthen the horizontal alignment at their institution for faculty development strategies. One provost expressed a desire to "move in a direction where we have more of a formal mentoring program. . . . [W]hat we realized is that we don't have any formal program [in which we] outline what the expectations are, nor do we have any formal training for the mentors. And that's the direction that we're heading." This provost confirmed our observations that at most LACs there was a dearth of mentoring available to posttenure faculty members by highlighting a "need in the mid-career area because we have had an assumption that once you get past tenure, you don't need any mentoring." This belief was shared by many of the academic deans we spoke with, and we perceived an assumption that mentoring was not needed after tenure. That perception assumption was shared by the mid- and late-career faculty members who participated in our research study.

Findings from our interviews with academic leaders supported findings from our analysis of P&T documents. Some colleges supported mentoring, while others had little to no focus on mentoring. For example, one president discussed the institution's lack of any plan for mentoring or socializing faculty members by saying, "You know there's no specific institutional plan within a larger strategic vision about [faculty] socialization." A dean at another institution noted that it was growing, with many new faculty members—who, it was hoped, would create a new culture: "So we are evolving, and the whole question of socialization that presupposes an existing system, existing tradition, existing norm, existing culture is really part of our own creation now." Based on our conversations, it was unclear how mentoring might fit into this plan.

Faculty Experiences

"Increasingly there's a lot of research on sort of coaching relationships where various senior people work with mid-career people. . . . I'm wondering whether that couldn't be formalized more."

—An associate professor of English

Mary Deane Sorcinelli (2000) wrote about decades of research findings that point to effective practices for supporting new faculty members, including mentoring by senior faculty members. She observed that mentoring must take place at the department level, but given the turnover in department chairs, it should be seen as an institutional activity. As we show below, in the liberal arts colleges we studied, most formal mentoring efforts targeted early-career faculty members.

We define mentoring as consisting of both psychosocial and career support (Kram 1988). Psychosocial support involves listening, confidence building, and role modeling. Career support includes sponsorship and protection, and advice on or coaching about how to navigate the mentee's job and career. We asked faculty members to consider the career support function when we surveyed and interviewed them.

Faculty-Student Mentoring

About 20 percent of faculty members we interviewed discussed the value of their mentoring relationships with students, even when our questions were aimed at their own developmental experiences. Faculty members saw the mentorship of students as part of their teaching and advising roles. When asked what was the most important role of a faculty member, some said that "mentorship is really important," Such mentoring takes place through honors experiences (for example, faculty-supervised honors theses), undergraduate research, classes, and advising.

However, new faculty members may not be fully prepared for the extent to which mentoring students is seen as part of their role at a LAC. As we explained in the introduction and chapter 4, graduate education rarely provides future faculty members with training on mentoring and advising students. One faculty member noted that mentoring undergraduates is an activity that he loves and values, and it is what keeps him at an LAC. But he noted that mentoring takes an amount of time that is "somewhat shocking to our new faculty members sometimes."

Mentoring Networks

Scholars of faculty development and mentoring have joined with their peers from the organizational and business fields in suggesting we need to rethink our notion of mentoring as a singular, one-on-one relationship. Such traditional mentoring relationships between faculty members are time intensive and unlikely to meet all the professional development needs that the mentee might have. Thus, the idea of mentoring networks has gained traction as a way to support faculty members (Sorcinelli and Yun 2007). Having a network of mentors who can provide complementary, but not overlapping, information can help faculty member mentees navigate their careers more successfully. Furthermore, research suggests that four or five is the right number of mentors to have in a network (Thomas, Lunsford, and Rodrigues 2015). For example, faculty members should seek out one junior and one senior faculty mentor at their institution and another junior and senior mentor outside of the institution. In addition, if these four mentors do not share a salient demographic trait such as religion or ethnicity that is important to the faculty member, then a fifth mentor who has that trait might be added to provide value and perspective. Thus, a mentoring network provides more in-depth strategic information and support than having a regular professional network of key contacts. We found that most faculty members who participated in mentoring were embedded in a network of developmental relationships. Over half (232) of the faculty members surveyed reported having at least one mentor, and the modal number of mentors was two, with a total of 1,295 mentors reported. About three-fourths (295) of the faculty members reported having at least one mentee, and the modal number was two, with a total of 1,700 protégés reported.

Our survey results confirmed two points we heard from administrators: the importance of the department as a source of mentoring, and the greater reliance on informal than on formal mentoring. In interviews, faculty members often noted that their campus was small, and people there got to know each other quickly. About one-third (373) of the mentors and nearly one-third (500) of the mentees were in the same department, suggesting that departmental mentors were important. This finding highlights the importance of proximity in forming mentoring relationships and suggests that guidance is needed about departmental norms, which greatly influence a faculty member's success. Almost half (570) of the mentors and about two-fifths (712) of the mentees were in the same institution but not the same department. Only thirty-eight faculty members had mentees who were outside of both their discipline and their institution.

A lack of mentoring at their own organization might be what would lead faculty members to engage in mentoring relationships outside their institution and discipline. It might also be the case that some mentor relationships were the result of personal relationships that began before the faculty member entered graduate school.

Informal mentoring characterized the majority of the reported mentoring relationships. In fact, formal, institutional mentoring programs were responsible for only 9 percent (113) of mentors and 12 percent (201) of mentees. Mentors in their same discipline but at another institution were reported more often than mentors from formal programs at their same school (159). Fewer protégés were from the same discipline as their mentors and at another institution (181).

Full Professors

Our study suggests that mentoring support might be most important for mid- and late-career faculty members for three reasons. First, many of the mentors were full professors but they did not seem to have much information (or appropriate training or mentoring resources) to support them in becoming excellent mentors. Early-career faculty members looked to full professors for mentoring support. One junior faculty member summarized this desire by saying, "I think senior people are in a place to help mentor you along the way and sort of let you know, 'this is how things are done, this is what the expectations really are.'" Yet some senior faculty members saw mentoring as a hierarchal relationship that would be inappropriate between faculty members. For example, one faculty member said, "So I don't really try to mentor the junior faculty because they are equal to me, right?"

Second, mentoring may help mid- and senior-level faculty members stay engaged even as they end their careers. The sense of leaving a legacy or being reenergized by these mentoring relationships was a motivation for full professors to mentor others. One faculty member said: "I also think it's important for the more senior faculty members to be involved in that mentoring system. Because I think it's what keeps people fresh. You know, at the end of their careers, to be fully engaged in bringing along the younger generation."

Our results show that full professors were not always available or supportive. For example, one faculty member "had to deal with these full professors who hated one another." Other faculty members reported a lack of full professors in their department or college. One person said, "There's relatively few tenure-track faculty, there really isn't anybody that's more senior than you that you can go to, to get support and mentoring and advice or even just a sounding board." Perhaps these faculty members would be more engaged if they were supported in mentoring earlier-career faculty members.

Third, mentoring may provide outside perspectives to mentees that promote the creative and integrative work expected of full professors. Boyer (1990) referred to this as the creativity contract, noting that faculty members may be more creative after working with mentors on other campuses to interpret and integrate their work into their existing faculty roles for the greater good. Full professors whom we interviewed expressed a desire to participate in formal work groups or collaborations to refresh their work. In some cases, they wanted support in navigating the last years before retirement and perhaps even after retirement. Reflecting Boyer's idea of the creativity contract, one faculty member said, "Having those mentors outside your department so you get to actually chat with other people—that . . . might be nice."

On average, our survey data (see table 5.1) showed that full professors saw their mentors at their institution as less a source of support than did assistant professors. Full professors did not receive advice very often from mentors at their institution. When they did receive such advice, it was related to teaching, or departmental or institutional policies. Full professors also were more likely than professors at lower ranks to perceive that their department had a

TABLE 5.1

Mentoring Perceptions and Activities by Rank across the Great Lakes Colleges Association (GLCA) Institutions

	Assistant professor	Associate professor	Full professor	NTT faculty member
Comfortable seeking career-related advice from my department chair.	4.5	4.0	4.0	4.8
My department has a mentoring culture.	4.5	4.5	4.8	4.1
My institution has a positive mentoring culture.	4.3	4.3	4.3	3.8
Comfortable seeking career-related advice from colleagues within my rank in my *institution*.	4.8	4.7	4.7	4.4
Comfortable seeking career-related advice from colleagues within my rank in my *department*.	4.5	4.6	4.7	4.7
Mentors at my institution have advised me about:				
my teaching/instructional activities.	4.5	3.5	2.8	4.0
departmental or institutional policies and politics.	4.5	3.6	2.8	4.0
promotion and my progress toward promotion.	4.2	3.4	2.5	2.4
my research, scholarly activities, and/or publications.	3.4	2.8	2.5	2.6

Notes: Responses are on a Likert scale from 1 (not at all) to 7 (a lot). A response of 4 means "sometimes," and a response of 5 means "often." NTT is non-tenure-track.

mentoring culture. Full professors sometimes felt their institution had a positive mentoring culture, and they often sought advice from other full professors in the department and institution.

Associate Professors

Mid-career faculty members are relatively neglected when it comes to mentoring support. Scholars have suggested that faculty members lack mentoring after the early-career stage, and that female faculty members may feel this lack most keenly (Austin and Sorcinelli 2013; Buch, Huet, Rorrer, and Roberson 2011), a point that we touched on in chapter 3. Faculty members at mid-career need assistance with intentional career planning to chart the next stages of their careers, though this seems to be infrequently recognized in practice. A quote from a study of mid-career faculty members at a research university characterizes the state of mentoring we also identified at LACs: "To sum it all up, you're pretty much left to your own devices" (quoted in Baldwin, DeZure, Shaw, and Moretto 2008, 50). Roger Baldwin and colleagues pointed to networking and collaboration with other faculty members as potentially promising practices for mid-career faculty members.

Faculty members at mid-career have considerably fewer institutionalized efforts to support them than do those at the early-career stage. As noted above, almost all of the college-supported mentoring in the GLCA institutions was intended for new assistant professors. The assumption appeared to be that after achieving tenure, faculty members knew what to do. Furthermore, it seemed that if associate professors were engaged in mentoring, it would be as mentors to assistant professors instead of as mentees themselves.

However, our interviews with faculty members highlighted their desire for support to navigate their career. The service loads increased for associate professors, and they needed help staying on track. One faculty member stated the situation clearly: "I think that we could probably do a better job—and this goes back to what I said before with mentoring faculty at different stages as far as how to get their research work done, how to engage in their scholarship while they're teaching six courses in a 3–3 load." Another faculty member echoed the need for more senior faculty members to think about the next step of their research: "We certainly drop the ball by mid- and late-career faculty." This person observed a need for "more opportunities to work with other people and be mentored in terms of how to set your research agenda or integrate your teaching and research in meaningful ways and how to plan for the last ten years of your career."

Furthermore, mentoring may help motivate faculty members, who often stall out at the associate rank. One faculty member said: "We have a whole lot of associate professors who've been here thirty years. Why hasn't somebody in the administration sat them down and said, 'Hey, here's what you need to do to take the next step'? Why don't they encourage, push, inform? They do nothing." Others expressed a need for targeted support for women who should have been promoted to associate professor but were not. These faculty members were no longer in their early career. A faculty member described how she had created an informal group to support these neglected women. She was nicknamed "Oracle," and she said: "I do a lot of mentoring with that group and it's just frustrating to see it over and over and over again. You can do all the training you want of women and pointing out to them how to be more assertive in negotiating, but it's not about us at this point in time."

Our survey data from associate professors showed that they sometimes felt that they could seek advice from their department chair (see table 5.1). They reported that a mentoring culture was sometimes present in their department and at their institution. Associate professors often felt comfortable seeking career advice from colleagues at the same rank in their department and institution.

Associate professors reported receiving advice less frequently, compared to assistant professors. However, the advice they received most frequently (though still not very often) was about teaching, departmental or institutional policies, and promotion or progress toward promotion.

The mid-career stage is the best time for mentoring and coaching to support developing the next generation of faculty and institutional leaders. The good news is that about 30 percent of associate professors in the GLCA reported being mentored in the past five years to take on leadership roles, and 40 percent of the associate professors reported having a well-developed mentoring network. Faculty members described the important role that mentors played in providing "insights on how to tackle challenging issues," "opportunities to see inside the challenges experienced by others," and ideas on "how to manage my expectations." Mentoring conversations can provide "tool kits" that are invaluable to faculty members who take on leadership roles. Another faculty member told us that she had received "guidance on interpersonal communicating, guidance on policy and procedures" and had had "frank conversations on the current status of the unit I was taking over." However, advice from mentors sometimes seemed counterproductive. One faculty member said, "I've learned from them [mentors] to be wary of leadership roles." Another commented, "It is difficult to find people to trust."

A lot of these mid-career faculty members are simply not being mentored for future leadership roles. Other faculty members described a lack of any type of mentoring. One said: "I don't really have any [mentoring]. There has been no preparation. People just say, 'Oh, you'll do fine.'" Half of the associate professors we spoke with had not been mentored for leadership positions, 40 percent do not actively seek out mentorship for formal leadership roles, and 30 percent did not have a well-developed mentoring network. In some cases, faculty members might be intentionally avoiding mentorship. One noted: "I have not had a mentoring relationship. I would not have found that to be useful."

Assistant Professors

Faculty members at this rank had more opportunities to participate in formal mentoring programs than did their senior colleagues. Formal mentoring for early career colleagues is associated with institutional expectations (and concomitant resources) and programs that connect faculty members with mentors who are more experienced. The aims of these formal programs include purposes such as retaining faculty members by orienting them to the institution, supporting them in the P&T process, and enhancing their writing and research activities (Law et al. 2014; Mayer, Files, Ko, and Blair 2009; Sawatzky and Enns, 2009). These programs are generally part of an orientation program and may be organized informally or formally at the department or college level (Sorcinelli 2000), as we discussed in chapter 2.

Most faculty members we interviewed said that formal mentoring, when it did occur, was for new faculty members. Such formal mentoring lasted from one year to several years (through P&T), depending on the institution. We considered any college-supported activity to be formal mentoring, even if it was not well structured or was voluntary. There was considerable institutional variability in mentoring activities for new faculty members as well as variation in how faculty members at the same institution perceived mentoring. One faculty member noted that her college had a mentoring program in place but admitted that mentoring availability varied by department. Another faculty member at the same institution thought that its mentoring efforts needed more formalization: "We sort of mentor people on an individual basis here. But I think there really needs to be a structure on campus."

Many new faculty members also engaged in naturally occurring mentoring relationships, and scholars report that about half of faculty members do so (Blood et al. 2012; Haynes and Petrosko 2009). However, much of this research has focused on faculty members at research institutions. Our study begins to fill in the gap concerning what we know about informal mentoring experiences for faculty members in LACs.

Some of the faculty members we interviewed felt that informal mentoring would take place spontaneously as a result of their campus climate and that formal mentoring was not needed. They expressed the sense that their campus was a small, collegial place where mentoring occurred naturally and informally. For example, at one college, faculty members described a "tradition of dinners" and faculty meetings as contributing to the socialization of new faculty. Indeed, some departments on this campus appeared to do mentoring well, and faculty members felt well supported and said that they had learned a great deal. For example, one said, "I've had a very good experience in my department, and my senior colleagues have really done a good job of, I think, providing a lot of mentoring, mostly informally." Another person at this institution noted that "at the same time, the system that we have seems to work, because the mentoring part, which is more off the radar and more unofficial, is part of the culture, and is effective." Faculty members also observed that mentoring was a role of the department chair, who "informally" mentored new faculty members.

Mentoring initiatives often appeared to be subject to the interests or desires of whoever happened to be in charge of faculty socialization or development. For example, several faculty members at one college mentioned that they had once had a formal mentoring program, but it seemed to have disappeared. One faculty member at that college explained that the program had been a "matchmaking process" facilitated by the faculty development person, who informally connected a new faculty member with someone from another department. Another faculty member at the same institution said: "We then had a mentoring program, which again we're doing sort of a little bit right now, but not in any real big formal capacity. It used to be a much bigger program." Yet the provost at this college said that the mentoring program had recently been restarted. Thus, even when formal mentoring was taking place, there were perception problems on campus, as some senior faculty members were unaware of available mentoring opportunities.

Faculty members at one college reported that it had a well-supported mentoring program for new faculty members, and the program was also described positively by the college's leaders. Each mentor received a stipend, and each new faculty member was assigned a mentor in his or her department, as well as a mentor outside of the department. However, we found that colleges varied widely in whether they assigned new faculty members a mentor from the same or a different department, or both.

Assistant professors were significantly less likely to mentor other faculty members than were associate or full professors, even though many assistant professors did act as mentors to colleagues. (χ^2 = 49.63, df = 3, p > 0.0001). Our survey data from assistant professors also showed that they sometimes felt they could seek advice from their department chair (see table 5.1). They felt that a mentoring culture was often present in their department and sometimes present at their institution. And they often felt comfortable seeking career advice from colleagues at the same rank in their department and institution.

We asked assistant professors about the frequency with which they engaged with mentors from their institution. The top-rated activity they reported was that mentors often provided meaningful advice about teaching, along with departmental or institutional policies and politics. The other two top-rated activities were advice about departmental or institutional policies and procedures and advice about promotion or progress toward it.

Non-Tenure-Track Faculty Members

As the number of non-tenure-track (NTT) faculty appointments increases, administrators in charge of faculty development wish to support them better (Austin and Sorcinelli 2013), but such support remains limited. One study reported that formal or structured mentoring appears to be available to about one-third of NTT faculty members, and that formal mentoring was more likely to be available to part-time faculty members when it was present for full-time faculty members (Gehrke and Kezar 2015). These scholars also found that institution type influenced mentoring support for NTT faculty members: private colleges were more likely than public ones to support such professional development. We found mixed support of mentoring of NTT faculty members at the institutions in our study.

For ease of reporting, we grouped faculty members with titles of visiting professor, lecturer, adjunct faculty, or instructor into one category called NTT faculty members. Many of these faculty members reported that collegiality was one of the positive aspects of their department. They made comments such as "the departmental environment is very supportive" and "friendly environment, open doors." Some of these NTT faculty members noted that the department appeared to have good intentions toward their faculty that did not actually result in action. For example, one person noted that "while [they are] welcoming, I don't always feel supported by the department in my work." Another reported that "everyone is so busy that, although I am officially supposed to be receiving some mentoring, it has been somewhat haphazard and passed around from person to person." Other NTT faculty members felt more excluded, noting that there was "not a sense of belonging."

Our survey results showed differences between the experiences of NTT and other faculty members (see table 5.1). NTT faculty members were more comfortable with going to the department chair as a resource or career support than were tenured or tenure-track faculty members. They also felt that a mentoring culture was less apparent in their department and institution than did other faculty members. Teaching is the main responsibility of NTT faculty members, and they reported receiving more support on their teaching than did associate or full professors, but not as much support as assistant professors received.

Bright and Dark Sides of Mentoring: Relationship Quality

"There's like a structural sickness in our faculty that no one wants to talk about. Everyone knows it's there. No one wants to talk about it. No one has the authority to do anything about it, and no one wants to do anything about it because it would involve potentially altering the landscape that people–the very foxholes that people have dug for themselves."

–An assistant professor of religious studies

Faculty members described positive mentoring experiences as well as challenging relationships. Interviews with faculty members highlighted the fact that positive mentoring relationships seemed to be transformative and energizing, while negative experiences were derailing and demotivating. For example, one faculty member noted that great mentors made a big difference: "[I] had some great mentors along the way, and I think they've been—you know, they certainly have been a good role model and pointed me in the right direction. What [this college] is and where we're trying to go and what we're trying to do." In contrast, a lack of mentoring motivated some faculty members to always be "looking" for another position elsewhere. For example, when one faculty member was asked to describe his experiences specifically within his department in terms of colleagueship, support, and development, he responded: "Okay. I'm so sorry that I really don't have good news to tell you." Later in the interview he noted that as a result, "it probably won't surprise you to learn that every year, I'm selectively testing the market. And one of the big things that has become more and more important to me every year when I look at places is, what's the collegiality like?"

Published research (Allen et al. 2004) is unclear about whether having a mentor is sufficient for the people involved to receive benefits from that relationship, or if the quality of that relationship makes a difference. Our survey results allowed us to examine what mattered when it came to a person's job satisfaction.

We drew on the work of Abraham Carmeli, Daphna Brueller, and Jane Dutton (2009), who theorized that high-quality relationships at work were characterized by their emotional tone, openness, and tensility. Emotional tone refers to the extent to which relational partners can celebrate achievements (good news) and share failures (bad news). Openness refers to how much the relationship connects individuals with new ideas and thoughts. And relationships with tensility enable the individuals to continue to interact even after a difficult conversation.

We used our GLCA survey data to analyze mentoring relationships and outcomes with ordinary least squares regression (see Appendix A for details on the measures). As relationship quality increased with a mentor ($F_{(4, 259)} = 18.55$,

$p < 0.001$; $R^2 = 0.22$) or a mentee ($F(1,287) = 32.81$, $p < 0.001$; $R^2 = 0.10$), so did job satisfaction. There was a bigger effect size for the mentees than for the mentors. Associate professors who had a relatively high-quality relationship with a mentor also reported more job satisfaction, compared to professors at other ranks who had a similar relationship with a mentor. (Job satisfaction did not matter for their relationships with mentees.)

Interestingly, we found that faculty members reported significantly higher relationship quality with mentors than with mentees (mean = 5.4 and 4.8, respectively; $t = 4.50$; $df = 563$; $p < 0.001$; 95 percent confidence interval: 0.32, 0.81). In other words, mentees felt they had a better mentoring relationship, on average, than did mentors. In our opinion, this is because mentees may share more with their mentors than mentors might be willing to share with their mentees. For example, a mentee may be more likely to discuss with a mentor a negative interaction with a colleague and ask for advice about how to deal with that colleague, while a mentor is unlikely to discuss similar matters and seek advice about them from a mentee.

What Can I Do? Advancing a Mentoring Culture

"It doesn't matter what stage of the career you're in. But we have to formulate—you know, exactly what do we mean by mentoring and, and how are we going to structure a mentoring program that allows people to be receptive?"

—A provost

"In advising, I asked the question when I first got here, about, 'Well, what kind of training will we get?' And the response from one of my colleagues was, 'You'll figure it out,' which I was really disappointed at, because I would have appreciated something more than that. . . . [T]his deep advising is important to us."

—An assistant professor of history

Strengthen Vertical Alignment

Mentoring was recognized by most GLCA administrators as a valued way to develop faculty members. However, it was difficult to tie mentoring initiatives to the overall institutional strategy. Strong vertical alignment of faculty development policies may help administrators use limited resources wisely on mentoring initiatives. The AFFD-LAC highlights opportunities to improve faculty development. Two recommendations flow from our study of the GLCA colleges:

connect institutional plans to faculty mentoring and develop strategies for mentoring for all faculty members.

We recommend that administrators connect faculty development initiatives to institutional strategic plans and fund-raising campaign plans. Faculty members are the heart of an LAC in terms of its teaching mission, and they desire to create knowledge and serve their communities. Thus, administrators will benefit from examining how mentoring is tied to these institutional goals so they can fit this valuable activity into faculty development plans. Administrators should examine their faculty development efforts annually to ensure that mentoring resources are devoted to those areas valued by the institution. A mentoring program for new faculty members might need to be revised to include goals for faculty development that align with institutional goals.

For example, Denison College's new strategic plan puts mentoring front and center in its first goal. The college website states that "first, we need to continually strive to provide a high-touch, high-quality experience" and that "central to this process is mentorship." Vertical alignment suggests that the development of a mentoring culture at Denison would best support a focus on mentoring experiences for faculty members to support their development as mentors and also provide them with mentorship. Thus, faculty members would benefit from developing their mentoring skills to support each other and students. Fund-raising plans could include goals to raise money for a faculty mentor award or a yearly faculty mentor-in-residence program.

We recommend that faculty development efforts include mentoring opportunities for all faculty types and career stages. For example, continuing with the Denison example above, even senior faculty members would benefit from briefings on optimal mentoring. Furthermore, having a mentoring culture means that mentoring interactions take place informally and frequently. Thus, full professors might benefit from being mentored themselves in learning how best to navigate their mentor roles, make decisions to move into formal leadership roles, and establish their legacy as they end their career. Across the GLCA, we found a strong focus on mentoring for faculty members early in their careers and a relative neglect for those in the middle or late stages of their careers. NTT faculty members reported even less of a sense of a mentoring culture in their department and institution. Given the greater reliance on NTT faculty members on most college campuses, we believe that they need to be included in mentoring programs and plans.

QUESTIONS FOR CONSIDERATION

1. Are formal faculty mentoring programs in place that directly promote activities and outcomes connected to the institution's strategic plan?

2. Do faculty mentoring programs provide opportunities for faculty members across career stages and ranks to participate as both a mentee and a mentor?

Developing Strong Horizontal Alignment

Horizontal alignment means that policies related to mentoring are well defined across departments and units. Such alignment provides accountability and sustainability in mentoring, which makes the program less vulnerable to the whims of whoever is in charge of faculty development or mentoring. We found that some colleges within the GLCA had strong horizontal alignment, and other colleges had inconsistent or nonexisting policies.

Our examination of horizontal alignment in the GLCA schools suggests that policies could be clearer about what language faculty handbooks should use, the role of the department chair, and the function of faculty mentor coordinators. We recommend that the language in faculty handbooks should describe the official campus policies and procedures related to mentoring for faculty members. There was relatively little discussion about mentoring in the documents we examined, even for new faculty members. Mentoring faculty members to become excellent teachers is an important aspect of mentoring in many colleges, and there is an opportunity to clarify the relationship of mentoring to teaching for faculty members in most of the faculty handbooks we examined. Relatedly, there should be language about whether mentoring students is a criterion for P&T. Some colleges mentioned the importance of faculty members' mentoring students, while other colleges did not have the word "mentor" in their faculty handbooks at all. It could be the case that advising is seen as mentoring in some colleges. However, a clear and consistent expectation about either advising or mentoring might increase the attention that all faculty members pay to mentoring.

We recommend that mentoring be an official part of the job description for a department chair. Department chairs were important in mentoring experiences for faculty members, especially those not on the tenure track. Job descriptions and annual review criteria for department chairs should reflect the importance of the people in this role in mentoring faculty members and should emphasize that the chairs need to connect faculty members with multiple mentors in the department and across the institution. All faculty members in a department should encourage mentorship as part of a departmental culture. Ideally, this will then facilitate faculty members' serving as mentors for peers in and outside of their departments.

We also recommend that campus leaders formally designate an administrator—such as the provost or someone in faculty affairs or development—as responsible for reviewing mentoring activities and outcomes on campus yearly, and include this responsibility in the annual review of that administrator. There should be someone in charge of mentoring who coordinates faculty mentoring initiatives. For LACs in a consortium such as the GLCA, this coordination might occur at the consortium level. The consortium as a whole might have a faculty member as a coordinator, a two- or three-year position that would rotate among member schools. Such an arrangement would raise awareness among the campuses about mentoring activities taking place across the consortium and might enable the coordinator to connect faculty members from different institutions in mentoring relationships.

QUESTIONS FOR CONSIDERATION

1. What is the right committee or office on your campus to initiate a review of the language in faculty handbooks about mentoring?
2. How might human resources work with deans to review the job descriptions of department chairs and ensure that mentoring is mentioned in those descriptions?
3. What is the right office on your campus to sustain and support mentoring efforts across the campus and perhaps to coordinate with other institutions on sharing the overhead to manage mentoring efforts?

Developing Strong Implementation

When we examined mentoring programs and related efforts, we found that the GLCA colleges were weakest in the implementation of mentoring programming and supports. There was little or no training or information about what optimal mentoring is or what activities might best support excellent mentoring experiences. Furthermore, at many institutions we detected a sink-or-swim attitude about faculty success, along with an overreliance on informal mentoring. We make three recommendations to address these issues: have more training, better assessment, and more engagement of faculty members.

We recommend that a high-quality mentoring training program be available to mentors and mentees. Training for mentors is the most obvious implementation activity that flows from the recommendations above. Given the importance of department chairs in the success of the endeavor, there should be evidence-based training of chairs on mentoring. An annual briefing or formal orientation for faculty mentors would improve mentoring efforts for both faculty members and for students. However, faculty mentees also benefit from a briefing or training to learn more about understanding their roles and responsibilities. In addition, this information should help them become the mentors of the future.

We recommend that a program coordinator assess mentoring programs (not participants!) annually. An evaluation of mentoring efforts, resources, and related outcomes will help administrators know when to remove, redesign, or create new professional development opportunities and programs for mentoring. As part of this assessment, administrators will have an opportunity to promote an institutional dialogue about what mentoring means on the campus for all students and employees. Faculty members across the GLCA schools did not report that a lot of faculty mentoring was happening at their institution. We believe that institutions would benefit from promoting the use of a common mentoring vocabulary and holding common expectations about mentoring. Clarity about what mentoring is at a faculty member's institution might also help him or her recognize it and engage in it. The goal is to create a culture of mentorship that is recognized by community members, and reported as happening in an effective way by faculty members on their campus.

It sometimes happens that an institution has a program "on the books" but not in reality. Annual assessment of mentoring or other development programs for faculty members will help administrators detect such problems. One faculty member told us, "our school hasn't supported it [mentoring] at all," and a faculty member at another college noted, "I don't see a lot of mentoring going on." Yet administrators on both campuses reported that there was a formal mentoring program for faculty members. We recommend that focus groups or committees be established with faculty members from across ranks and appointment types who can identify the mentoring needs of faculty members.

Mentoring programs need to meet the needs of faculty members and to deliver evidence-based content effectively. On average, we found that faculty members were undecided—4.6 on a scale from 1 (very unlikely) to 7 (very likely)—about participating in faculty mentoring as a formal faculty development initiative. It is critical that faculty members be part of conversations on campus about what they need to motivate them to participate in programming that is developed based on what they most need. We know it is frustrating to develop mentoring programs that are not well attended. One faculty member reflected this reality when describing a mentoring program through the GLCA consortium as a "pretty interesting . . . opportunity," and then wryly observing, "but this is so ironic. I couldn't find the time." The fact is that many faculty members are drawn to LACs for their unique environment. Steve, the professor featured in the vignette at the beginning of this chapter, told us: "I know I've brought up a few negative things, but my experience is almost entirely positive. And when I can spend time with students and other faculty members, especially across campus but mostly in my own department, it's a very rewarding, interesting, fascinating, useful life." More attention to and intention about mentoring may help LACs attract talented faculty members like Steve and help keep them there to become the next institutional leaders.

Conclusion

In this chapter we advocated for the development of a mentoring culture at LACs that will support formal mentoring initiatives and promote an increase in the number of informal mentoring relationships. Faculty members desire and value mentoring and gain from being a mentor, yet mentoring appeared to be haphazardly implemented across departments and colleges. Somewhat surprisingly, we found that faculty members—even full professors—are often engaged in mentoring as both mentors and mentees, and that colleges need to do a better job of helping faculty members develop the tools for and understand the importance of creating strategic mentoring networks as critical for career supports. Ensuring that mentoring activities are aligned with institutional goals and strategies is the first step to creating more strategic and effective practices across the campus. Assessment is also needed to make certain that mentoring takes place in ways that are valued by faculty members.

6

◦◦

Trends and Exemplars

After class Sally, an associate professor in the performing arts, heads to her office. There she reads the weekly e-mail noting the faculty development programs available in the upcoming weeks. As she scans the listings with great interest, Sam, a full professor in social sciences, walks into her office on his way to a committee meeting. He asks if she has seen the e-mail and whether she plans to attend any of the programs being offered. Sally believes the faculty development offerings to be plentiful, and she praises the Center for Teaching and Learning (CTL) on her campus to Sam: "We have a very active CTL, run by a wonderful sociology professor. There are many events, and the topics of those events are quite diverse—as are the times such programming is offered." However, Sally continues: "Since the center's establishment several years ago, not a single one of its activities has been oriented toward arts teaching. The topics addressed are virtually irrelevant to what I do."

Sam replies that every semester there are always three to four dedicated programs covering more general topics that she might like, from syllabus development to teaching with technology. Yet Sam's overall assessment of the CTL is not positive, either: "I appreciate the effort, and I know the center director works very hard to offer these programs. However, these workshops tend to be very time-consuming for the benefits accrued, at least for me. I need support beyond teaching and learning. I would appreciate more of an opportunity to connect with my peers across campus to talk about our teaching and classroom experiences and our scholarship, as opposed to sitting through a workshop about it."

Unfortunately Sally's and Sam's views represent what our data on faculty development reflect—good intentions that fail to be fully materialized and, at times, a misunderstanding of what faculty members truly want and need in the way of professional development. This vignette illustrates tactic speak (Gratton and Truss 2003). Tactic speak occurs when the faculty development function of a college or university focuses on the implementation of faculty development programming aimed at the faculty as a whole, with limited connection to the overall aims and objectives of the institution, departments, or disciplines. Paying attention to tactic speak is important for faculty development offices because of the implications it has for improving faculty development. Our study shows that there are opportunities to provide faculty development that better addresses:

1. Career-stage needs and perspectives;
2. Comprehensive support for teaching and learning, scholarship, and service;
3. Disciplinary or departmental needs; and
4. Institutional goals and strategic initiatives.

We wrote this book to help campus leaders, faculty developers, and faculty members in liberal arts colleges (LACs) identify opportunities to build the institution's most strategic and expensive resource—faculty members. A strategy and process approach offers the most benefit for faculty development efforts. Such an approach is rooted in personnel policies aligned with institutional goals and strategies, with the goal of effective implementation once buy-in is secured from all parties involved. Furthermore, a strategy and process approach to faculty development may create a strategic advantage for liberal arts and other small colleges in the struggle to rein in spending through the more efficient and effective deployment of resources.

In this chapter, we provide a snapshot of participation trends in faculty development programs, and faculty members' preferred professional development formats by career stage and appointment type. We then feature strong faculty development initiatives already in place across the Great Lakes Colleges Association (GLCA) that are working toward a strategy and process approach to faculty development.

Trends in Faculty Development Participation: Career Stage and Rank

The good news is that, as we noted in chapter 4, nearly 60 percent of the faculty members who participated in our study believe that someone on their campus was working to meet their needs through faculty development programming.

The bad news is that the remaining 40 percent did not think anyone was in charge of faculty development for all GLCA institutions combined, suggesting that either some faculty members are unaware of faculty development programs on their campuses or that they did not perceive the offerings to be targeted to their needs.

Individuals are motivated to participate in and benefit from professional development activities when such activities meet their perceived needs. Unmet needs lead to frustration and demotivation for everyone involved in faculty development programming, as well as to the ineffective use of financial resources and faculty members' and administrators' time.

It is probably common across campus for a well-planned workshop for faculty members to be poorly attended. Organizers and other key campus leaders then point to the workshop as one more example of how they are meeting faculty needs, but that faculty members are not engaged. The lack of participation becomes the excuse for leaders not to invest more time and resources in such programs because "faculty don't show up anyway." However, the faculty members view the experience as another example of how campus leaders and program developers fail to meet their needs. As a result, they either don't go to future sessions that are patently of no use to them, or they go but conclude: "That was a waste of my time. That had zero relevance to me. I could have been grading papers instead."

How can campus leaders and faculty developers achieve a strategy and process approach to faculty development? They must have a clear understanding of trends in faculty development participation on their campus, including what obstacles prevent attendance and engagement, which activities that faculty members have engaged in, and what training format and content are preferred—all according to the ranks and appointment types of faculty members.

Trends in Participation by Career Stage and Rank

Full Professor

> "At this point in my career, I find I enjoy engaging with my colleagues, my
> peers, as we think about the final act of our careers."
>
> —A full professor of religious studies

As discussed throughout this book, heavy workloads and the changing nature of academic work create challenges for faculty members. Those challenges are experienced and managed differently by professors depending on what stage of their career they have reached.

OBSTACLES. Unsurprisingly, workload was the number one reason that full professors cited for their lack of participation in faculty development programming (49 percent of our full professor respondents mentioned it). For faculty members, workload translates into energy spent learning to reinvent themselves in the classroom and to mentor junior colleagues through the promotion and tenure (P&T) process and help them navigate the formal and informal rules of the institution. As we discussed in chapter 4, sometimes full professors have the ability to engage in these tasks, and sometimes they do not—due to a lack of resources, knowledge, or needed supports. Time was another major obstacle that prevented full professors from participating in faculty development programming. One explained: "I have become more protective of my time, and I am sure that's motivated by the career and life stage I am in. But I am not giving up more time away from other passions outside of work to come in on the weekend for another workshop." The third most significant obstacle preventing full professors from participating in the programming was its lack of relevance. Full professors lamented that it was clearly geared toward early-career scholars. One stated: "I don't need to attend yet another syllabus-building workshop. The content is important, but irrelevant for me. If I don't know how to draft a syllabus at this point, it's time to retire."

PREFERRED FACULTY DEVELOPMENT ACTIVITIES. Full professors identified professional conferences, college-sponsored workshops and presentations, and publication as the top three faculty development activities they had participated in over the past three years. Forty-one percent of our respondents at the rank of full professor noted professional conferences in their disciplinary areas as the most important faculty development experience available to them. Such conferences were described as "a great way to connect with colleagues from other institutions," "a way to receive feedback on your work," and "a way to combat the isolation of being the only person on your campus who does what you do." Professional conferences also enable faculty members to stay engaged in and up-to-date on the current state of their discipline and profession. From the stories we heard from LAC faculty members, it seems that this sort of engagement was particularly crucial given that they worked in small departments and institutions and were often the only person on their campus studying a specific topic. Combined with the traditional cultural emphasis on teaching prevalent at LACs, that made contact with disciplinary colleagues at professional association and academic meetings an essential type of professional development for LAC faculty members.

While full professors considered having supports outside of the institution important to achieving relevance in their field, they were also interested in internal opportunities that showcased their work and that of their colleagues.

Thirty-eight percent of our full professor respondents discussed college-sponsored workshops and presentations organized on their respective campuses as "important," "useful," and "a great way to stay informed about colleague scholarship or teaching," depending on the focus of the event. One stated: "I really appreciate it when [my institution] hosts symposia that features the great work of my colleagues. Despite our size, it's so easy to be out of the loop when it comes to the great work happening on this campus. What a great way to showcase the work of colleagues."

Finally, engagement within and outside the institution allowed full professors to turn those efforts into deliverable outcomes. Thirty-five percent of our full professor respondents discussed their scholarship, specifically publication, as an activity they have participated in that was important to their continued engagement in their work and their remaining "active in the discipline." One noted: "I am finally at a place in my career where I enjoy the research and publication process. Before, it was a necessary aspect to my work. Now, it's a place to do some good thinking and take some risks I was unable to do before achieving my promotion."

PREFERRED FACULTY DEVELOPMENT FORMATS. It became apparent that full professors were most interested in faculty development that was built around engagement with peers, ranging from peer-to-peer exchanges of ideas (mentioned by 33 percent of our full professor respondents), organized informal discussions with colleagues (29 percent), and structured discussions with colleagues (25 percent). One noted: "At this point in my career, I find I enjoy engaging with my colleagues, my peers, as we think about the final act of our careers. And it's in those conversations that I feel I gain the most." Full professors also noted that they are responsible for "leaving the institution in a better position compared to when we arrived," which meant deliberately prioritizing their roles and—perhaps more important—how they approached their roles on campus. It was during conversations with peers that allowed full professors to be deliberate about their responsibilities and their interactions with junior colleagues and administrators.

Full professors appreciated discussing relevant topics with peers, particularly retirement and preparing for the last five to ten years of their careers. One said: "I have been asked many times by my junior colleagues when I plan to retire, and I never answer that question. But I will discuss it with my cohort, if you will, because it's something that is very personal, and I save that for a select group of individuals outside of my family." Other full professors in our study had similar feelings. They were happy to engage in a variety of faculty development programming, but the programming they found most relevant to them involved their full professor peers and topics that were specific to their career stage. Therefore, we were not surprised to learn that full professors found support both inside and outside of their respective institutions.

SOURCES OF SUPPORT. Fifty-one percent of our full professor respondents noted the importance of departmental colleagues (see chapter 2 for more details on the role of departmental relationships), 42 percent mentioned collaborators outside of the institution, and 37 percent mentioned colleagues in professional associations (see chapter 5 for more details on supportive relationships). Full professors are often seen as mentors or guides to early-career faculty members. Yet as we mention in chapter 5, they often lack the support and training they need to fulfill those roles effectively. Faculty members are essentially left to their own devices to figure out what works or how to fulfill institutional expectations of mentoring communicated by provosts or department heads. There also appears to be a need for mentoring, or at least coaching, for full professors as they wind up their career. Full professors noted a desire for mentoring and coaching support in learning new teaching or research techniques and ending their career well.

Associate Professor

> "Not one faculty development offering in the past three years or more has featured topics like this [administrative support] to help us think about our roles in these areas."
>
> –An associate professor of biology

Our findings mirror those in the literature, which highlights the challenges associated with mid-career faculty members (Austin 2010; Baldwin, DeZure, Shaw, and Moretto 2008; Mathews 2014). Increases and changes in expectations, with little or no meaningful available support, seem to characterize the experiences of associate professors.

OBSTACLES. Workload was the greatest barrier to engagement in faculty development programming (reported by 48 percent of our associate professor respondents), closely followed by time (46 percent). Associate professors described "time creep," saying that more and more personal time was being "hijacked" to accommodate attendance at institutional programs—given that there are not enough work hours in the day to accomplish all the work needed to be done (see chapter 3 for a discussion of work-life balance and related challenges). One associate professor stated: "These faculty development workshops are consistently being offered on evenings, weekends, and during the summer. It creates this tension of trying to maintain some balance and personal life outside of work while taking advantage of the needed supports. At times, I get frustrated [because] the administration keeps encroaching on my personal time, and when I choose to pass, I fear that's being monitored."

Associate professors were also "disappointed" in the topics addressed in faculty development programming, with 34 percent citing interest and relevance as an issue. One commented: "I find it odd that at this stage we are heavily steeped in administrative duties and service, yet not one faculty development offering in the past three years or more has featured topics like this to help us think about our roles in these areas." Several associate professors described the current faculty development programming on their respective campuses as "a missed opportunity," "irrelevant," and "more useful for one's early career." We see this as a real opportunity for faculty development offices to be strategic about future faculty development offerings for LAC associate professors.

PREFERRED FACULTY DEVELOPMENT ACTIVITIES. Much like their full professor colleagues, associate professors identified professional conferences (mentioned by 43 percent) and college-sponsored workshops and presentations (39 percent) as the top two faculty development activities they engaged in. Publications and grants were tied for third (28 percent each). However, despite the fact that both full and associate professors identified similar activities, the two groups viewed these activities and the role they play in a professor's career growth very differently. While full professors discussed the utility of engagement in such activities, associate professors regarded professional conference attendance as "vital," "necessary," and "the most important way to gain credibility in the field." One noted: "Despite the lack of financial resources at [my institution] to attend conferences, I see the importance of investing my own resources to attend. My colleagues don't know this line of work, so it's imperative I attend if I want to advance in my career either here or elsewhere."

And while full professors described college-sponsored workshops and presentations as useful and a means of staying informed about colleagues' work, associate professors saw these events more strategically. "Members of the community serve on the faculty personnel committee, and they also attend these events. I participate to get the campus exposure and a greater awareness of my work," one associate professor said. Others expressed similar opinions, describing these events as "networking opportunities" that can provide "critical exposure" and as "necessary." The work that associate professors accomplish through publication and grant-funded research could be disseminated at professional conferences and college-sponsored workshops and presentations. Associate professors viewed this faculty development activity as "vital to promotion," "the key to full professorship," and "a differentiator" among their associate professor peers at other institutions and between those who are promoted and those who aren't. However, this was also the faculty development that associate professors felt was the most challenging to achieve, given the increased service and campus leadership expected of them at this career stage. One commented: "I know I need to publish and bring external money to [the institution], and thank goodness I have been successful in these areas. But it's not easy when you're department chair, mentoring two new professors in the department, and managing the committee work." Furthermore, a lack of resources such as access to a full-time grants administrator made winning external grants a challenge, as noted by several of our associate professor participants.

PREFERRED FACULTY DEVELOPMENT FORMATS. Associate professors also appreciated opportunities to interact and engage with peers at the same rank, but they found workshops useful only if the content was focused and relevant to their pursuit of promotion. The career development formats most valued by our associate professor respondents were workshops (mentioned by 41 percent), peer-to-peer exchanges of ideas and discussions (33 percent), and organized informal discussions with colleagues (29 percent). Once again, they were quick to point out that the content and goals of the programming, regardless of delivery, were most important. Rather than attend a general microteaching workshop, associate professors wanted training on how to be a department chair, how to manage up when engaging with administrators and manage down when working with junior colleagues, how to be an effective mentor, and how to reenvision the next stage of one's career. Such topics were characterized as "more relevant," "more useful," and "better connected to the skills needed to succeed and advance."

SOURCES OF SUPPORT. Peer-to-peer exchanges and organized informal discussions with colleagues appeared to serve two purposes: career support, as in the "sharing of best practices" and "lessons learned," and critical emotional support, by creating that feeling of "I am not the only one struggling" or "thank goodness I'm not going crazy." Given their desire to advance, associate professors still felt a need for impression management and preferred to save certain conversations for peers, rather than have them with senior colleagues. After being promoted to associate professor, they also felt a change in how their junior colleagues related to them, realizing that those colleagues too were managing impressions by pulling back a bit in terms of their engagement with people who were now more senior colleagues. Therefore, having the support of those in a similar career stage and the dedicated time and space to have conversations with them was what associate professors most needed, valued, and appreciated. Given these realities, we were not surprised to learn that they identified as the top three sources of support were departmental colleagues (38 percent), collaborators outside of the institution (31 percent), and colleagues in professional associations (28 percent).

Associate professors appear to be the most at risk when it comes to mentoring. It is assumed they have mastered their role as they attain P&T. Yet many of these faculty members noted confusion about how to navigate the next stage of their career. Formal mentoring support is lacking for mid-career faculty members. Yet associate professors expressed a strong desire for mentors or guides to help them navigate their heavier service load, reinvigorate their teaching and research, and sometimes even advise them on balancing family and professional demands. According to our survey data, the department chair and other colleagues sometimes provide mentoring support, but not nearly enough.

Assistant Professor

> "I will not be here in five years if I do not publish."
>
> —An assistant professor of sociology

Early-career professors face the steep learning curve that is associated with taking on a new position in a new environment, particularly an environment that differs from graduate school. Expectations surrounding their roles, responsibilities, and work-life balance can sometimes conflict, thus increasing the importance of faculty development programming for these faculty members.

OBSTACLES. Like full and associate professors, assistant professors cited workload as the greatest barrier to engagement in faculty development programming (reported by 49 percent of our assistant professor respondents). However, their workload challenges were related not so much to increased expectations but to understanding and managing the myriad roles, responsibilities, and expectations of being an early-career faculty member, while working toward and understanding the P&T process. Having a heavy workload was related to work-life balance issues (see chapter 3), and thus timing (mentioned by 38 percent) was cited as the second greatest obstacle. Much like associate professors, assistant professors expressed disappointment in the ever-increasing commitments they were expected to make to evening, weekend, and off-contract summer events, which were exacerbated by the ever-increasing workload faculty members are expected to manage. But the assistant professors acknowledge the challenge of finding the right times to offer such support, given "there are only so many hours in the day."

Interest and relevance was the third most cited obstacle by assistant professor participants, mentioned by 27 percent. They were eager for programming more tailored to their needs and milestones. In particular, they wanted programming more specifically related to working toward interim and tenure reviews, how colleagues had recently successfully passed those milestones, and what to expect next.

PREFERRED FACULTY DEVELOPMENT ACTIVITIES. Interestingly, like full professors, assistant professors reported college-sponsored workshops and presentations (45 percent), professional conference attendance (40 percent), and publication (38 percent) as the three most important faculty development activities in which they had engaged during the past three years. But once again, they viewed these opportunities quite differently than full and associate professors. For example, college-sponsored workshops or presentations were an opportunity to "increase campus visibility" and "begin to make a name for oneself." More senior colleagues often suggested that assistant professors participate in some development programs. As one faculty participant explained, "My department chair really suggested I participate, given this is viewed as one of the most important faculty development activities supported by [the institution]. I appreciated her letting me know how this event is viewed by the larger campus community. It's open to faculty, staff, and members of the board of trustees. I want to be viewed as an active scholar, so this is one opportunity to do that."

Assistant professors also echoed comments made by associate professors about being the one person in a department or on a campus who works in a specific area of research or study. As a result, assistant professors regarded professional conference attendance as vital, but they saw as "necessary to maintain relationships with key collaborators." Assistant professors were still working to create their on-campus and local community networks, thus making relationships with colleagues and peers from their graduate institutions important. Professional conference participation supported "face to face collaborations," "facilitated important networking opportunities," and "served as an important motivator of scholarship." Participating in professional conferences makes publication more likely, and having publications is important for getting tenure, as one faculty respondent noted, "publications will make or break the tenure decision." While all the institutions in our study are LACs whose missions focus on strong teaching, publication and scholarship was increasingly necessary for P&T, and this reality was not lost on assistant professors. One said: "I will not be here in five years if I do not publish. No matter how strong a teacher I am, scholarship appears to be the defining factor in getting tenure."

PREFERRED FACULTY DEVELOPMENT FORMATS. Assistant professors nearly mirrored associate professors in terms of preferred formats, with 46 percent of assistant professors mentioning workshops, 38 percent citing peer-to-peer exchanges of ideas and discussions, and 31 percent mentioning structured discussions. However, the two groups' focus and intended outcomes once again differed greatly. For example, assistant professors were very interested in workshops that covered the main areas in which they were expected to engage. Examples we heard included syllabus development, best practices in advising, teaching with technology, and balancing teaching and research.

Similar to associate professors, assistant professors were also eager to have opportunities to engage with peers at their same level. One assistant professor commented: "I just wish I knew what my peers were doing, how they were organizing their dossiers, and how they are managing everything we have to do. I feel like I am so busy that I don't have the opportunity to ask these simple but important questions." Assistant professors saw exchanges with peers as a "safe space" in which to ask questions about balance, scheduling, and juggling of responsibilities. Assistant professors felt such interactions would create a sense of "we're in this together" among peers in the same career stage. They looked to senior colleagues, however, to engage by way of structured discussions on specific topics such as understanding and navigating the P&T process. One assistant professor said: "I would love to have a panel, for example, where recently tenured faculty from across campus talk us through their experience, how they managed the process, and the best and worst advice they received. I can learn from others' experiences."

SOURCES OF SUPPORT. Finally, like their senior colleagues, assistant professors found sources of support in departmental colleagues (mentioned by 38 percent of assistant professor respondents) and collaborators outside the institution (31 percent). The difference was that the third most important source of supports for assistant professors was peers from graduate school (28 percent). Departmental colleagues were viewed as the "make it or break it" group of individuals who served as the bridge to P&T. Without their support, assistant professors knew that their prospects for earning P&T were slim or nonexistent. Collaborators and peers from graduate school were viewed as critical to assistant professors' being productive and engaged scholars within their disciplines. These individuals served as "conduits to the discipline and profession" and provided "professional accountability" to ensure productivity and achievement of proposed research agendas.

Most of the LACs in our study provide some formal mentoring for new assistant professors. In fact, most formal mentoring efforts across the GLCA were targeted at early-career faculty members. Colleges varied in terms of the expectations and amount of support they provided, and our assistant professor respondents noted that while expectations were clear about mentoring, how mentoring actually took place was unclear. Assistant professors were more likely to seek mentoring support from department chairs as compared to their departmental colleagues. The mentoring support they received focused on teaching practices, learning institutional policies, and dealing with promotion at this career stage.

Non-Tenure-Track Faculty Member

"We need a workshop on how to do more with less, given we are not eligible for internal supports despite managing the same responsibilities and expectations."

–A non-tenure-track (NTT) faculty member in physics

NTT faculty participants in our study identified the same primary obstacles that prevented their participation in faculty development programming on their respective campuses as their tenured and tenure-track colleagues did.

OBSTACLES. Workload was the dominant challenge faced by NTT faculty members (mentioned by 61 percent), given their lack of job security and the fact that they worked just as much as, if not more than, other faculty members in terms of teaching and scholarship to "appear worthy" of a full-time tenure-track position in the institution where they are employed. Time (mentioned by 51 percent) also created challenges for many of our NTT faculty respondents, because they were also employed as NTT faculty members at nearby institutions—which made it impossible for them to be fully immersed in one campus and its surrounding community. Several described their daily grind and the need to leave one campus to be on time to teach at the next. Finally, NTT faculty members cited interest and relevance (mentioned by 38 percent) as the third most important obstacle to their participation in faculty development programming. One remarked: "We need a workshop on how to do more with less, given we are not eligible for internal supports despite managing the same responsibilities and expectations. That is more relevant to me at this stage, unfortunately."

PREFERRED FACULTY DEVELOPMENT ACTIVITIES. Our NTT faculty participants were quite active in faculty development activities, and those activities mirrored those of their tenured and tenure-track colleagues. NTT faculty respondents put professional conference attendance (mentioned by 60 percent) first and publication (38 percent) third. Their second most cited activity was participation in summer institutes or workshops (41 percent). Their participation in professional conferences was all about "networking, networking, networking," given the "lack of job security from one year to the next." Professional conference attendance supports the job search process and enables NTT faculty members to stay in the "minds of hiring institutions and departments."

Summer institutes and workshops were viewed in a similar way, but those were less about disciplinary motivations and more about the development of skills in areas such as leadership, writing, and improving teaching skills. One NTT faculty member noted that "these are skills that transcend institution type, and the stronger I can be in these areas, the better." Finally, publication was considered the "currency needed to get a tenure-track job."

PREFERRED FACULTY DEVELOPMENT FORMATS. NTT faculty members were the most diverse group in terms of their preferences for faculty development formats, indicating that the most important were workshops (mentioned by 46 percent), peer-to-peer exchanges of ideas and discussions (38 percent), and classroom observation (30 percent). They preferred workshop content that was related to improving teaching techniques and organization, maintaining a productive scholarly agenda, and managing the job search process. While NTT faculty members were committed to their institutions, the lack of job security meant that they had one foot on campus and the other foot elsewhere as they sought to earn full-time, tenure track faculty appointments. They were also eager to have faculty development programs that would help them secure such a position, regardless of location.

NTT faculty members were also interested in faculty development centered on engagement, which could occur either through exchanges with other NTT faculty members or with professors in full-time positions at higher ranks. One NTT faculty member noted: "I attend as many of these functions as time permits. The topics may not always be relevant, but I see the networking opportunities as very relevant to my goals." They also were interested in classroom observations, both as an observer and as the one being observed. Given the teaching focus of LACs, the desire to improve teaching capabilities was strong, and classroom observation by veteran faculty members considered exemplary teachers was a critical resource for NTT faculty development. One commented: "I welcome as many people in to my class as possible. I get some great feedback, and it shows an investment in my growth, which I hope translates into a full-time offer. I also have observed four colleagues already this term, trying to get as many examples [of others' teaching] as possible." The focus on skill development and relationship building were important criteria for faculty development.

SOURCES OF SUPPORT. The relationships that were of most value and served as important sources of support for NTT faculty members paralleled those of full and associate professors: departmental colleagues (mentioned by 43 percent of our NTT faculty respondents), collaborators outside the institution (34 percent), and colleagues in professional associations (26 percent). NTT faculty members hoped that departmental colleagues would advocate turning the currently contingent position into a full-time one, while collaborators outside the institution and in professional associations were seen as important for networking and productivity.

Mentoring was valued by NTT faculty members, who looked more to the department chair for support than did other faculty members. Some NTT faculty members reported a strong sense of collegiality in their department, while others felt relatively neglected and isolated. Surprisingly, even though teaching was their main responsibility, they did not receive support for their teaching as often as assistant professors did.

Summary

We cannot stress enough the importance of understanding the how, why, what, and who of developing and delivering relevant and desired faculty development programming. We find faculty members to be rational and pragmatic about how they spend their time. They participate in faculty development, despite their workload concerns, but only when they perceive value in, and a professional (or perhaps personal) connection to, the content being delivered. As the saying goes, "when something is important to you, you make it a priority." But faculty members fail to participate in many current faculty development efforts because they believe that the content does not add value and/or the method of delivery does not meet their needs. During our discussions with faculty members, we heard the same comment over and over: "I don't have time for another workshop. They take too much time away from my actual work." On some level, we agree. We have all found ourselves sitting in workshops and retreats that left us thinking, "I could be so productive if I wasn't sitting here" or "Gee, that was six hours of my life I will never get back."

We advocate for the development of a balanced portfolio of faculty development programming, one that includes offerings of interest to all faculty members, regardless of career stage. However, a balanced portfolio also means that there should be programming specific to different career stages and appointment types. We found that faculty members seek outside support to supplement what they do or don't receive at their respective institutions. Many of the faculty members who participated in our study focused on faculty development opportunities outside of their institutions, such as at professional conferences or through collaborators. This focus only further exacerbates faculty members' disengagement from their institution and pushes them to develop greater commitment to and affiliation with their discipline. Faculty members who begin to see themselves as just a full-time equivalent on their campus, or someone who could teach anywhere, do a disservice to the mission and intent of LACs. Regardless, administrators—particularly those tasked with managing faculty development programming—should engage in a regular assessment to track trends in faculty members' participation in that programming, both internal and external to their institutions.

Featured Faculty Development Programs and Supports in the GLCA

We had two goals in writing this chapter. The first was to provide insights into faculty development participation trends by career stage, rank, and appointment type as a necessary step to aligning institutional priorities and individual needs. The second was to provide faculty development programming examples from across the GLCA that we believe address critical needs. We organize this section by first noting the institutional challenge and then discussing the faculty development program that seeks to address it.

Too Much Focus on the Early-Career Stage

Mentoring was a support that all our faculty respondents discussed as important. In particular, mid- and late-career faculty members were eager to receive more of it to help them navigate their changing roles and expectations. However, the majority of effort across the GLCA was on early-career faculty mentoring.

An example of strong horizontal and vertical alignment for programming that addresses the needs of all faculty members and that has been effectively implemented is the Seasons program at the College of Wooster. Seasons was created to provide a venue for faculty members to share and discuss challenges, concerns, or suggestions for the various stages of their careers, as a means of addressing those challenges not typically covered by usual faculty development programs such as new faculty members' orientation. Seasons includes informal gatherings meant to give College of Wooster faculty members an opportunity to talk about anxieties and concerns in a safe environment.

Over the years topics have included: "I'm Tenured: Now What?," "Finding Mentors at All Stages of Your Career," "Balancing Work and Family," "Thinking about Retirement," and "Switching Gears: How Do We Reinvent Ourselves as Teachers and Scholars?" Seasons has also had reading circles in which faculty members have discussed *Presumed Incompetent* (Gutiérrez y Muhs, Niemann, González, and Harris 2012), an edited volume about the experiences of faculty members of color, and *Lean In* (Sandberg 2013), about women in leadership.

We really appreciate this program at the College of Wooster, because it is designed to bring together faculty members across and within career stages to discuss issues that they face. The content addresses career-stage issues head-on, while fostering peer-to-peer exchanges and structured, informal discussions. These are formats that faculty members have told us they want.

Lack of Support for Multiple Mentors in Career Progression

When it came to mentoring support, some colleges had strong horizontal alignment, while others had weak vertical and horizontal alignment. As shown in chapter 5, few colleges had effective implementation of mentoring, even for new faculty members.

Kenyon College's Early Career Developmental/Mentoring Network is a good example of effectively implemented mentoring initiative that provides multiple sources of mentoring support for early-career faculty members. Under the initiative, all faculty members must organize a group of mentors by the first of November in the first semester of their employment. The mentoring group traditionally includes the department chair, a tenured departmental colleague, and one additional faculty member who may or may not be a member of the same academic department. The associate provost is informed of who is in the group. The purpose of the developmental/mentoring network is to provide regular feedback to the new faculty member in the three primary areas of evaluation, according to the handbook: teaching, scholarship, and citizenship. Members of the group are expected to meet occasionally with the new faculty member and to attend at least two of his or her classes each semester to observe the teaching. At the end of the first academic year, the group is expected to meet with the new faculty member to discuss his or her strengths, areas for improvement, and goals and strategies for the upcoming year. Summaries of his or her course evaluations from the first semester and a curriculum vitae are also made available to and reviewed by the mentoring group. A summary of this meeting is shared with the provost. The same requirements apply for the faculty member's second year.

We were pleased to learn more about this faculty development support—and to feature it here—given our interest in mentoring research and the outcomes of mentoring. One of the benefits of this support is that it creates a network of individuals, both inside and outside of a faculty member's department, to provide guidance and developmental assistance. That assistance also engages individuals at a higher rank, which helps early-career faculty members develop relationships with individuals who can serve as advocates in their pursuit of P&T. But peer-to-peer exchanges are included, too, as are structured discussions related to the advancement of an early-career colleague.

Policies and Procedures Not Aligned with Emphasis on Teaching

Guided by the assumption that sharing and discussing faculty and staff members' role in student learning helps enable all community members to acknowledge the distinctive contributions of faculty and staff members, Albion College's Symposium on Teaching and Student Learning offers a variety of formats that encourage discussion and engagement on the part of all community members.

Formats include "flag-table" discussions, in which participants rotate through a series of brief, loosely moderated discussions about relevant topics; poster sessions, including the traditional conference poster and works of art or a letter from a parent; and a "Five and Done," which features a limited number of individuals who share insights about teaching and student learning—for example, through a mini-lecture or monologue.

The institutions in the GLCA are LACs, and all of their missions are deeply rooted in effective and innovative teaching practices. We value and understand the importance of programming that supports, highlights, and recognizes the substantial efforts faculty members, administrators, and other staff members provide in the area of teaching and learning (T&L). This program at Albion College features lessons learned about, techniques for, and critical topics related to T&L that are of great importance to the twenty-first century LAC. The format is similar to that provided at a professional conference, allowing faculty members to engage with their peers in formal and informal ways around the broad, but structured, topic of T&L.

Policies Not Aligned with Appropriate Practice

Allegheny College embarked on a faculty handbook revision steered by a few faculty members. The revision was focused on faculty members' engagement in what they termed "high-impact practice"—particularly related to undergraduate research, scholarship, and creative activity (URSCA). A faculty member commented: "As we pursued incorporating URSCA into our P&T guidelines, we took that opportunity to include other high-impact practices. Although the faculty as a whole could not agree on the use of the term 'high-impact practice,' we listed those efforts individually in the language (. . . community engagement, international experiences, etc.). We also explicitly added the value of work done on the scholarship of T&L." The revised handbook language now reads:

> Excellence in research, scholarship, and creative activity rests on the capacity to develop significant findings from investigation or original thought. This excellence may be pursued individually or as part of a collaboration with academic peers, *students*, or community members. It may be demonstrated through a wide range of efforts to advance knowledge or understanding, including research projects, descriptions and analyses of a field, the scholarship of teaching and learning, and the development or improvement of analytical tools. It may also be demonstrated through teaching and by mentoring, encouraging, and collaborating in research, scholarship, creative activity, including work undertaken with students and community members.

We applaud Allegheny College for its efforts to make this much-needed revision in its handbook language. Such efforts are groundbreaking. It took approximately four years from the time the faculty group began advocating the incorporation of URSCA into the P&T guidelines to the faculty vote that approved the new language. Allegheny College is one of the few institutions in the GLCA to require a senior thesis or project for graduation. This requires faculty members to engage with students in research, yet this engagement traditionally had not counted in evaluation for P&T (it still is not remunerated). Such efforts recognize and, perhaps more importantly, reward faculty members for the work they do in terms of T&L, scholarship, and mentoring or advising students who engage in scholarly inquiry.

The programs featured here are just a few examples of faculty development programming across the GLCA that seek to achieve horizontal and vertical alignment while also successfully implementing that programming. As we conclude this chapter with our recommendations, we return to concepts described by Lynda Gratton and Catherine Truss (2003)—particularly the three primary approaches to development: tactic, process, and strategy—and we situate those ideas in the context of faculty development. While using these approaches can achieve components of alignment, they fail to achieve the strategy and process approach we discussed at the beginning of this chapter. Our recommendations seek to identify the missteps in faculty development programming as a means of reaching a strategy and process approach to a faculty development portfolio.

What Can I Do?

Leaders who view faculty development as an investment that is aligned with institutional goals, vision, priorities, and other strategic imperatives are more likely to have an engaged, highly performing faculty. The institutions in the GLCA invest a great deal of time and resources in faculty support. However, as evidenced in this chapter, such initiatives in LACs could be more valuable if they accounted for preferences of faculty members across career stages and ranks and the holistic needs that faculty members experience in their lives and careers. Just as administrators and faculty members assess student behavior, we believe that the same sort of efforts should be made to understand trends in faculty members' participation in career development efforts to ensure that time and resources are being invested as wisely as possible.

To frame this discussion, we define and illustrate the three most common tactics we found across the GLCA by sharing examples from actual faculty development programming and/or recommendations of how to move beyond these tactics toward the achievement of horizontal and vertical alignment and implementation. By sharing trends in faculty development participation and preferred formats, as well as featuring exemplary programs at GLCA institutions, we seek to help LACs achieve a strategy and process approach to faculty development.

The tactic approach—in which there is little discernible relationship between the various faculty development programs or policies across areas, and little understanding of how some programs and policies may undermine others—characterizes all of the mentoring programs supported in the GLCA institutions, especially the early-career mentoring programs. Most of these mentoring initiatives lack clear direction and support. We make two recommendations for focusing efforts on mentoring programs. First, administrators should clarify the goals of mentoring programs. Second, administrators should develop evidence-based briefings and training for mentors of faculty members to improve their relationships with their mentees and lead to positive outcomes such as greater job satisfaction and faculty retention. This might also improve the experiences of previously untrained early-career and senior faculty members engaged in the mentorship and reduce the burden on them.

We urge administrators to set goals and make sure those goals are accounted for in key campus documents. For example, Denison College's faculty handbook includes clear expectations about the role of department chair and other faculty members in mentoring colleagues. The codification of these tactics in the college's processes strengthens vertical alignment and makes horizontal alignment and implementation more likely.

We also saw examples of a process approach to faculty development that is characterized by a tightly integrated set of goals at the individual level that are disconnected from the institutional objectives. All the GLCA institutions maintain faculty development programming through structures, supports, and evaluations, as described in chapter 1. Administrators and campus leaders know that they need to invest in their faculty development programming. However, we saw little or no explicit mention of faculty development in strategic planning, no language about faculty development supports in mission or vision statements, and no concerted efforts to connect faculty development priorities to development or institutional advancement initiatives. And we saw limited connections between CTLs and grants officers or other committees working on internal funding decisions or sabbaticals, for example. Administrators and faculty and staff members are missing a critical opportunity to be strategic about investing in their institution's faculty members.

The Mid-Career Task Force and Mid-Career Faculty Development Program initiative at Hope College is an example of moving past a process approach. The college's provost convened a mid-career task force consisting of mid- and late-career faculty members to think strategically about supporting mid-career faculty members on the campus. Goals set by the provost for the task force members included providing opportunities for continued growth in teaching, scholarship, and service for mid-career faculty members; offering opportunities at the institution to allow them to explore new avenues of scholarship and creative performance (including work with students); and creating an environment in which candid discussions about the challenges particular to mid-career faculty members (such as work-life balance; sabbatical planning; and service to the college, the local community, and the academy) could be supported. The provost believes that achieving these goals will help Hope College realize its strategic plan, particularly as it relates to the goal of "rearticulation of the vocation of the whole college."

Members of the task force prepared a proposal for external funding, which was approved. That proposal stated: "We [Hope College] face the challenge and opportunity of renewing the whole college's focus on vocation as a means of implementing the college's new Strategic Plan, especially its goals for students. Nurturing vocational reflection among midcareer faculty is a crucial strategy for strengthening our ability to provide opportunities for vocational reflection and discernment among students." The funding was awarded in spring 2016, so the initiative has not yet been fully implemented. However, this is an example of an effort to achieve both horizontal and vertical alignment to support strategic planning at an LAC. In other words, investing in mid-career faculty members will help the college better support students and cultivate a rich understanding of vocation in the context of a Christian school, which is a key goal in Hope's strategic plan.

Lastly, a strategy approach to faculty development is best described as programming that consists of clearly articulated ideals but neither translated into a coherent set of faculty development policies nor fully implemented by those responsible for faculty development initiatives. The strategy approach, to some degree, was apparent across all the GLCA institutions. By all accounts, these institutions are investing in their faculty, and in some cases that investment is quite large: yearly faculty development budgets in the GLCA range from $90,000 to $1.8 million. But that investment might not always be as intentional and strategic as it could be. The majority of faculty development programming across the GLCA is in workshop format, and the topics included are generalized so as to appeal to a broad range of faculty interests. We agree that there is a place for such programming in a faculty development portfolio, but that focus should be only a small portion of it.

Faculty members prefer opportunities to engage with their peers and colleagues both in formal and informal settings, and to have both structured and unstructured discussions. Many of them told us, "I am not attending another damn workshop." Furthermore, supports need to be aligned with expectations. We recommend a thorough review of policy and practice to ensure, for example, that faculty handbook language accurately represents current and future practice. Are the current programs the right ones, and who are they intended for? A review of policy and practice should also examine the expectations, as described in handbooks and other documents about evaluation, surrounding P&T in conjunction with a review of the faculty development offerings. As recommended in chapter 4, there should at least be supports offered that address the primary areas in which faculty members are evaluated (teaching, scholarship, and service). Within those categories, career stage and rank as well as divisional and/or disciplinary needs and supports should be accounted for in faculty development programming.

We briefly return to the example above about Allegheny College's revisions of its faculty handbook language to appropriately recognize the work faculty members do when engaging in high-impact practices. This effort moved beyond a mere strategy approach to connect all the pieces in a strategy and process approach to faculty development.

Conclusion

To truly invest in the human capital of an organization, it is imperative that the individuals responsible for that investment and its development, delivery, and assessment be aware of the intended population and its members' needs. Furthermore, we argue that development programming should be informed by and aligned with institutional initiatives and strategies. In this chapter, we showed the participation trends, sources of support, and preferred faculty development formats across the GLCA by career stage and appointment type. Such knowledge can be used to ensure that programming provides value to faculty attendees—which will result in higher participation rates that, in turn, will repay the time and investment that went into its creation. Such outcomes are critical to supporting faculty learning and development. We were pleased to highlight, as models for future offerings, some of the amazing faculty development programming across the GLCA institutions that were working toward a strategy and process approach. An important common feature of those examples is that they were informed by faculty members.

PART FOUR

At the Intersection

A Space for Innovation and Competitive Advantage

7

The Alignment Framework for Faculty Development in Liberal Arts Colleges

In effective department meetings, institutional and unit-level priorities drive the discussion and agenda. Imagine what it might look like for faculty support and development to be similarly aligned with institutional priorities. Is the term "faculty excellence" about understanding and supporting the faculty experience and academic work, or merely a way of incorporating faculty work into conversations with potential donors?

These questions are squarely situated at the all-important, yet often neglected, intersection of faculty needs and organizational goals. A failure to recognize this intersection and respond well to the issues located there contributes to the feelings of frustration that participants in our study reported to us and that we describe throughout this book. Administrators express disappointment at faculty members' low participation rates in faculty development programming, while faculty members describe their irritation because such programming fails to meet their needs.

In the course of writing this chapter, one of us received an e-mail about her institution's "welcome back faculty" retreat to kick off the fall semester, which illustrates our point perfectly. Within minutes of receiving the same e-mail, a colleague posted a message to a social media account that read, "For this year's back to school faculty meeting team building activity, I suggest we play, 'go back to your classroom and get ready for the first day.'" Another of us received a text message from a colleague at a faculty retreat asking, "Why do we keep appointing the same ineffective people to represent us on faculty needs?" And the third author overheard a comment from a nearby colleague who was pretending to be the dean as they awaited the start of the opening faculty meeting: "I will now tell you things you already know and read to you from the following twenty slides."

Such responses humorously reiterate the need to reenvision similar faculty programs, given the perception that they add no value and take productive time away from faculty members' preparations for the coming semester.

In "Angst and Hope for Liberal Arts Colleges," Scott Jaschik (2016) described a dialogue at the College of Saint Benedict among nearly two hundred professors and provosts whose aim was to examine the vulnerability of liberal arts colleges (LACs). A tornado warning was issued during a session, which caused all attendees to move to the basement. Jaschik wryly noted that the warning may have been prescient for this type of institution in the higher education landscape in the years and decades to come. The value of LACs was acknowledged by many people who attended the discussion, yet professors and administrators also described the risks that LACs need to navigate.

Terms such as "accountability," "learning outcomes," "assessment," and "vocationalism" now dominate conversations about LACs, as stakeholders attempt to quantify the outcomes of a liberal arts education. Yet sometimes the processes and activities that are most difficult to measure matter most in achieving individual and organizational outcomes. Investment in human capital, especially faculty development, has a return in the form of faculty retention leading to professors staying longer on a campus than the average college president does (Padilla and Ghosh 2000). Thus, it is critically important that administrators and faculty leaders think about faculty development in a way that aligns resources and activities with both institutional and individual goals. As we have noted above, there is a body of scholarly literature and practice-based evidence on faculty development, but it has mostly focused on universities and colleges with strong research missions. The absence of resources to guide thinking about faculty development and support in LACs was our motivation for writing this book.

Over the last four years, faculty members and administrators from the thirteen LACs in the Great Lakes Colleges Association (GLCA) have shared with us their experiences, needs, and ideas. Our aim has been to provide a greater appreciation for the changing and expanding roles and responsibilities that come with belonging to the academy, specifically to working at LACs. The research shared in this book provides insights into faculty life in the twenty-first century LAC, an institution type that has been neglected in research and practice related to academic work and the faculty experience.

We have attempted to better understand the connection between institutional and individual priorities as they relate to the successful development of faculty members. By crafting faculty development strategies that recognize this intersection of priorities and outcomes, LACs can help achieve their mission. This emphasis on the intersection is one of the unique contributions of this book and will help administrators and faculty members develop, implement, and assess a diversified portfolio of faculty development programming that takes into account faculty members' career stage, rank, and appointment type. This approach to faculty development may provide a strategic and sustainable competitive edge for this sector of higher education. The right investment in the development of faculty members will ensure high-quality learning experiences for faculty members and students alike.

The higher education landscape is changing quickly, which requires administrators and faculty leaders to draw on multiple perspectives in decision making. Our interdisciplinary perspective integrates scholarship from higher education, organizational studies, and psychology. The organizational scholars Lynda Gratton and Catherine Truss (2003) provided insights into the study and understanding of the connection between and among macro- and micro-level and implementation considerations that informed the research presented in this book. The ideas in their three-dimensional people strategy of organizational goals and priorities, personnel policies, and action were developed based on years of research and practice in business settings. We integrated their strategy with existing work by researchers and practitioners of faculty experiences and academic work (Gappa, Austin, and Trice 2007; Levin 2006; Neumann 2005). We adapted and expanded their work in the context of higher education, specifically LACs, to develop what we call the alignment framework for faculty development in liberal arts colleges (AFFD-LAC).

Integration of Key Findings

In this section, we review and integrate the key findings presented in each chapter to present the conclusions, rooted in the AFFD-LAC framework, and the next steps that administrators and faculty members may wish to take as they apply the framework to their contexts and needs. The book is divided into four parts to highlight the role of context, individual needs, and available resources and clarify how these intersect to provide opportunities for faculty development. The final section, this chapter, addresses the implications and the utility of the AFFD-LAC.

Part 1 of this book highlighted the importance of the LAC context and supporting faculty work in this institution type. Chapter 1 laid the groundwork from an institutional perspective of the structures, supports, and evaluation systems that undergird faculty development programming and delivery across the GLCA. Many individuals, committees, offices, and centers are involved in supporting faculty members and academic work. Orchestrating collaborations between and among these stakeholders can be challenging. Our recommendation is to take an institutional view of the areas in which faculty members are expected to engage and excel. Thus, a close examination of how institutional goals are communicated through promotion and tenure (P&T) processes and other evaluative criteria is needed to ensure that faculty members in each career stage and appointment type are well supported to meet challenges and take advantage of opportunities. This chapter prompts questions such as: Do we have the right supports in place? Are there redundancies among committees or positions that can be streamlined? and Is faculty development connected to broader institutional initiatives? Understanding this intersection supports the development, delivery, and assessment of faculty development programming.

Chapter 2 highlighted the significance of the academic department as a location of faculty work, development, and support, particularly in LACs. The experiences of our study participants revealed the important role faculty members play not only in the functioning of their departments, but also in collective tasks; individual careers; and faculty members' morale, motivation, and perceptions of their institutions. Faculty development must extend beyond teaching and learning to support faculty members in the myriad ways in which they contribute to their institutions, departments, and students. The academic department may provide previously overlooked opportunities to invest in and support the faculty.

In Part 2, we turned to individual experiences and focused on faculty work lives and needs. Chapter 3 provided a view of faculty life in LACs. Changing demographic characteristics—including a more diversified academy and a greater reliance on non-tenure-track faculty members—have changed the face of the professoriate. Personal and professional considerations influence the degree to which faculty members experience fulfillment in their lives and careers. Relationships matter greatly, and creating a culture of collegiality is an important building block for an effective faculty development portfolio. Policies are vital but insufficient to account for the human side of faculty life—particularly the balancing act that describes the lives of the faculty members who participated in this research.

Chapter 4 established the groundwork for facilitating conversations between faculty members and administrators about faculty development supports. Our findings revealed an unfortunate, but perhaps not surprising, reality of faculty development. Both faculty members and administrators spoke of the same priorities and needed investments for faculty development programming. However, such alignment was unusual in practice. Greater transparency and collaboration is needed to overcome the frustration expressed by faculty members who know that campus leaders and administrators are aware of the challenges yet fail to act or are very slow to do so. Similarly, administrators expressed frustration about dwindling budgets and low participation rates in faculty development programming—which faculty members suggested wasn't meeting their needs. Continual engagement in conversations, development, and assessment among administrators and faculty and staff members is needed to ensure that policies and practices are aligned to achieve institutional and individual outcomes.

Part 3 focused on how to align institutional resources and faculty development. Resources include tangible assets such as money, as well as intangible resources such as time invested in relationships. Chapter 5 shed light on mentoring programming and engagement in mentoring relationships (both as a mentor and mentee). We learned that formal mentoring needs to be more clearly aligned with the institution's strategic plans. Most faculty members say mentoring is a hit-or-miss activity that depended greatly on their department's leadership. The absence of a strong alignment between institutional goals and a mentoring culture makes it difficult for administrators to engage their key human resource, faculty members, in achieving institutional goals.

Chapter 6 featured trends in faculty development participation, preferred formats, and sources of support and exemplary programming across the GLCA. To support a successful faculty development portfolio, it is imperative to understand the ways in which faculty members engage in faculty development both on and off campus. Across the GLCA, we saw a great deal of engagement in off-campus faculty development. However, beyond the early career years, there was limited stage-specific support for faculty members. This should be cause for a reassessment of faculty development programming on campuses. Our findings highlight that faculty members find disciplinary-based programming to be of most value, and that they prefer delivery formats centered on dialogue with colleagues. This knowledge suggests that faculty members' needs are specific to their career stage and type of appointment, and faculty development programming should be as well. To that end, we highlighted programming in existence or being developed at GLCA institutions that illustrates how alignment between institutional priorities and strategic initiatives and faculty development programming can be improved.

The GLCA is to be commended for the faculty development programming featured in this book. The investments made to support faculty development are substantial in some areas, particularly teaching and learning. As we took stock of the knowledge gleaned from our study, we found that LAC faculty members expressed four basic needs. To best engage in their work and have sustainable and rewarding careers, they need financial resources; supports that are a good use of their time and meet their needs; recognition and acknowledgment of their work; and opportunities to connect with colleagues. The dominant format for faculty development was workshops, which have a time and place in the faculty development landscape but are often poorly attended. We urge institutional leaders and faculty developers to invest in programming that meets the four needs listed here.

The Initiative for Faculty Development in Liberal Arts Colleges

Investing in human resources throughout career trajectories is not a new concept. In fact, many professional fields recognize the importance of such an investment and achieve it through the use of professional certifications. For example, the accounting profession supports the certified public accountant examination series, and golf professionals earn and maintain certification through the Professional Golf Association. In primary and secondary education, teachers and administrators participate in continuing education to maintain certifications and update skills. These fields have built-in requirements to ensure that their professionals continue to enhance their knowledge and skills and adapt to changes.

However, the professoriate does not have such a system. The academy is the place of employment for PhDs, and there are no requirements for continuing education or professional development after graduate school to help academics continue to evolve as teachers and scholars. Professional development and faculty development programming is vital for these individuals' growth and knowledge creation and to ensure that their skills are adequate to prepare the next generation of scholars who sit in their classrooms. Strategic investment in faculty members is necessary to support vitality and engagement in the academy and to safeguard the institutions that serve as their employers.

Why Alignment?

Institutional leaders, faculty members, and administrators invest a great deal of time and resources in strategic planning and institutional branding. Such a process, on average, occurs once every five years (Goldman and Salem 2015) or whenever a new president arrives on campus (whichever is shorter). Strategic plans serve as the foundation for future campus and programming development, as well as fund-raising initiatives (either stand-alone efforts or part of capital campaigns). Strategic planning typically touches on the student experience, community engagement, institutional facilities, and campus infrastructures. The number of hours alone associated with such planning and implementation is substantial. These efforts affect an institution's ability to fulfill its mission and to attract, recruit, and retain a talented and diverse student, faculty, and staff body. Given the work associated with strategic planning and institutional branding initiatives, we find it discouraging that greater efforts are not made to align faculty development programming (including its development, delivery, and assessment) to strategic planning priorities and institutional missions.

A cursory review of the "about" links on websites of the GLCA institutions reveals a desire to attract students who are curious, creative, life-long learners interested in and open to new ideas. Faculty members employed across these institutions are described as "outstanding scholars" who "place teaching first" among their many roles as "advisors, mentors, and friends." An examination of practice across the GLCA institutions reveals that the greatest investment made in faculty development is to support teaching and learning, largely at the early-career stage. As our data showed, far fewer tailored supports are available to help faculty members engage in scholarship, be effective mentors, or receive adequate mentorship themselves later in their careers. Faculty development programming needs to invoke feelings of creativity, curiosity, and lifelong learning to help faculty members feel enriched and capable of creating the experiential learning opportunities in and out of the classroom that promote these same feelings in students. Institutional leaders, faculty developers, and faculty members are missing a critical opportunity to align faculty development programming with institutional strategic planning efforts and institutional missions.

The Alignment Framework for Faculty Development in Liberal Arts Colleges

A primary outcome of the research presented in this book is the AFFD-LAC (see figure 7.1). This framework illustrates why and how vertical and horizontal considerations can be connected to achieve a more strategic, deliberate, and focused faculty development agenda at LACs. These efforts will require conversations among key stakeholders who rely on the priorities and mission of the institution as a guide. We agree with Mary Deane Sorcinelli, Ann Austin, Pamela Eddy, and Andrea Beach, who noted that "one model or framework for faculty development will not be appropriate for all institutions" (2005, 163). Judith Gappa, Ann Austin, and Andrea Trice (2007) connected faculty development to outcomes in their book about faculty development in colleges and universities. Yet as we reflected on our findings, we found that their framework did not fully explain the role of career stages, mentoring relationships, and departmental experiences in supporting and developing faculty work in LACs. Similarly, Gratton and Truss's (2003) thinking about people strategies was informative but incomplete when applied as a tool for understanding faculty work in higher education.

The AFFD-LAC focuses on how competing, and sometimes conflicting, faculty members' and institutional priorities might be best met at the intersection of individual and institutional goals and needs. Faculty development programming provides a nexus to creatively support both the institution and its faculty members. This framework acknowledges that faculty members are essential partners in faculty development; it is not something that is done to them, but rather is developed in concert with them.

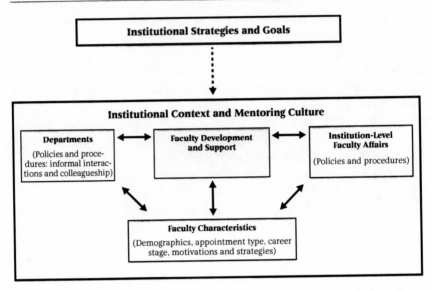

FIGURE 7.1. The Alignment Framework for Faculty Development in Liberal Arts Colleges

Faculty development is more than helping faculty members become good teachers and scholars. It is also about helping them advance the goals, strategic imperatives, and mission of the institution in which they work. To provide the right mix of tailored support, there must be consideration of how institutional goals are aligned with faculty work (vertical alignment—the dashed line in figure 7.1) and how policies and procedures are formalized across units (horizontal alignment—the solid horizontal lines in figure 7.1). Finally, plans and procedures must be implemented. This implementation will promote the development of a mentoring culture in the institution that will support the achievement of individual and organizational outcomes.

Elements of the Model

INSTITUTIONAL AND INDIVIDUAL CONSIDERATIONS. Our focus on the intersection of institutional and individual considerations is an important one, since faculty development that is not informed by or in support of institutional priorities and missions is not strategic. Additionally, faculty development that neglects individual needs or does not consider career stage and appointment type does not add value. Without these considerations, programs cannot motivate faculty members, create a sustainable competitive advantage for the institution, or developing its talent and intellectual capital to achieve both institutional and individual outcomes. Faculty members and administrators should not operate on parallel tracks but should engage in thoughtful conversations with each other to inform the development of faculty-focused programming.

A closer look at the intersection allows for an examination and the inclusion of key horizontal factors at the institutional level. At a minimum, initiatives that stem from strategic planning should serve as the foundation for current and future faculty development. The institutional mission, strategic goals, and institutional priorities should be some of the primary drivers that inform that development.

Administrators, campus leaders, and faculty developers should seriously consider the target audience of faculty development programming—the faculty members. Researchers (Pascarella and Terenzini 2005) have revealed the important influence of student demographic characteristics on the student experience, and the same is true for faculty members. Personal characteristics, previous professional and academic experiences, and personal responsibilities (for example, as caregiver or parent) influence one's willingness to engage in and need a variety of faculty development supports (Pifer and Baker 2016).

DEPARTMENTAL INFLUENCE. As we explored in chapter 2, the academic department is an important—in fact, the central—context both of informal faculty colleagueship, mentoring, and collaboration and of formal development, policy implementation, and mission fulfillment. Thus, it has a prominent place in our framework. It may be assumed or implied that institutional goals and policies, as well as efforts to support faculty work, are channeled through the department. Yet we learned that effective departments invested a substantial amount of resources and work in the cultivation and sustainability of that effectiveness, often with little institutional support. And departments that lacked both institutional support and the internal resources and motivation for excellence were not always able to overcome challenges and create processes and cultures that guaranteed faculty success. It is imperative that all stakeholders in faculty success and mission fulfillment consider the roles that the department and its leaders and members might play in those areas.

CAREER STAGES. Our framework acknowledges the importance of career stage, specifically the time associated with moving within and between career stages and ranks, and appointment type. The faculty trajectory does not merely include the three phases of assistant, associate, and full professorship. Within each career phase are milestones, such as the assistant professor's interim review, the associate professor's assumption (not always voluntarily) of a leadership role such as department chair, and the full professor's planning for retirement. What we learned from our study participants is they seek out opportunities to invest in themselves, but that more often than not, those opportunities draw them outside of the institution. And for some, that external engagement keeps them continually on the job market.

MENTORING CULTURE. Mentoring is at the heart of a classic liberal education and was clearly valued by faculty members and administrators on the campuses we studied. Yet informal mentoring activities were largely department-driven and left to the whim of department leaders and senior faculty members. Departments and divisions with faculty members who had longer tenures and supportive climates reported effective informal mentoring. But informal mentoring practices were not uniform across the campuses. Formal mentoring programs were supported by provosts, and sometimes through institutional policies that also clarified the role of mentoring in departmental or divisional leadership roles and in P&T processes. But even these institutional supports often focused only on early-career faculty members and rarely reflected policies and procedures about faculty work that were well aligned. Faculty members will be better mentors to students if they themselves are well mentored.

How Can This Model Inform Faculty Development on My Campus?

The AFFD-LAC has several implications. First, when it comes to faculty development, as with many aspects of higher education, the institution type matters. In this book, we reengage in conversations about the professoriate that were initiated by Burton Clark (1987). He explored a range of institutional settings and concluded that the hallmark of American higher education is its diversity of institution types. Furthermore, he noted the importance of institutional type in understanding and supporting faculty members. Twenty years later, Gary Rhoades (2007) argued that the the faculty experience and academic work were largely seen and understood as those at research universities—a trend that has persisted. While the faculty experience in research universities is important, a narrow focus of that experience fails to adequately acknowledge or portray the variety of institutional settings in which newly minted PhDs are employed, nor does it account for the institutional nuances, unique features, or realities that influence faculty development across institution types. The development of AFFD-LAC was informed by faculty members' experiences in LACs and applies to that context.

Second, career stage matters—a lot. We argue that a one-size-fits-all approach to faculty development is not only antiquated, but it is also demotivating for faculty members who take such an institutional approach as signaling a lack of real investment in their development and growth. Furthermore, we believe a one-size-fits-all approach to faculty development is counterproductive for an institution's mission and strategic priorities. Educational leaders cannot continue to invest in creating pseudo-customized educational experiences that rely on high-impact practices for students yet offer what appears to be cookie-cutter faculty development programming that supports only those faculty members in the first quarter of their careers in the academy.

As the data from our research reveal, career stage matters, and each career stage and appointment type is associated with different challenges, needs, and hurdles to overcome. Those challenges, coupled with faculty members' personal realities and responsibilities at home, make customized faculty development programming essential to support different career stages and appointment types and promote the continued learning, advancement, and vitality of the faculty members at an institution.

We firmly believe that it is time for the academy to take a cue from other fields that invest in the life-long learning of their professionals throughout the trajectory of their careers. This belief causes us to return to the College of Wooster's Seasons program (discussed in chapter 6), which brings together faculty members across career stages and also within career stages to talk thoughtfully and honestly about the challenges they faced and ways to overcome those challenges. Not only is the content specific to various career stages and appointment types, but the format allows for dialogue among colleagues. It also creates a "we're in this together" feeling and capitalizes on the cohort model.

Third, faculty development and related supports in LACs must reflect a commitment to faculty members shared by many stakeholders, such as provosts, deans, associate deans, and department chairs. Faculty development must span units and centers (including centers for teaching and learning and scholarship), institutional structures (including committees, both standing and ad hoc), and offices (such as those for institutional advancement and grants). A shared commitment requires deliberate efforts and collaboration to coordinate and manage all the moving parts and pieces. It's no wonder that despite their best efforts, administrators, other campus leaders, and faculty and staff members may not be strategic in their investment in and delivery of faculty development and support that account for career stage, rank, and appointment type. Faculty development efforts need to be situated at the juncture of institutional and individual needs and goals.

Fourth, administrators and other campus leaders need to create a mentoring culture on campus. Mentoring is a valued activity at LACs and was frequently mentioned on the websites of the GLCA institutions and by faculty members and administrators in our study. Our findings show the critical importance of collegial relationships in faculty engagement and retention and the spotty nature of great mentoring. Excellent formal mentoring programs can promote a culture of mentoring that will lead to both formal and informal mentoring interactions that support faculty members' development.

The AFFD-LAC reveals where mentoring relationships can be strengthened in LACs. All LACs value mentoring as part of the undergraduate experience.

However, an examination of mentoring's place in institutional priorities or its use to support institutional goals can provide insights into where it might be better supported. For example, there is an opportunity to support faculty members in developing an explicit mentoring philosophy as part of an existing institutional requirement, such as a teaching statement or participation in a new faculty orientation or mentoring experience. Discussions early in a faculty member's tenure about mentoring and how to do it well can increase faculty members' reflections about and engagement in informal mentoring with students and colleagues.

Administrators could also examine institutional policies and procedures across departments or divisions to foster mentoring interactions and conversations. Furthermore, our findings showed that it is critical for mentors be available to new faculty members who are outside of their department or division. Support for faculty members from multiple mentors can help protect them from a dysfunctional colleague or department.

The development of a mentoring culture also places a focus on faculty members in non-tenure-track appointment and at the associate and full professor ranks. Our findings showed an emphasis on mentoring for new faculty members and little or no support for faculty members after their first few years at an institution. Yet faculty who move to new ranks or to or from administrative positions also need mentoring. Thus, the implementation of formal mentoring would help administrators and faculty members design formal supports for all faculty members and fill in the current gaps. Mentoring can be recognized as a valued activity through the inclusion of that activity as part of service or teaching and through annual awards for mentoring at the division or college level given by the provost or president.

Finally, the department must be part of any holistic conversation about supporting faculty work. There is room for improvement in how colleges select, train, support, and assess department chairs. Given the burden of responsibility on today's department leaders, it is imperative for institutions to properly invest in the success of these individuals, who must advance both academic and administrative priorities across stakeholder groups and individuals. Institutional leaders must also be clearer about the consequences of ineffective, nonresponsive, or unethical behavior by department chairs. One very clear source of support for faculty work is placing the right people in positions of authority and responsibility in academic units. If department leaders are insufficiently supported or permitted to be ineffective, the effects on the unit and its faculty members can be drastically negative and long lasting. Ultimately, these effects on morale, productivity, and motivation extend to students' experiences, campus climate, mission fulfillment, and institutional reputation. The department is also the hiring unit for academic positions, which highlights an opportunity for faculty support and development through policies related to faculty recruitment, selection, onboarding, promotion, tenure, and development. Finally, as the site of informal mentoring, professional collaborations, and friendships, the department is a crucial component of any institution's faculty development strategy, and the institution should invest in creating and supporting healthy departments.

Next Steps: Refining and Applying the Framework

Existing models could not adequately explain the gaps in faculty development support that we observed in our study of LACs and their faculties. Thus, we developed the AFFD-LAC to acknowledge the importance of career stages and departments and to highlight the weight of institutional contexts and mentoring cultures. This framework also places faculty development at the intersection of individual and institutional goals and needs. Our overarching aim is to give faculty members and administrators new perspectives on and help them be active partners in implementing effective faculty development.

The contribution of this model is that it can help administrators and faculty members think deeply about the intersection of faculty work and institutional goals and needs. Such reflection may help you think about institutions in the future. While all types of higher education institutions may benefit from a focus on the intersection of individual and institutional goals and needs, we believe that such a focus is especially important for LACs. Compared to other educational institutions, they have fewer resources, smaller faculties, and perhaps a more manageable opportunity to tailor faculty development activities—and thus increase their competitive advantage in higher education. The goal is to foster faculty members' collaboration and creativity; create proactive, rather than reactive, faculty development programming; and engage faculty members in supporting the strategic imperatives of their institution.

There is an opportunity to develop this model further by adapting it to other institutional contexts. For example, departments are important for all faculty members, yet we believe they play a greater role in influencing faculty work at LACs than at other institutions. The development of a mentoring culture is also valued across institutional types, but it too plays a more central role at an LAC, where low student-faculty ratios and mentoring are defining features. While we hope that our model and the research presented in this book will inspire administrators, other campus leaders, and faculty members to apply and adapt these ideas and recommendations at their institutions, our aims in studying the faculty experience in LACs were to address the lack of knowledge and understanding about what faculty work in LACs looked like; to provide insights into how institutional leaders at LACs were investing in faculty support and development; to determine how this institutional type differed from others; and to assess whether institutional programming in LACs was aligned with faculty members' needs. We believe that we achieved our aims, as evidenced by the data, featured examples of faculty development programming, and the voices and experiences of administrators and faculty members presented throughout this book.

Faculty members are active actors in the intersection of individual and institutional goals and needs, which means they also need time for reflection on creative models for faculty development and support that go beyond a one-off workshop. We urge administrators and faculty and staff members to be creative in envisioning and implementing faculty and staff development. The number one challenge that participants in our study reported (and that we experience in our professional lives) is a lack of time. We cannot add more minutes to the day, but we believe that reflection is needed on which activities are critical to the mission and which might best be discontinued. Investment in faculty development should help faculty members make better decisions about how to spend their time. We believe that faculty development that is effective and energizing will lead to reducing inefficiencies and redundancies and encourage collaboration, innovation, and creativity. It is worth noting that these attributes and skills are exactly the ones we hope to develop in our students, and we want to help faculty members model them well.

The work we have shared here can also be of value to recent and prospective faculty members. Perhaps more than you realize, you can influence your career trajectory and forge your own path. Yes, you need support in that process, and yes, your institution, department, and colleagues have a responsibility to support (or at least not hinder) your growth. However, if you are not getting the support you need or want, it may be time to reevaluate and broaden your network as a critical step toward taking an active role in your professional development. Learning to be your own best advocate is a skill—one that is well worth developing to foster others' confidence in you as well.

Administrators and faculty developers reading this book might take away a seemingly simple but powerful lesson. Engage in frequent conversations with faculty members. Ask them what they need and want and be transparent in working to provide it. If finances or some other obstacle prevent you from acting on what you learn from those conversations, then consider offering a short- and long-term plan of how and when you will be able to provide the needed support. Most faculty members are reasonable people and will understand that all needs cannot be addressed at any one time. But such plans, with budgets attached, are rarely presented. Of course, some implementation is a must. The only behavior worse than not asking your employees for feedback is to ask for it and doing nothing with it. These conversations need to be frequent and genuine to ensure that faculty development activities meet changing needs. Furthermore, faculty members are more likely to be engaged and empowered to participate in faculty development when they have had an active role in designing it. Such an environment creates buy-in, respect, and trust, all of which also contribute to a mentoring culture in the institution.

We are strong advocates of creating accountability, and that holds true for faculty development programming both in terms of its development and participation in it. But accountability does not occur until you do what we just suggested. Ask faculty members what they need, engage them in conversations about how to best meet those needs, and draw from the expertise on campus to support the creation and marketing of faculty development programming. Then faculty members will have a responsibility to engage in it, especially when needs are met. Additionally, administrators and faculty developers need to create safe spaces in which faculty members can discuss their needs. For example, junior colleagues are likely reluctant to voice concerns or frustration about processes on campus in front of senior colleagues, especially when those senior colleagues are responsible for the creation and/or implementation of those policies. In these instances, opportunities are necessary for early-career colleagues to discuss their concerns only in the presence of a trusted liaison. A seemingly minor, yet powerful, message would be conveyed through the presence of such a liaison, and this person could serve as the voice of early-career faculty members to senior colleagues without fear of negative reprisal.

Conclusion

We are passionate about understanding the faculty experience and supporting faculty members in their work, and the Initiative for Faculty Development in Liberal Arts Colleges has supported our own development and allowed us to be the voice of the faculty members who participated in our study across the GLCA. Collectively, we have over forty-five years of experience as tenured faculty members, higher education administrators, and consultants who seek to help our peers and clients address the many challenges we highlighted in this book. We have been the early-career colleagues working to navigate the tenure track, and we have been (or currently are) the associate professors and mid-career colleagues working to envision the next phase of our careers while also mentoring early-career peers toward tenure and our students toward graduation. We have also been mentored by senior colleagues who have more knowledge than we do and insights to share. What we learned in the process of this research is our experiences are not unique. All faculty members—regardless of life circumstance, career stage, rank, appointment type, or institution—manage challenges, and they must articulate their needs and advocate for their own advancement.

Campus leaders and administrators have the often unenviable task of allocating resources, managing cultures, and creating programming and policies under various constraints. But we firmly believe that faculty development created at the intersection of institutional priorities and individual needs can serve as a strategic advantage and a solid foundation for supporting and developing the greatest resources of postsecondary institutions—the faculty. LACs are particularly poised to answer this call, given their unique blend of tradition, innovation, and prominence in the higher education landscape.

ACKNOWLEDGMENTS

The research featured in this book was inspired by heated debates in faculty meetings at Albion College and by conversations at the Global Liberal Arts Alliance meeting in Athens, Greece, in the summer of 2012. Topics such as how to better support faculty members and the changing nature of faculty expectations in liberal arts colleges in the United States and abroad resonated deeply among the academics there, as we thought about how to create our own networks of support to navigate our careers and lives.

This research was possible only because of the enthusiasm and support of Rich Ray (former provost at Hope College), Michael McDonald (provost at Kalamazoo College), Susan Conner (former provost at Albion College), and Richard Detweiler (president of the Great Lakes Colleges Association [GLCA]), who provided us with initial access to the GLCA campuses for focus groups and funds for associated expenses. This work and the resulting book would not have been possible without the support, participation, and additional assistance we received along the way.

We thank all of the faculty members who participated in this research across the GLCA. We know time is precious, and we are grateful to you for so willingly and thoughtfully sharing your experiences, hopes, and disappointments with us. We hope that we honored your stories and insights in this book.

We are grateful to the academic deans and provosts (past and present) at the GLCA schools for their continued support. They granted us access to their campuses, faculty members, and other institutional resources, and we appreciate their willingness to allow us to feature their campuses, perspectives, and goals.

Two people helped us shape the narrative of faculty work presented in this book. Thank you, Ann Austin, for agreeing to be the discussant at a symposium based on our research that became the basis of this book. Your generosity in offering your time and guidance about how to write a compelling and useful book about the faculty experience were instrumental in this undertaking.

Thank you, Brad Johnson, for your mentorship and invaluable advice as we learned to write book proposals, navigate contracts, and write a book.

Thank you, Kim Guinta, our amazing editor at Rutgers University Press. Your support, words of encouragement, and developmental reviews helped us immeasurably. You set the bar high for other editors to meet, and we appreciate your confidence in us.

We are grateful to Sarah Ashlock for superb editing and master formatting, Ryan Arey for helping us with data collection at the last minute and with only short notice, and Joe Worth for reviewing references and final details.

We also thank our institutions for providing financial support to cover travel and data collection expenses. Without those faculty development funds, there would be no book.

We collectively acknowledge our present and past colleagues and students, who have inspired, pushed, questioned, and supported us: thank you for everything. It made our work better.

Vicki wishes especially to thank her mother, Mary Ann Osborne; husband and coauthor in life Bryan Harris; and two beautiful children, McKenna and Henley. Your inspiration, encouragement, and love are what motivates this academic mother. She also thanks her late grandfather, Dr. Anton J. Brence, for instilling in her a passion for education and supporting others in their pursuit of their dreams, and her two amazing coauthors for bringing joy and laughter to the research process. Laura is grateful to have found two smart, witty, hardworking, and fun women with whom to think, write, and celebrate. She thanks her husband, Art, for putting up with the extra hours she needed to finish this book. Meghan thanks her coauthors for their drive, passion, skill, care, and humor throughout this project and all aspects of life. She is especially grateful for the humor.

APPENDIX A
STUDY OVERVIEW

Sample and Methods

This book draws on a mixed-methods study, the Initiative for Faculty Development in Liberal Arts Colleges, which began during the 2012–13 academic year and ended in spring 2016. The study's data set has transcripts from focus groups and interviews and the results of two surveys, all of which are described below.

The institutional review board (IRB) at Albion College provided initial approval for all data collection, and the twelve IRBs at the institutions in the Great Lakes Colleges Association (GLCA) provided secondary approvals for each data collection site.

Focus Groups

Fifteen focus groups in total were conducted at five GLCA institutions (Albion, Denison, Earlham, Kenyon, and Hope Colleges) in 2012–13. The information from these focus groups provided the evidence needed to warrant further exploration of the faculty experience in liberal arts colleges.

Administrator Interviews

We conducted interviews with all academic deans in the GLCA and four GLCA presidents during the summer of 2013. Interview questions centered on four themes: institutional priorities; formal and informal socialization on campus; faculty development and socialization practices; and available support for faculty members related to teaching, scholarship, and service. The interview questions are listed in Appendix C.

Survey of Faculty Members

An invitation to participate in a faculty development survey was emailed in spring 2014 to all 2,492 faculty members at twelve GLCA institutions, including full- and part-time faculty members and those in both tenure-track or non-tenure-track (NTT) positions. For the remaining GLCA institution, administrators shared the college's data from the most recent Higher Education Research Institute survey, and we integrated that informatoin into our analysis. There were 541 completed surveys and 299 partially completed surveys, giving us a 20 percent response rate from tenured or tenure-eligible faculty. Areas addressed by the survey were faculty development structure and needs, participation in faculty development activities, mentoring support, satisfaction, and demographic characteristics. The questions are listed in Appendix B.

Faculty Interviews

At the end of the survey, faculty members indicated whether or not they were willing to be interviewed. During the fall 2014 and spring 2015 semesters, we conducted seventy-seven faculty interviews across the thirteen GLCA institutions. In addition, faculty interviews were conducted with key personnel who held leadership positions on campus, such as directors of centers for teaching and learning and department chairs. Interviews were in person or over the phone and were taped and then transcribed verbatim. Interviews focused on five areas: the interviewee's professional background, his or her primary roles on campus, support provided by or desired by the GLCA and the institution, personal aspects that support or hinder success in the professoriate, and programming and supports needed to attract and retain talented faculty members. The interview protocol is provided in Appendix C.

Associate Professors Survey

During spring 2016 we invited all 599 associate professors employed at the GLCA institutions to complete a survey about professional needs and supports at mid-career. The response rate was 46 percent ($n = 278$) for partially completed surveys and 34 percent ($n = 203$) for completed surveys. The survey had five sections, with forty questions overall. Questions focused on leadership preparation, coaching and mentoring, nonprofessional needs, and demographic characteristics. Faculty members who were then or had recently been department heads also answered questions about their preparation for and needs in that role.

Specific Measures

Relationship Quality

We developed a three-item measure of relationship quality based on the three characteristics of high-quality relationships. Relationship quality was assessed by computing an average score from the three-item Likert scale, which ranged from 1 (never) to 7 (all of the time). Emotional tone was measured with the item, "I can express my feelings (good or bad) to my mentor/mentee" Tensility was measured with the item, "I can count on my mentor (protégé) even after difficult conversations." Openness was measured with the item, "I think about new ideas as a result of interactions with my mentor/mentee."

Protégés' mean scores for each item on the relationship quality scale were 5.40 for emotional tone, 5.47 for tensility, and 5.23 for openness. Mentors' mean scores for each item on the scale were 4.84 for emotional tone, 5.25 for tensility, and 5.13 for openness. Alphas were acceptable for the relationship quality with the mentor (alpha = 0.92) and the protégé (alpha = 0.79).

Job Satisfaction

The Cronbach alpha for the twelve-item job satisfaction scale was 0.91.

We analyzed our survey data and computed several models using ordinary least squares regressions.

APPENDIX B

FACULTY SURVEY

Albion College Consent to Participate in Research

Study Title: Helping faculty make the critical transition from research-intensive institutions to faculty life at liberal arts colleges: A look across career stages (IRB F12–13)

Researcher(s):

PI [principal investigator]: Dr. Vicki L. Baker, associate professor of economics and management, Albion College

Co-PI: Dr. Laura G. Lunsford, assistant professor of psychology, University of Arizona

Co-PI: Dr. Meghan J. Pifer, assistant professor of higher education, Widener University

Sponsors: Great Lakes Colleges Association and Hewlett-Mellon Fund for Faculty Development at Albion College

This is a consent form for research participation. It contains important information about this study and what to expect if you decide to participate.

Your participation is voluntary.

Please consider the information carefully. Feel free to ask questions before making your decision whether or not to participate. If you decide to participate, you will be asked to indicate as such and are encouraged to print a copy of the form for your records.

Please note that by clicking on the "I agree" button at the bottom of this form, you agree that:

You have freely volunteered to complete a survey questionnaire.

You may call or e-mail questions to the researcher before, during, or after the survey.

You may contact the researcher at any time to obtain information about the project.

You may withdraw from the project at any time without penalty.

You are encouraged to print this form/screen for your records.

Purpose: The research addresses two primary areas: faculty development support (and needs) and socialization into liberal arts colleges. This survey contains questions about your current faculty development activities and needed support and your socialization experiences as a faculty member in a liberal arts college. This information will be used to better support faculty across the career stages at your institution as well as across the GLCA [Great Lakes Colleges Association]. Additionally, information gathered will be used to help faculty assimilate into successful careers in a liberal arts college environment.

Procedures/Tasks: You will complete an online survey that will take approximately 15 minutes to complete. Topics addressed on the survey include: Faculty Development Assessment, Faculty Development Participation, Professional Relationships and Mentoring Support, Socialization into Liberal Arts College life, Satisfaction, and Demographics.

Duration: The survey will take approximately 15 minutes to complete. If you self-select as part of the survey, we may contact you to conduct a 45 minute interview as a follow up to your survey responses. You may leave the study at any time.

Risks and Benefits: There are no known risks of participating in this research. Summary data will be shared with your institution and the GLCA to support future faculty development and socialization programming to better support faculty. No comments or responses will be ascribed to you.

Confidentiality: Efforts will be made to keep your study-related information confidential. All data will be secured via password and kept in a locked, secure location as per IRB [Institutional Review Board] policy.

Participant Rights: You may refuse to participate in this study without penalty or loss of benefits to which you are otherwise entitled. If you choose to participate in the study, you may discontinue participation at any time without penalty or loss of benefits. By signing this form, you do not give up any personal legal rights you may have as a participant in this study. If you decide to stop participating in the study, there will be no penalty to you, and you will not lose any benefits to which you are otherwise entitled. Your decision will not affect your future relationship with your institution, Albion College, the GLCA, or any of the researchers.

An Institutional Review Board responsible for human participant research at Albion College reviewed this research project and found it to be acceptable, according to applicable state and federal regulations and College policies designed to protect the rights and welfare of participants in research.

Contacts and Questions

For questions, concerns, or complaints about the study you may contact Vicki L. Baker, research PI at vbaker@albion.edu or via cell at 814–932–5580.

For questions about your rights as a participant in this study, you may contact the chair of IRB at IRB@albion.edu.

By clicking I agree below I indicate that I have read (or someone has read to me) this information and I am aware that I am being asked to participate in a research study. I have had the opportunity to ask questions and have had them answered to my satisfaction. I voluntarily agree to participate in this study.

☐ I am not giving up any legal rights by "clicking" the "I agree" button. I am encouraged to print a copy of this information.

☐ I agree / I do not agree.

We hope to learn more about how to help faculty succeed in a liberal arts college environment. Thus, we appreciate your assistance by completing this survey. The questions are about the current faculty development activities, support and socialization experiences at your institution. This information will be used to better support faculty across career stages on a per-institution basis as well as across the GLCA. There are 5 sections to the survey, which should take approximately 15 minutes to complete.

Section 1: Faculty Development

Think about your institution's support of faculty development in answering the questions in this section. Select the best response for each question. Faculty development is any form of organized support to help faculty members develop as teachers, scholars, or institutional citizens.

1. What best describes your institution's faculty development structure? (choose one)

☐ A centralized unit with dedicated staff that offers a range of faculty development programs

☐ A clearinghouse for programs and offerings that are sponsored across the institution, but offering few programs itself

☐ A committee charged with supporting faculty development

☐ An individual faculty member or administrator charged with supporting faculty development

☐ I don't know.

☐ Other (please describe below)

2. Faculty development programs may be influenced by a variety of factors. Please indicate the extent to which each factor below influences the focus and activities of your program.

[Response options: not at all, slightly influences, moderately influences, greatly influences, not sure.]

☐ Faculty interests and concerns

☐ Priorities of department chairs and deans

☐ Priorities of senior-level institutional leaders

☐ Priorities of the director or person leading your faculty development program

☐ Immediate organizational issues, concerns, or problems

☐ Institutional strategic plan

☐ Your faculty development program's strategic plan

☐ Priorities suggested by the higher education or faculty development literature

3. How likely would you be to participate in the following faculty development initiatives? Click on or slide the indicator to provide your response to each item.

[Response options from 1 (very unlikely) to 7 (very likely).]

☐ Assessment of student learning outcomes

☐ Teaching underprepared students

☐ Integrating technology into classroom learning

☐ Team teaching

☐ Pre-tenure review

☐ Post-tenure review

☐ Course/teaching portfolios

☐ New faculty development

☐ Developing students' critical thinking skills

☐ Incorporating active learning strategies into my courses

☐ Increasing student motivation

☐ Course and curriculum development

☐ Developing leadership skills

☐ Faculty mentoring
☐ Classroom management
☐ Grant writing
☐ Writing manuscripts and conference proposals
☐ Department chair training
☐ Committee chair training
☐ Peer-review of teaching
Incorporating active learning strategies into my classroom

4. Please rate the likelihood of your participation in professional development initiatives in these formats at your institution. Click on or slide the indicator to provide your response to each item.

[Response options: 1 (not at all), 2 (slightly), 3 (moderately), 4 (very likely).]
☐ Hands-on workshops
☐ Peer-to-peer exchanges of ideas/dialog
☐ Web-based resources
☐ Structured discussions with colleagues
☐ Organized informal discussions with colleagues
☐ Guest speakers
☐ "Brown-bag" meetings
☐ Lecture series
☐ Classroom observations with feedback
☐ Peer networks including faculty from other GLCA institutions
☐ Retreats (1–2 days)

5. Thinking about the *current* academic year (last fall, this spring), which obstacles prevent you from attending workshops, events, and other professional development opportunities offered by your institution? (select all that apply)
   a. Timing of event
   b. Workload
   c. Location
   d. Topics
   e. Departmental support
   f. Awareness of event
   g. Interest / Relevance
   h. Other (please explain)

Departmental Support

6. To better describe the challenges and needs you face at your career stage (early, mid, late), please answer the following open-ended questions:
   a. Describe the greatest professional challenges you face currently.
   b. How might the institution better support you to effectively manage this/these challenge(s)?

c. Describe briefly institutional policies or programs that negatively contribute to those challenges.

d. Describe briefly institutional policies or programs that reduce those challenges.

Section 2: Participation in Faculty Development Activities

Think about your participation in faculty development activities as you answer the following questions.

7. Please indicate which activities you have participated in at your *current institution* during *the last 3 years* (under columns 2/3). Yes responses will ask you to also rate the benefit of participation to you and to your students (1= lowest benefit, 4 = highest benefit).

   ☐ Sabbatical leave

   ☐ Published article/book based on research or teaching

   ☐ Summer institute(s), workshops, etc.

   ☐ Retraining for fields in technology

   ☐ Internship or exchange in business/industry or back-to-practice

   ☐ Conducted funded research or development projects

   ☐ University credit courses

   ☐ Professional Conferences

   ☐ Training in computer skills

   ☐ College-sponsored presentations, workshops, etc.

   ☐ Academic exchanges

   ☐ Other (please specify).

8. Think about your primary faculty responsibilities (e.g., teaching, research, service, advising, etc.). Then indicate how influential the sources of support below are to your professional development. Click on or slide the indicator to provide your response to each item.

   [Response options from 1 (not at all) through 4 (somewhat) to 7 (a lot).]

   ☐ Departmental colleagues

   ☐ Divisional colleagues (humanities, social science, fine and applied arts, natural sciences, etc.)

   ☐ Colleagues outside of division but within institution

   ☐ Colleagues within GLCA Consortium

   ☐ Institutional resources (outside your division; e.g., sponsored program through Center for Teaching and Learning)

   ☐ Graduate school advisor or mentor

   ☐ Peers from graduate school

☐ Colleagues within disciplinary or professional association

☐ Colleagues from prior academic appointment as faculty, instructor, post-doc, etc.

☐ Collaborators outside institution

☐ Other (please explain below)

9. During the past three years at this institution, have you taken advantage of the following professional development opportunities?

[Response options: yes, no, not eligible/applicable to me.]

☐ Paid workshops outside the institution focused on teaching

☐ Travel funds paid by the institution

☐ Internal grants for research

☐ Training for administrative leadership

☐ Incentives to develop new courses

☐ Incentives to integrate new technology into your classroom

☐ GLCA-sponsored programs (e.g., workshops, grants)

☐ Departmental/unit mentoring program

10. In the past three years indicate how many of the following items you have earned/participated in.

Write the number (whole number, e.g., 0 or 3)

☐ Peer-reviewed articles PUBLISHED in academic or professional journals

☐ Peer-reviewed articles IN PRESS in academic or professional journal

☐ Chapters in edited books or volumes

☐ Books, manuals, or monographs

☐ Technical papers

☐ Intellectual property events, patents, or computer software products

☐ Essays, poems, etc.

☐ Exhibitions or performances

☐ PI or co-PI on a grant proposal (under review or not funded)

☐ PI or co-PI on a FUNDED grant proposal

11. During the current academic year (last fall, this spring), how many hours per week, on average, do you spend on each of the following activities?

Hours per week (round to whole number, e.g., 0 or 1)

☐ Scheduled teaching (actual hours, not credit hours)

☐ Preparing for teaching, grading, course development

☐ Advising and counseling students, working with student organizations

☐ Supervising undergraduate research

☐ Research, scholarly writing, keeping up with the literature in your field

☐ Developing other creative products/performances

☐ Grant writing, grant administration, or efforts to secure funding

☐ Preparing for professional conferences or meetings

☐ Participating in or attending institutional events (fundraisers, sporting events, etc.)

☐ Committee work and meetings

☐ Other administration

☐ Disciplinary service (editor or reviewer, task forces, etc.)

☐ Outreach/service (related to profession)

☐ Community or public service (personal, not related to profession)

☐ Outside consulting, freelance work, other employment

☐ Socializing, mentoring, and friendship with institutional colleagues

☐ Household/childcare duties

☐ Hobbies or personal interests, social time with friends or family

☐ Other activities not listed (please describe below)

Section 3: Mentoring

12. This set of questions is about activities you may have engaged in with a mentor or mentors at your current institution. Please select the best answer for each question. If you have not engaged in any of these activities or have no one who is a mentor, then select "Not at all." At least one of my mentors has. . . . Click on or slide the indicator to provide your response to each item.

[Response options from1 (not at all) through4 (occasionally) to 7 (a lot).]

☐ Provided meaningful advice about my teaching/instructional activities

☐ Reviewed my teaching as part of my formal evaluation for retention or promotion

☐ Provided meaningful advice about my research, scholarly activities, and/or publications.

☐ Provided meaningful advice about obtaining external funding and resources.

☐ Reviewed my clinical work.

☐ Provided meaningful advice about promotion and my progress toward promotion.

☐ Advised me about departmental or institutional policies and politics.

☐ Advised me about disciplinary policies or politics.

☐ Introduced me to key scholars in my field.

☐ Invited me to important networking or work-related social events to enhance my visibility.

☐ Advised me about balancing work and personal life.

☐ Nominated me for awards.

☐ Alerted me to professional opportunities.

13. Think about your impressions of your department and institution. Click on or slide the indicator to provide your response to each item. If you are unsure, then the answer is likely never in your experience.

[Response options from 1 (never) through 3 (rarely), and 4 (sometimes), and 5 (often) to 7 (all of the time).]

☐ My department has a mentoring culture (e.g., senior faculty members and department chair help junior faculty members).

☐ My institution has a positive mentoring culture (e.g., senior faculty members and department chair help junior faculty members).

☐ I feel comfortable seeking career-related advice from senior colleagues in my department.

☐ I feel comfortable seeking career-related advice from colleagues within my rank in my department.

☐ I feel comfortable seeking career-related advice from senior colleagues in my institution.

☐ I feel comfortable seeking career-related advice from colleagues within my rank in my institution.

☐ I feel comfortable seeking career-related advice from my department chair.

☐ There are barriers to success for underserved faculty in my academic department.

☐ Some of my colleagues perceive barriers to success for underserved faculty in my department.

☐ Within my department, senior colleagues help remove barriers to inclusion.

☐ My department chair promotes an equitable and inclusive climate.

☐ My president promotes an equitable and inclusive climate.

14. Think about the current academic year (last fall, this spring). Consider if anyone provided you with career support. Type below how many mentors you have (e.g., 0 or 2).

[If the number was greater than 0, the respondent was asked questions a–f.]

Of these mentors how many . . .

a. originated from a FORMAL institutional program

b. are in your department

c. are in your institution

d. are in your discipline but at another institution

e. are outside of your discipline and your institution

f. are from elsewhere (describe organization)

Think of the primary mentoring relationship you have NOW. Indicate your agreement with these items. Click on or slide the indicator to provide your response to each item.

[Response options from 1 (never) through 3 (rarely), and 4 (sometimes), and 5 (often) to 7 (all of the time).]

    g. I can express my feelings (good or bad) to my mentor.

    h. I can count on my mentor even after difficult conversations.

    i. I think about new ideas as a result of interactions with my mentor.

15. Think about the current academic year (last fall, this spring). Consider if you have provided anyone with career support. Type below the number of faculty members you MENTOR? (e.g., 0 or 2)

[If the number was greater than 0, the respondent was asked questions a-i.]

Of the people you mentor how many . . .

    a. originated from a FORMAL institutional program

    b. are in your department

    c. are in your institution

    d. are in your discipline but at another institution

    e. are outside of your discipline and your institution

    f. are from elsewhere (describe organization)

Think of the primary mentoring relationship you have NOW. Indicate your agreement with these items. Click on or slide the indicator to provide your response to each item.

[Response options from 1 (never) through 3 (rarely), and 4 (sometimes), and 5 (often) to 7 (all of the time).]

    g. I can express my feelings (good or bad) to my mentee.

    h. I can count on my mentee even after difficult conversations.

    i. I think about new ideas as a result of interactions with my mentee.

Section 4: Satisfaction

16. Think about your current position as you answer the following questions. Please select the best response for each item. Click on or slide the indicator to provide your response to each item.

[Response options from 1 (very dissatisfied) through 3 (dissatisfied), and 4 (neutral), and 5 (satisfied) to 7 (all of the time).]

How satisfied are you with:

Appropriate recognition for your contributions

A sense of personal accomplishment from your work

Your direct supervisor

Your overall job security

The institution as a place to work

Your job overall

Interest colleagues take in your success

Amount of professional interaction with colleagues at higher rank

Amount of personal interaction with colleagues at your rank

Amount of professional interaction with colleagues at lower rank

Sense of fit in your department

Sense of fit in your institution

17. What are the two (and only two) best aspects of working at your institution?

18. What are the two (and only two) best aspects of working in your department?

19. What are the two (and only two) most challenging aspects of working at your institution?

20. What are the two (and only two) most challenging aspects of working in your department?

Section 5: Demographics

Your responses to these questions will help us understand needs of faculty by career and life stage and to examine any disciplinary or other demographic differences.

21. I am:

☐ Male

☐ Female

☐ Self-identify (please describe below)

☐ Prefer not to answer

22. The year I received my first academic appointment was (select year from list):

23. The year I received my academic appointment at current institution was (select year from list):

24. My first academic appointment at my current institution was:

☐ Professor

☐ Associate Professor

☐ Assistant Professor

☐ Visiting Assistant Professor

☐ Lecturer

☐ Adjunct Faculty

☐ Instructor

☐ Other

25. My present academic rank is:
- ☐ Professor
- ☐ Associate Professor
- ☐ Assistant Professor
- ☐ Visiting Assistant Professor
- ☐ Lecturer
- ☐ Adjunct Faculty
- ☐ Instructor
- ☐ Full time administrator
- ☐ Other

26. My present academic appointment is:
- ☐ Full time, tenured/tenure track
- ☐ Full time, non-tenure-track
- ☐ Part-time, tenured/tenure track
- ☐ Part-time, not tenured/tenure track
- ☐ Full time administrator with teaching responsibilities

27. My division is:
- ☐ Natural Sciences
- ☐ Social Sciences
- ☐ Fine Arts
- ☐ Humanities
- ☐ Dual Appointment (please list the areas below)

28. My discipline is (select from a list of available disciplines in the GLCA):

29. My department is (select from a list of available departments in the GLCA):

30. My ethnicity is:
- ☐ American Indian or Alaskan Native
- ☐ Asian
- ☐ Asian American
- ☐ Black or African American
- ☐ Caribbean/West Indian
- ☐ Indian (subcontinent)
- ☐ Latino/a or Hispanic
- ☐ Middle Eastern
- ☐ Native Hawaiian or Pacific Islander
- ☐ White
- ☐ Self-identify (please describe)
- ☐ Prefer not to respond

31. Do you identify with any of the following groups (select all that apply)?
- ☐ Persons with documented disabilities
- ☐ Persons who identify as LGBTQ
- ☐ International Faculty

☐ No

☐ Prefer not to respond

32. What is your relationship status?

    ☐ Married/Domestic Partnership

    ☐ Divorced

    ☐ Widowed

    ☐ Single

    ☐ Prefer not to respond

33. Indicate your current parental status (select all that apply).

    ☐ No children

    ☐ Pregnant

    ☐ Pre-school children

    ☐ School-aged child(ren)

    ☐ Adult child(ren)

    ☐ Single parent

    ☐ Co-parent with a partner/spouse

    ☐ Co-parent with an ex-partner/spouse

    ☐ Other (please specify)

    ☐ Prefer not to respond

34. Indicate if you have any other dependents (select all that apply).

    ☐ Parent

    ☐ Grandparent

    ☐ Sibling

    ☐ Other (please specify)

    ☐ Prefer not to respond

    ☐ No other dependents

35. If you would be willing to be contacted for a follow up conversation you will be asked to provide your email and contact information after you submit the survey.

36. Hope College asked us to include four additional questions, otherwise you will be directed to the survey end. Thus, please indicate your institution (select from a list of GLCA institutions). [If Hope College was selected, four additional questions were asked about faculty development programming. The answers were supplied to Hope College but not used in our study.]

APPENDIX C
FACULTY AND ADMINISTRATOR INTERVIEW PROTOCOLS

GLCA [Great Lakes Colleges Association] Faculty Interview Protocol

1. Tell me a bit about yourself and your academic/professional history (e.g., graduate degree/granting institution, prior places of employment, etc.).
2. Why did you choose to work at [institution]?
   a. What opportunities exist for you here?
   b. What challenges to your professional success do you see?
   c. How is [institution] similar to or different from other institutions where you were trained or have worked?
3. What role does the GLCA consortium have in supporting your career success and satisfaction?
   a. Do you have any recommendations for ways in which the consortium, or your institution through its membership, could best support faculty work?
4. What are the main roles you engage in through your academic position?
   a. How do you divide your time between teaching, research, and service?
   b. Are there any roles that particularly affect your time or your work (e.g., department chair, executive search committee, PI [principal investigator])?
   c. What do you see as your most important role/function as a faculty member at [institution]?
5. What support do you need to effectively engage in those roles?
   a. What support exists currently?
   b. Do you utilize these resources (why/why not)?
   c. What support would you like to see in the near future?

6. Is there anything else about your career that affects your ability to be successful and satisfied at [institution] (e.g., disciplinary culture, departmental size, research projects, etc.)?

    a. How might your institution better support you in response to those factors?

7. Is there anything about your personal life that affects your ability to be successful and satisfied at [institution] (e.g., caregiving responsibilities, dual-career couples, health/wellness issues, etc.)

    a. How might your institution better support you in response to those factors?

8. How are new faculty socialized into life at [institution]?

    a. What traditions exist for helping new faculty members settle into the institution?

    b. Can you give me an example of a way in which faculty members support new hires?

9. How can [institution] attract and retain strong faculty?

    a. How can you, as a faculty member, ensure that [institution] continues to attract and retain strong faculty?

GLCA Administrator Interview Protocol

1. What are your institutional priorities?

    a. How are those priorities communicated?

    b. How are those priorities supported?

    c. When, if at all, were those priorities reevaluated or reenvisioned?

    d. What were some of the associated conversations?

2. What are the venues in which socialization occurs (both official and unofficial)?

    a. What kinds of programs orient faculty to the campus?

    b. What kinds of programs engage faculty in campus life?

    c. In what ways are faculty supported in engaging in institutional priorities?

    d. In what ways do faculty help socialize other faculty in your opinion?

3. Key documents, rituals, etc. that exist that serve to socialize faculty into life of the campus.

    a. What are the guiding documents that help establish the values/culture on your campus?

    b. What are the faculty rituals that are accepted practice/common place on campus?

    c. Are there any accepted faculty traditions that serve to socialize faculty?

4. What support is provided to faculty to support teaching, research, and service?

    a. In what ways are faculty supported (financially, personnel-wise) in the areas of teaching, research, and service?

REFERENCES

Albion College. 2017. "Faculty Mentor Guidelines." Accessed January 31, 2017. http://www
.albion.edu/academics/student-research/fursca/faculty-mentor-guidelines.

Allen, T.D., L. T. Eby, M. L. Poteet, E. Lentz, and L. Lima. 2004. "Career Benefits Associated
with Mentoring for Protégés: A Meta-Analysis." *Journal of Applied Psychology* 89:127–36.

American Association of University Professors. 2014a. "Background Facts on Contingent Faculty." Accessed August 20, 2015. https://www.aaup.org/issues/contingency/
background-facts.

———. 2014b. "Contingent Appointments and the Academic Profession." Accessed
August 25, 2015. http://www.aaup.org/file/Contingent%20Appointment.pdf.

Association for Women in Science. n.d. Mentoring and coaching. Accessed February 14,
2017. http://www.awis.org/?Mentoring.

Austin, A. E. 2002. "Preparing the Next Generation of Faculty: Graduate School as Socialization to the Academic Career." *Journal of Higher Education* 73 (1): 94–122.

———. "Supporting Faculty Members across their Careers." 2010. In *A Guide to Faculty
Development*, edited by K. H. Gillespie, D. R. Robertson, and associates, 363–78. San
Francisco: Jossey-Bass.

Austin, A. E., and Rice, R. E. 1998. "Making Tenure Viable: Listening to Early Career Faculty."
American Behavioral Scientist 41 (5): 736–54.

Austin, A. E., and M. D. Sorcinelli. 2013. "The Future of Faculty Development: Where Are We
Going?" *New Directions for Teaching and Learning* 133:85–97.

Baker, V. L., and R. G. Baldwin. 2015. "Liberal Arts Colleges in the 21st Century: An Integrative Approach to Understanding Organizational Change and Evolution in Higher
Education." *Innovative Higher Education* 40 (3): 247–61.

Baker, V. L., R. G. Baldwin, and S. Makker. 2012. "Where Are They Now? Revisiting Breneman's Study of Liberal Arts Colleges." *Liberal Education* 98 (3): 48–53.

Baker, V. L., L. G. Lunsford, and M. J. Pifer. 2015. "Systems Alignment for Comprehensive
Faculty Development in Liberal Arts Colleges." *To Improve the Academy* 34 (1–2): 91–116.

Baker, V. L., M. J. Pifer, and L. G. Lunsford. 2015. "Faculty Challenges across Rank in Liberal
Arts Colleges: A Human Resources Perspective." Paper presented at the Annual Meeting of the American Educational Research Association, Chicago, IL, April.

Baker, V. L., M. J. Pifer, L. G. Lunsford, J. Greer, and D. Ihas. 2015. "Faculty as Mentors in
Undergraduate Research, Scholarship, and Creative Work: Motivating and Inhibiting
Factors." *Mentoring and Tutoring* 23 (5): 394–410.

Baldwin, R., and R. T. Blackburn. 1981. "The Academic Career as a Developmental Process:
Implications for Higher Education." *Journal of Higher Education* 52 (6): 598–614.

Baldwin, R., and D. A. Chang, 2006. "Reinforcing Our 'keystone' Faculty: Strategies to Support Faculty in the Middle Years of Academic Life." *Liberal Education* 92, (4): 28–35.

Baldwin, R., D. DeZure, A. Shaw, and K. Moretto. 2008. "Mapping the Terrain of Mid-Career Faculty at a Research University: Implications for Faculty and Academic Leaders." *Change* 40 (5): 46–55.

Barney, J. B., and P. M. Wright. 1997. "On Becoming a Strategic Partner: The Role of Human Resources in Gaining Competitive Advantage." CAHRS Working Paper No. 97–09, 1997. Ithaca, NY: Cornell University, School of Industrial and Labor Relations, Center for Advanced Human Resource Studies. Accessed January 30, 2017. http://digitalcommons .ilr.cornell.edu/cahrswp/150.

Bates, S. 2015. "Making CEOs Most Likely to Succeed." *HR Magazine*. Accessed March 4, 2017. https://www.shrm.org/hr-today/news/hr-magazine/pages/0116-ceo-succession.aspx.

Blackburn, R. T., and J. H. Lawrence. 1995. *Faculty at Work: Motivation, Expectation, Satisfaction*. Baltimore: Johns Hopkins University Press.

Blanchard, K. D. 2012. "I've Got Tenure. How Depressing," *The Chronicle of Higher Education*, January 31. Accessed May 15, 2015. http://www.chronicle.com/article/Ive-Got-Tenure -How/130490.

Blood, E. A., N. J. Ullrich, D. R. Hirshfeld-Becker, E. W. Seely, M. T. Connelly, C. A. Warfield, and S. J. Emans. 2012. "Academic Women Faculty: Are They Finding the Mentoring They Need?" *Journal of Women's Health* 21 (11): 1201–8.

Boice, R. 1992. *The New Faculty Member: Supporting and Fostering Professional Development*. San Francisco: Jossey-Bass, 1992.

———. 2000. *Advice for New Faculty Members: Nihil Nimus*. Boston: Allyn and Bacon.

Bordes, V., and P. Arredondo. 2005. "Mentoring and 1st-Year Latina/o College Students." *Journal of Hispanic Higher Education* 4 (2): 114–33.

Boyer, E. L. 1990. *Scholarship Reconsidered: Priorities of the Professoriate*. Princeton, NJ: Carnegie Foundation for the Advancement of Teaching.

Breneman, D. W. 1990. "Are We Losing Our Liberal Arts Colleges?" *AAHE Bulletin* 43 (2): 3–6.

Buch, K., Y. Huet, A. Rorrer, and L. Roberson. 2011. "Removing the Barriers to Full Professor: A Mentoring Program for Associate Professors." *Change* 43 (6): 38–45.

Carmeli, A., D. Brueller, and J. E. Dutton. 2009. "Learning Behaviours in the Workplace: The Role of High-Quality Interpersonal Relationships and Psychological Safety." *Systems Research and Behavioral Science* 26 (1: 81–98).

Carpenter-Hubin, J., and L. Snover. 2013. "Key Leadership Positions and Performance Expectations." In *Organization and Administration in Higher Education*, edited by P. J. Schloss and K. M. Cragg, 27–49. New York: Routledge.

Chopp, R., S. Frost, and D. H. Weiss, eds. *Remaking College: Innovation and the Liberal Arts*. Baltimore: Johns Hopkins University Press, 2013.

Clark, B. R. 1987. Introduction to *The Academic Profession: National, Disciplinary, and Institutional Settings*, edited by B. R. Clark, 1–10. Berkeley: University of California Press.

Cook, C. E., and M. Marincovich. 2010. "Effective Practices and Research Universities." In *A Guide to Faculty Development*, edited by K. H. Gillespie, D. R. Robertson, and associates, 277–92. San Francisco: Jossey-Bass.

D'Abate C. P., and E. R. Eddy. 2008. "Mentoring as a Learning Tool: Enhancing the Effectiveness of an Undergraduate Business Mentoring Program." *Mentoring and Tutoring* 16 (4): 363–78.

Douglas, L., and A. George. 2003. "The Academic Therapist. Treating Post-Tenure Depression." *The Chronicle of Higher Education*, February 21. Accessed May 15, 2015. http://www .chronicle.com/article/The-Academic-Therapist-/2614/.

Faulkner, W. 1951. *Requiem for a Nun.* New York: Random House.

Felten, P., D. Little, L. Ortquist-Aherns, and M. Reder. 2013. "Program Planning, Prioritizing, and Improvement: A Simple Heuristic." In *To Improve the Academy: Resources for Faculty, Instructional, and Organizational Development,* vol. 32, edited by J. Groccia and L. Cruz, 183–98. San Francisco: Jossey-Bass.

Ferrall, V. E., Jr. 2011. *Liberal Arts at the Brink.* Cambridge, MA: Harvard University Press.

Fries-Britt, S. 2000. "Developing Support Networks and Seeking Answers to Questions." In *Succeeding in an Academic Career: A Guide for Faculty of Color,* edited by M. Garcia, 39–56. Westport, CT: Greenwood.

Gappa, J. M., A. E. Austin, and A. G. Trice. 2007. *Rethinking Faculty Work: Higher Education's Strategic Imperative.* San Francisco: Jossey-Bass.

Gehrke, S. J., and A. Kezar. 2015. "Supporting Non-Tenure-Track Faculty at 4-Year Colleges and Universities: A National Study of Deans' Values and Decisions." *Educational Policy* 29 (6): 926–60.

Golde, C. M., and T. M. Dore. 2001. "At Cross Purposes: What the Experiences of Today's Doctoral Students Reveal about Doctoral Education." Accessed March 4, 2017. http://www.phd-survey.org/.

Goldman, C. A., and H. Salem. 2015. "Getting the Most Out of University Strategic Planning: Essential Guidance for Success and Obstacles to Avoid." Accessed March 4, 2017. http://www.rand.org/pubs/perspectives/PE157.html.

Gratton, L., and C. Truss. 2003. "The Three-Dimensional People Strategy: Putting Human Resources Policies into Action." *Academy of Management Executive* 17 (3): 74–86.

Gutiérrez y Muhs, G., Y. Niemann, C. González, and A. Harris, eds. 2012. *Presumed Incompetent: The Intersections of Race and Class for Women in Academia.* Boulder: University of Colorado Press.

Haskins, C. H. 1965. *The Rise of Universities.* Preface by T. Mommsen. Ithaca, NY: Cornell University Press.

Haynes, R. K., and J. M. Petrosko. 2009. "An Investigation of Mentoring and Socialization among Law Faculty." *Mentoring and Tutoring* 17 (1): 41–52.

Hearn, J. C., and M. S. Anderson. 2002. "Conflict in Academic Departments: An Analysis of Disputes over Faculty Promotion and Tenure." *Research in Higher Education* 43 (5): 503–29.

Hendrickson, R. H., J. E. Lane, J. T. Harris, and R. H. Dorman. 2013. *Academic Leadership and Governance in Higher Education: A Guide for Trustees, Leaders, and Aspiring Leaders of Two- and Four-Year Institutions.* Sterling, VA: Stylus.

Hill, R., and P. Reddy. 2007. "Undergraduate Peer Mentoring: An Investigation into Processes, Activities and Outcomes." *Psychology Learning and Teaching* 6 (2): 98–103.

Hughes, A. 2014. "Tenure at Small Colleges." *Inside Higher Education,* August 11. Accessed January 24, 2017. https://www.insidehighered.com/advice/2014/08/11/essay-earning-tenure-small-liberal-arts-colleges.

Hyers, L. L., J. Syphan, K. Cochran, and T. Brown. 2012. "Disparities in the Professional Development Interactions of University Faculty as a Function of Gender and Ethnic Underrepresentation." *Journal of Faculty Development* 26 (1: 18–28).

Jaschik, S. 2012a. "Disappearing Liberal Arts Colleges." *Inside Higher Education,* October 11. Accessed May 15, 2015. https://www.insidehighered.com/news/2012/10/11/study-finds-liberal-arts-colleges-are-disappearing.

———. 2012b. "Unhappy Associate Professors." Inside Higher Education, June 4. Accessed May 15, 2015. https://www.insidehighered.com/news/2012/06/04/associate-professors-less-satisfied-those-other-ranks-survey-finds.

———. 2016. "Angst and Hope for Liberal Arts Colleges." *Inside Higher Education*, July 13. Accessed January 24, 2017. https://www.insidehighered.com/news/2016/07/13/meeting -discusses-challenges-facing-liberal-arts-colleges.

Kanter, M. J. 2010. "The Relevance of Liberal Arts to a Prosperous Democracy: Under Secretary Martha J. Kanter's Remarks at the Annapolis Group Conference." June 22. Accessed May 25, 2015. http://www.ed.gov/news/speeches/relevance-liberal-arts -prosperous-democracy-under-secretary-martha-j-kanter%E2%80%99s-remarks -annapolis-group-conference.

Kezar, A. 2001. "Understanding and Facilitating Organizational Change in the 21st Century: Recent Research and Conceptualizations." *ASHE-ERIC Higher Education Report* 28 (4): 1–162.

Kezar, A., and S. Gehrke. 2014. "Why Are We Hiring So Many Non-Tenure-Track Faculty?" *Liberal Education* 100 (1): 44–51.

Kiley, K. 2012. "Making the Case." *Inside Higher Education*, November 19. Accessed May 15, 2015. https://www.insidehighered.com/news/2012/11/19/liberal-arts-colleges-rethink -their-messaging-face-criticism.

Kimball, A. B. 1986. *Orators and Philosophers: A History of the Idea of Liberal Education*. New York: Teachers College Press.

King, J., and G. Gomez. 2007. *The American College President 2007*. Washington: American Council on Education.

Knapp, P. 1965. "Changing Functions of the College Professor." In *The American College: A Psychological and Social Interpretation of the Higher Learning*, edited by N. Sanford, 290–311. New York: Wiley.

Kram, K. E. 1988. *Mentoring at Work: Developmental Relationships in Organizational Life*. Lanham, MD: University Press of America.

Lane, A. 2013. "Liberal Arts Colleges Add Degrees, Sports, Incentives to Contend in Highly Competitive Market." *Crain's Detroit Business*. June 2. Accessed on May 15, 2015. http:// www.crainsdetroit.com/article/20130602/NEWS/130609994/liberal-arts-colleges-add -degrees-sports-incentives-to-contend-in.

Law, A. V., M. M. Bottenberg, A. H. Brozick, J. D. Currie, M. V. DiVall, S. T. Haines, and E. Yablonski. 2014. "A Checklist for the Development of Faculty Mentorship Programs." *American Journal of Pharmaceutical Education* 78 (5): 1–10.

Lee, V. S. 2010. "Program Types and Prototypes." In *A Guide to Faculty Development*, edited by K. H. Gillespie, D. R. Robertson, and associates, 21–33. San Francisco: Jossey-Bass.

Levin, J. S. 2006. "Faculty work: Tensions between Educational and Economic Values." *Journal of Higher Education* 77 (1): 62–88.

Lopatto, D., and S. Tobias. 2010. *Science in Solution: The Impact of Undergraduate Research on Student Learning*. Washington: Council on Undergraduate Research.

Macdonald, R. "Academic Development." 2009. In *The Routledge International Handbook of Higher Education*, edited by M. Tight, K. Mok, J. Huisman, and C. Morphew, 427–39. New York: Routledge.

Mathews, K. R. 2014. "Perspectives on Midcareer Faculty and Advice for Supporting Them." Cambridge (MA): Harvard Graduate School of Education, Collaborative on Academic Careers in Higher Education. Accessed January 30, 2017. http://scholar.harvard.edu/ files/kmathews/files/coache_mathews_midcareerfaculty_20140721.pdf.

Mayer, A. P., J. A. Files, M. G. Ko, and J. E. Blair. 2009. "The Academic Quilting Bee." *Journal of General Internal Medicine* 24 (3): 427–29.

Miller, E. R., and R. A. Skinner. 2012. "Passionate Traditionalist or Pragmatic Visionary?" *Inside Higher Education*, March 7. Accessed May 20, 2015. https://www.insidehighered .com/advice/2012/03/07/essay-next-generation-liberal-arts-college-presidents.

Mooney, K. M., and M. Reder. 2008. "Faculty Development at Small and Liberal Arts Colleges." In *To Improve the Academy: Resources for Faculty, Instructional, and Organizational Development*, vol. 26, edited by D. R. Robertson and L. B. Nilson, 158–72. San Francisco: Jossey-Bass.

Neumann, A. 2005. "Observations: Taking Seriously the Topic of Learning in Studies of Faculty Work and Careers." *New Directions for Teaching and Learning* (102): 63–83.

Nilson, L. B., E. B. Nuhfer, and B. B. Mullinix. 2011. "Faculty Development as a Hazardous Occupation." In *To Improve the Academy: Resources for Faculty, Instructional, and Organizational Development*, vol. 30, edited by J. E. Miller, 290–305. San Francisco: Jossey-Bass.

O'Meara, K., and R. E. Rice. 2005. *Faculty Priorities Reconsidered: Rewarding Multiple Forms of Scholarship*. San Francisco: Jossey-Bass.

O'Meara, K., A. L. Terosky, and A. Neumann. 2008. *Faculty Careers and Work Lives: A Professional Growth Perspective*. San Francisco: Jossey-Bass.

Padilla, A. and S. Ghosh. 2000. "Turnover at the Top: The Revolving Door of the Academic Presidency." *Presidency* 3 (1): 30–37.

Pascarella, E. T., and P. T. Terenzini. 2005. *How College Affects Students*. Vol. 2. San Francisco: Jossey-Bass.

Pifer, M. J. "His, Hers, and Ours: Gendered Roles in Departmental Networks." Forthcoming. *NASPA Journal about Women in Higher Education*.

Pifer, M. J., and V. L. Baker. 2016. "Professional, Relational, and Personal: A Preliminary Framework for Exploring the Salience of Identity in Academic Careers." *Identity Journal* 16 (3): 190–205.

Reder, M. 2007. "Does Your College Really Support Teaching and Learning?" *Peer Review* 9 (4): 9–13.

———. 2010. "Effective Practices in the Context of Small Colleges." In *A Guide to Faculty Development*, edited by K. H. Gillespie, D. R. Robertson, and associates, 293–308. San Francisco: Jossey-Bass.

Reder, M., and E. V. Gallagher. 2007. "Transforming a Teaching Culture through Peer Mentoring: Connecticut College's Johnson Teaching Seminar for Incoming Faculty and the Scholarship of Teaching and Learning." In *Resources for Faculty, Instructional, and Organizational Development*, edited by D. R. Robertson and L. B. Nilson, 327–44. Bolton, MA: Anker.

Reder, M., K. Mooney, R. A. Holmgren, and P. J. Kuerbis. 2008. "Starting and Sustaining Successful Faculty Development Programs at Small Colleges." In *Resources for Faculty, Instructional, and Organizational Development*, edited by L. Nilson and J. Miller, 267–86. San Francisco: Jossey-Bass.

Rhoades, G. "The Study of the Academic Profession." 2007. In *Sociology of Higher Education: Contributions and Their Contexts*, edited by P. J. Gumport, 113–146. Baltimore: Johns Hopkins University Press.

Sandberg, S. 2013. *Lean In: Women, Work, and the Will to Lead*. New York: Random House.

Sawatzky, J. A. V., and C. L. Enns. 2009. "A Mentoring Needs Assessment: Validating Mentorship in Nursing Education." *Journal of Professional Nursing* 25 (3): 145–50.

Schuster, J. H., and M. J. Finkelstein. 2006. *The American Faculty: The Restructuring of Academic Work and Careers*. Baltimore: Johns Hopkins University Press.

Scott, W. R., and G. F. Davis. 2007. *Organizations and Organizing: Rational, Natural, and Open System Perspectives*. Upper Saddle River, NJ: Pearson Prentice Hall.

Solem, M., K. Foote, and J. Monk, eds. 2009. *Aspiring Academics: A Resource Book for Graduate Students and Early Career Faculty*. Upper Saddle River, NJ: Prentice Hall.

Sorcinelli, M. D. 2000. "Principles of Good Practice: Supporting Early-Career Faculty. Guidance for Deans, Department Chairs, and Other Academic Leaders." Washington:

American Association for Higher Education. Accessed January 30, 2017. http://files.eric.ed.gov/fulltext/ED450634.pdf.

Sorcinelli, M. D., A. E. Austin, P. L. Eddy, and A. L. Beach. 2005. *Creating the Future of Faculty Development: Learning from the Past, Understanding the Present.* Bolton, MA; Anker.

Sorcinelli, M. D., and J. Yun. 2007. "From Mentor to Mentoring Networks: Mentoring in the New Academy." *Change* 39 (6): 58–61.

Thelin, J. R. 2011. *A History of American Higher Education.* 2nd ed. Baltimore: Johns Hopkins University Press.

———. 2014. *Essential Documents in the History of American Higher Education.* Baltimore: Johns Hopkins University Press.

Thomas, D., L.G. Lunsford, and H. A. Rodrigues. 2015. "Early Career Academic Staff Support: Evaluating Mentoring Networks." *Journal of Higher Education Policy and Management* 37 (3): 320–29.

Turner, C. S. V., J. C. González, and K. Wong. 2011. "Faculty Women of Color: The Critical Nexus of Race and Gender." *Journal of Diversity in Higher Education* 4 (4): 199–211.

US Department of Education. 2016. Institute of Education Sciences, National Center for Education Statistics. IPEDS Institutional Comparisons.

Wilson, R. 2012. "Why Are Associate Professors So Unhappy?" *The Chronicle of Higher Education*, June 3. Accessed May 15, 2015. http://www.chronicle.com/article/Why-Are-Associate-Professors/132071/.

Zemsky, R. 2013. *Checklist for Change: Making American Higher Education a Sustainable Enterprise.* New Brunswick, NJ: Rutgers University Press.

INDEX

ABOUT THE AUTHORS

VICKI L. BAKER is a professor of economics and management at Albion College and an instructor in business administration at the Pennsylvania State University's World Campus. She is cofounder of Lead Mentor Develop, LLC (www .leadmentordevelop.com). Before becoming a faculty member, Baker held administrative positions in Harvard Business School's Executive Education Division and worked at AK Steel Corporation. Baker studies the role of relationships (mentoring and developmental) in professional and personal development, with a particular focus on graduate students and faculty members. She also studies liberal arts colleges, both in terms of institutional change and the faculty experience. Baker is the principal investigator for a study called the Initiative for Faculty Development in Liberal Arts Colleges and the development of an Academic Leadership Institute for mid-career faculty members at the Great Lakes Colleges Association, funded by the Henry Luce Foundation. The National Science Foundation and Chemical Bank have also funded her work. Baker's most recent research has appeared in the *Journal of Higher Education*, *Identity Journal*, *Mentoring and Tutoring*, and *Journal of Faculty Development*. Her current work continues to focus on the faculty experience in liberal arts colleges, with a particular focus on mid- and late career stages. She has published over fifty peer-reviewed journal articles as well as book chapters. Baker consults with corporations and higher education institutions in the areas of leadership development, change management, mentoring programming, and faculty development.

LAURA GAIL LUNSFORD is director of the Swain Center at the Cameron School of Business, at the University of North Carolina at Wilmington. Before returning to administrative work, she was a tenured associate professor of psychology at the University of Arizona. She has also worked in admissions and residence life, and as the alumni relations director at Duke University's Fuqua School of Business and director of the Park Scholarships at North Carolina State University. Her scholarly interests focus on the psychology of mentoring and leadership development. She has published over thirty peer-reviewed articles, as well as case studies and book chapters on toxic leadership, leadership development, mentorship dysfunction, optimizing mentoring relationships, and evaluating mentoring. Her work has appeared in journals such as *Mentoring and Tutoring*, the *Journal of Higher Education Policy and Management*, and *To Improve the Academy*. She authored the *Handbook for Managing Mentoring Programs* and coedited the *SAGE Handbook of Mentoring*. She has presented her work at conferences sponsored by the European Mentoring and Coaching Council, American Psychological Association, Association for Psychological Science, and American Educational Research Association, among others. The Department of Education, National Science Foundation, and the Henry Luce Foundation has funded her work. She received the 2009 International Mentoring Association's Dissertation Award for her work on doctoral student mentoring and advising. She frequently consults with organizations about mentoring and leadership development and is cofounder of Lead Mentor Develop, LLC (www .leadmentordevelop.com).

MEGHAN J. PIFER is an associate professor of higher education in the Department of Educational Leadership, Evaluation, and Organizational Development at the University of Louisville, where she is also assistant director of the Cadre and Faculty Development Course. She earned a PhD in higher education from Pennsylvania State University, an EdM in higher education administration from Boston University, and a BA in philosophy and literature from the University of Pittsburgh. Pifer studies colleges and universities as organizational contexts and is interested in ways in which identity and individual characteristics, as well as interpersonal networks and relationships, in those contexts shape both individual and organizational outcomes. She has held administrative positions in multiple institutional and disciplinary contexts, including theology, business, and education. Her previous research includes studies of the mentoring experiences of students from underrepresented groups in the geosciences, doctoral students across disciplines and identity characteristics, and faculty members at various career stages. Her work has been published in such periodicals as the *Journal of Higher Education*, *American Journal of Education*, and *Journal of Diversity in Higher Education*. Her current research includes studies of faculty behavior in the organizational contexts of academic departments, faculty experiences in liberal arts colleges, and identity-based experiences in the academy.